THE DIARY OF A HUNTER FROM THE PUNJAB TO THE KARAKORUM MOUNTAINS

First published 1863
This edition published by Lector House in 2023

ISBN: 978-93-5800-737-4

Lector House LLP
Registered Office: H. No. 96, Block C, Tomar Colony,
Burari, Delhi – 110084, India
info@lectorhouse.com
www.lectorhouse.com

THE DIARY OF A HUNTER FROM THE PUNJAB TO THE KARAKORUM MOUNTAINS

AUGUSTUS HENRY IRBY

2023

LECTOR HOUSE LLP

THE DIARY OF A HUNTER FROM THE PUNJAB TO THE KARAKORUM MOUNTAINS

BY

AUGUSTUS HENRY IRBY

PREFACE.

It is hoped that the circumstances under which this volume appears may be considered such as to excuse its imperfections. It is—with some omissions and completions of sentences but with hardly a verbal alteration—the copy of a journal, not written with a view to publication but simply as a private record, kept up from time to time as opportunity offered in the midst of the scenes which it describes. The hand that wrote it is now in the grave. And it is solely in compliance with the wishes of many relatives and friends who were anxious to obtain such a memorial of one whom they loved, that it is now committed to the press by a brother.

CONTENTS

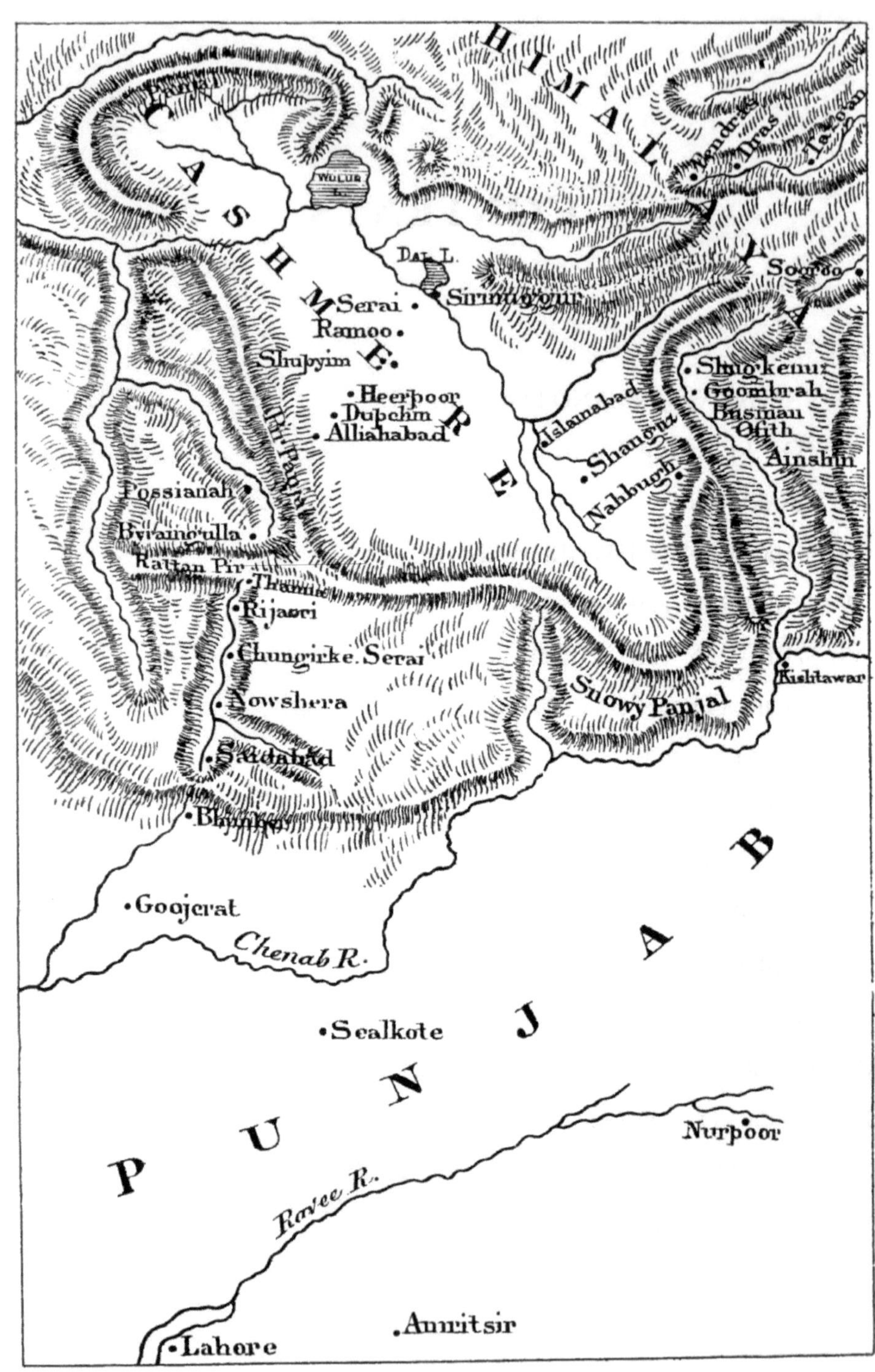

Browne. Lith. Norwich.

CHAPTER I.

PREPARATIONS AND EQUIPMENTS.

POSSIANAH, PIR PANJAL,
29th *April*, 1860.

An attempt at a Diary, with the intention of recording my adventures and experiences in an excursion contemplated in Cashmere and adjacent countries—that of Ladâk being a principal object—during six months' leave from my duties at Amritsir.

Several times in former days have I resolved to keep a journal, or jot down briefly the incidents and experiences of each passing day. But as often, after the lapse of a few days, have I failed to persist in the undertaking: whether from infirmity of purpose, or idleness, or from an utter contempt of the 'small beer' I had to chronicle, I do not myself know; and whether I shall be more successful in this present effort remains to be seen. Primary indications are not promising, as I have now been 'en route' from Amritsir, from the 16th to the 29th, thirteen days, and have excused myself, on one ground or other, from making a commencement until now.

To be in order, I must note my preparatory arrangements, detail my supplies—their quality and quantity—the number and office of my attendants—the extent of my stud, and the amount and nature of my sporting equipments; especially this latter, as the chase, or, as it is called in India, 'shikar,' is with me a sort of mania, and all that appertains thereto is to me of very great importance. Therefore, as a guide for myself, or to advise others on some subsequent and similar occasion, I must minutely specify my shooting apparatus and fishing appointments, and, in the course of my diary, especially take note of efficiences and deficiences in this respect, as occasion may demand.

To commence with the most important part of my travelling establishment,—the servants,—there was, First in consideration, the khansamah, who unites the duties of caterer, cook, and director general of the ways and means. Secondly, the sirdar or bearer,—the individual who, in this land of the minutest division of labour, looks after the clothes, bedding, &c., and assists in dressing and washing. He was a new hand, hired for the occasion, as my regular sirdar had to remain behind in charge of my property. Thirdly, the bheestie, who, in addition to his ordinary duties of fetching water, undertook to assist in cooking, washing up dishes, &c., for the consideration of three rupees additional wages, which I thought preferable to hiring a mussulchee, as the fewer attendants one has on the road to Ladâk the better, considering that for some marches all provisions and food have to be carried for the whole party. Fourthly, the classee, in whose charge were the tents and their belongings, &c.—his duty to accompany and pitch them. Fifthly and sixthly, two syces, grooms, in whose charge were my two ponies: one of which was a stout animal from Yarkand, a famous animal for mountain travelling: the other a good-looking, good sort of pony from Cabul, which I bought at hazard, taking him according to description in an advertisement, and he seems likely to justify fully the account given of him.

In addition to these attendants, I agreed, after consultation with my excellent friends, the missionaries of Amritsir, to attach to my party a native Catechist, who by birth claims to be a Cashmiri. He has been, however, brought up and educated in the Punjab; where, when serving as a khitmudgur or sirdar, he became a convert to Christianity, and has for some years been in the employment of the Amritsir Mission. He has been in Cashmere and Ladâk, and understands the language of the former country. The object of his accompanying me is to circulate the Gospel in Bibles, Testaments, and tracts, which I received for that purpose from the missionaries, having myself first suggested the possibility of my being able to promote the spread and knowledge of the Christian Faith and Hope, by means of these books, in the heathen lands to which I was going,—intending to distribute them personally should opportunities offer. But the co-operation of the Catechist was a sudden after-thought of one of my good friends, the missionaries; which, as it only had birth two days before I started, was rather embarrassing to mature and act upon. But after the project had almost lapsed, owing to some misunderstanding resulting from the excited and unsettled state of mind of Suleiman, the Catechist, consequent on so sudden a summons to start, with little or no preparation, on such an arduous journey, leaving, too, a wife and family—she in a delicate state—it was finally arranged that Suleiman should accompany me at my charges.

My retinue was again unexpectedly increased by engaging a Cashmiri who presented himself to me as I was returning home from breakfast at mess. He shewed me a certificate of character, stating him to be an useful servant, capable of any personal attendance required by a traveller and hunter. He had the strong recommendation, too, of an intimate acquaintance with the country of Ladâk, and the routes north and east of Cashmere, together with the sporting localities, the haunts of the yâk (wild cattle), and the kyang (wild horse); so thinking him an acquisition I closed with him at twelve rupees per month, and directed him to proceed to the rendezvous at Bhimber.

Having thus enumerated my personal attendants, I must now mention my coolies, Cashmiries, twenty of whom I engaged at five rupees a month to convey my baggage to Sirinuggur, the capital of Cashmere.

My stores, and all articles that could be so disposed, were packed in long baskets, called kheltas, which the Cashmiries hoist on their backs, strapping them to their shoulders: and with them they carry a stout crutch about two feet high, on the cross-piece of which they rest their load when pausing on the road, and taking breath in ascending mountains—an excellent mode of relief as it does not cause them to shift or put down their load. They only straighten their backs, so that the khelta rests on the crutch; and when refreshed again bend to their burden and trudge on, often—too often for the early arrival of one's baggage—repeating this process.

This mode of hiring coolies answers admirably. They are returning to their homes in Cashmere from Amritsir, to which grand emporium for Cashmere goods they had brought loads of merchandise in the commencement of the cold season, and it is to them, of course, a piece of good luck getting return loads. They all appeared strong, sturdy, well-limbed men, and got away with my traps, my servants and horses in company, the whole under charge of my khansamah, Abdoolah, on the evening of the 8th April.

I must not forget, in my catalogue of live stock, two little dogs, of no particular merit, but dear to me as affectionate companions after their kind.

I had made ample provision for my creature comforts, having been told by an experienced traveller, and having gleaned from books of travel, that the Ladâk country is sterile in the extreme, and consequently possesses little of what constitutes by habit the necessaries of an European.

I took 4 tins of bacon, 1 case of maccaroni, 1 ditto vermicelli, 2 ditto biscuits, 1 tin of cheese, 3 pots of jam, 7 bottles of pickles, 24 lbs. of tea in 3 tins, and 3 lbs. for immediate use, two 8-lb. boxes of China sugar, and some 5 or 6 lbs. I had by me, 3 bottles essence of coffee, 7 lbs. raw ditto, 2 bottles fish sauce, 4 various ditto, 3 bottles lime juice, 2 vinegar, 2 oil, 6 lbs. candles, besides which Clarke's patent lamp, and lots of candles, 6 bottles brandy, 12 sherry, 12 beer, to which I added, carrying with me, 6 bottles of hock and 6 claret—some of a batch arriving the day I left, which, having ordered expressly for the mess myself, I was anxious to taste. I took, by way of medicines, 12 drams of quinine, a box of Peake's pills, one phial chloridyne, some Holloway's ointment and sticking-plaister, with some odds and ends I do not remember. This was my stock.

Of fire arms, I took a double rifle by Blissett, 10 bore—one heavy double Enfield, ditto—one rifle, military pattern, by Whitworth—one double-barrelled Westley Richards for shot; 8 lbs. powder, good supply of bullets, shot No 3 and 6, caps, wads, &c.

These guns were taken from their cases and placed in a woollen case, then in a leathern case respectively, this being, I think, the most convenient way of carrying them, four of my servants having charge, each of one. Two Colt's revolvers and ammunition, shikar knife and belts, knives for skinning, four boxes arsenical paste, from Peake and Allen, cleaning rods, bullet moulds, and all the paraphernalia of a sportsman.

Of fishing-tackle, a large salmon-rod, a common trout-rod, a gaff, two large winches, one small; stout plaited silk line, and hair for the small rod, a variety of flies, and a good supply of spinning tackle and hooks, on which, from past success, I principally depended. Being without good spinning gear, I had some hooks, or rather the spinning contrivance to which they were fitted, made by a 'maistry' in Amritsir, after a model I had given him; and very well he succeeded. The system of hooks was devised and fitted by a young brother officer, an ardent devotee of the gentle craft, and clever at all kinds of fishing gear.

Having the year previous killed some good fish in a fine stream 'en route' to Cashmere, I anticipated some sport this time.

My tents were, the one a small two-poled shikar tent made very light, about 12 ft. long by 7, which for the present trip I had covered so as to resemble, in some degree, what is called a Swiss cottage tent; the other was a small thing, just big enough to put a bed in, and carried altogether by one coolie: the bigger one takes four. I had also a folding wooden bed, and lots of bed clothes, &c.

I have now enumerated all I recollect of my equipment, a good stock of suitable clothes being understood.

CHAPTER II.

TO SIRINUGGUR.

I had hoped to have received intelligence of the Commander-in-Chief's sanction of my application for leave ere the 15th. I only heard from the Assistant Adjutant General at Lahore that it had been forwarded: so, being in command at Amritsir, I gave myself leave in anticipation, and, having some days previously arranged my 'palki dâk,' I entered it about 4.30 P.M. on Monday the 16th, and making up my mind for a grilling, it being extremely hot, off I started amid the farewell salaams of my deserted retainers. The heat was very great, but the prospect before me of, ere many days, plunging into the eternal snows rendered endurance easy.

I reached the Sealkote bungalow about twelve next day: bathed, breakfasted, made another meal at 4 P.M., after which I again jogged on along the dusty road, keeping down my disgust and refreshing my weary spirits, by conjuring up visions of snowy regions, and glorious sport as before. And thus I arrived at Goojerat, after crossing the Chenab at 5 A.M. on the morning of the 18th.

Here I halted, breakfasted, and dined. Pursuing my hot and dusty route at 4.30 P.M., I arrived at Bhimber about twelve midnight, received good accounts of my belongings from Abdoolah, was almost devoured by my two little pets, found Suleiman had arrived, but no tidings of the Cashmiri, Jamhal Khan. I turned into bed in my tent, feeling a delightful sensation at being really out of the scorching plains of the Punjab; though I could hardly be said to be so, for the following day,—

Thursday, 19th April, the heat was excessive, thermometer in the day 96°, and at 9 P.M. in my tent, 90°. This day was employed in arranging loads, and selecting such articles as I needed on the road. Jamhal Khan joined, and made salaam. Suleiman went into Bhimber, a large straggling town, and endeavoured to create a desire for the knowledge of the Gospel. He encountered opposition, and found none willing to receive books.

20th April. I made a good start before day had well dawned. It was a miserable day's march, having a river to be crossed about ten times, the bed of which, and indeed the road itself, is composed of boulders and stones innumerable. There is also a steep ascent to climb, which is no easy job, the path up it being merely indented in the naked rock by continual footsteps. I may as well remark here, that this road is the whole way abominable, nothing being ever done to improve it, although there is a large amount of traffic along it with the Punjab; and the Maharajah, with his usual avarice, takes good care to have heavy dues levied on all imports and exports—bad luck to him, for a horrid screw! The track is nothing more than a watercourse, and up and down the steep hills is really dangerous.

The path this day leads over the said hill, on which is a station of the rajah's in a narrow pass, where are officials to examine passengers and take toll. The path thence descends roughly and irregularly to a small valley, in which is the halting place, the 'baraduri' being a repaired portion of one of the old 'serais,' built, I believe, by the Emperor Akbar. Many of them still exist, as also remnants of bridges, also the work of that mighty potentate.

This place is called Saidabad, and though, perhaps, as hot as the Punjab, being very confined, the pines and firs, the variety of foliage, green crops, and verdant grassy slopes, with hills around you, and mountains in the distance, tend much to lessen the sense of heat. There are officials and sepoys here, and supplies in moderation—tattoos, perhaps, coolies, fowls, &c. to be had.

21st April. I made a good start for Nowshera, sending on a coolie with a basket containing breakfast.

The first part of the road is rough and difficult, lying by the stream, interrupted by rocks; but it now opens into a pretty narrow valley, from which you ascend a stiff steep hill of rock, but well wooded, and, at this season, clothed with varieties of flowering shrubs and plants, dog-roses abounding, by which the air was pleasantly perfumed. On the summit of the hill is an old piece of solid masonry, now inhabited by an old couple who supply excellent milk and eggs to wayfarers.

There is a beautiful and very extensive view from this eminence of a fertile valley in which, on a small hill, is situate Nowshera, its white buildings conspicuous. But the object of interest is the snowy ridge of the Panjal range, and interposing itself midway, so as to exclude from sight all but the upper ridges of the Pir Panjal, lies the Rattan Panjal, its upper crests partially and thinly covered with snow. The whole scene is charming as viewed at early morning, ere the dews, ascending in misty vapours—in themselves beautifying the landscape by their varied and many-tinted effects—are dissipated by the sun.

At the foot of the hill the path proceeds through ups and downs of a more or less stony character, until you descend into the valley of the Tooey, a fine rapid brawling stream, in some places one hundred yards wide, but averaging perhaps fifty: possessing some deep still pools, at the turbulent entrances to which an angler would wager good fish would be found, were there any in these waters. Nor would he be far wrong. There are fish, and huge ones, too, in those promising pools. Nor are they quite insensible to the wiles of the crafty angler, who may with moderate skill enjoy good sport along this river. But here, as elsewhere, fish have their moods and whims, their times and seasons, so that some practice and observation are requisite.

You cross this river, and some two hundred yards on the 'baraduri' is situated in the middle of a densely-planted garden. Not liking its appearance—thinking it would, at least, be prolific of insects and of fever—I went on through the town of Nowshera, and, descending again to the river, encamped under a 'tope' of mulberry trees, in a long grassy plain, lying between a range of hills of moderate height and the river. There is little to notice in Nowshera, a long street with the ordinary bazaar shops, and, on the right-hand, a castellated gateway, leading into an old serai, one of the series of Akbar, I suppose.

I tried fishing in the evening at a splendid looking pool, very deep, in which the rushing waters bury themselves, as it were, for a time, pausing ere they again pursue their onward troubled course. This pool lies under a precipitous cliff, just beneath the town; it is of considerable extent, and of unknown depth, and in its dark recesses lurk mahseer of monstrous bulk, I am told. My fortunes were at their worst this evening, as far as catching a dish of fish went. I tried spinning, having been provided with most tempting minnow-like bait by some small boys, eager for 'backsheesh': and I tried 'atta' in a sticky lump on a large-sized salmon-hook—a bait of reputed irresistibility—but without effect. Numbers of fish, small and some evidently of goodly size, to set one longing, rose and actually floundered on the surface; but not a run could I get. A heavy thunderstorm, bursting in the distance, was rapidly approaching, which was, perhaps, the unlucky evil influence: so, tired of trying to get anything out of the water, I took a header in, and enjoyed a most refreshing and cooling swim.

22nd April. Sunday. Halted and passed the Sabbath in repose.

23rd April. To Chungir-ke-Serai—a long and tedious march, the path leading over rocks which hedge in the river, on turning an angle of which I overtook Abdoolah, who had preceded me with the breakfast things, standing gazing back in my direction. I told him it was not yet time for breakfast, supposing that to be his meaning, when he pointed upwards, and, suspended from the projecting limb of a tree, some little way up the hill shutting in the river, hung the still-mouldering body of a man, his lower limbs still in his clothes, the ghastly face denuded of flesh, yet with a matted felt of hair straggling here and there over the glistening bones, grinning horribly down upon us.

This wretch, it appeared, had in the most treacherous, barbarous, and cowardly manner murdered an old man and child, close to the spot where he expiated his crime. Being a sort of rural policeman in the employ of the Maharajah, he was armed with a sword, which, of course, excited no suspicion in his victims, whom he joined on the road as they journeyed from Nowshera, and ascertaining that they possessed a few rupees' worth of property, the miserable caitiff, yielding to the suggestions of the Tempter, cut them down, and threw their bodies into the river. Suspicions followed their disappearance: other circumstances pointed to this man, who was arrested, and confessing his guilt was executed where the bloody deed was committed.

I left this gloomy spot full of reflections of the most depressing nature: but with that rapidly revolving mental process, which so soon exchanges our train of thought, I was soon almost as though the repulsive object had not been met with.

I soon afterwards arrived at a pool, where I proposed stopping to breakfast, and also to fish, having in this pool, when passing last year, whilst occupying a seat on a rock overhanging it, observed some monstrous great fish basking; for it was a scorching hot day, and the sun at high meridian at the time.

I tried the 'atta' bait—merely paste made very adhesive—but without more than one or two nibbles which came to nothing: so knocked off and comforted the inner man. While so employed, came by a 'gent' riding, whom I saluted. I knew him to be in my rear, proceeding to join the Trig. survey party which was before me some days: asked him to dinner, and he accepted.

Arrived at Chungir-ke-Serai, an old Akbar serai, on the top of a hill overhanging the river—a fine view of the snowy range—the features of the country rough, but picturesque. I tried fishing again without success: enjoyed a cool swim: returned and had to wait about three-quarters of an hour for my guest, although he was close at hand, and I sent to him two or three times. But, lo! he at length appeared, got up rather considerably, quite abashing me, who was sitting in a flannel shirt and corresponding nethers. We had a pleasant chat together. He informed me that he had never been out of India, was born in the country, and educated at Landour, whence he was appointed direct to the Survey department. I do not know his name.

24th April. Rijaori. I made an early start as usual, and had a rough scrambling march of it. The road following the trend of the river, here and there crosses steep stony hills, where the track is only a watercourse. We crossed the river just below Rijaori. This passage is at times very difficult and dangerous, and never very pleasant, as there is a great body of water, and strong current at all times, but after the rains a roaring flood.

The camp-ground of Rijaori is very pretty, in a garden, one of much note, there being remains of aqueducts and fountains, a summer-house on an eminence overlooking the river, and the town on the other side. In the garden are some magnificent plane trees, called 'chunar' in Cashmere, affording good and pleasant protection from the sun.

I found a young officer of the 24th encamped here, and asked him and my former guest to dinner.

I prepared my tackle, and was provided with small fish by youngsters who remembered me the year before, and started to fish, full of expectation, at 4.30 P.M.—the sun broiling. I tried the nearest pool under the temple, where last year a mighty fish had got off, breaking my line and robbing me of my best spinning tackle—no run, nothing stirring. I went down to another fine pool, where two streams blend their waters, situated under a lofty hill, steep and well-wooded down to the precipitous rocky bank of the river—a lovely piece of water; had an offer or two, and hooked and landed an impudent little brat of 2-lb. weight; then had some little sport with a nice little chap of 5-lb. or so, when, having disturbed the pool, I went lower and fished two or three likely spots, without moving anything.

So I struggled back over the bothering boulders to my pet pool, where I strove long and ineffectually, and was actually on the point of leaving off, when—Whirr, whirr, whirr, whirr went the reel, the rod bent double, the line smoked again, and the still waters of the pool rose in swells, as the sogdollager I had hold of darted violently down the stream. Fifty yards were out in no time, when I butted him strongly, and turned him, only then getting an idea of his weight, and joyfully exclaimed he was a twenty-pounder. The young officer of the 24th was with me;

he and the native attendants were greatly excited.

I was conscious of having work cut out for me, and intensely eager to secure the prize I knew to be at stake. The struggle was long and stout. At one time the fish turning up stream, made direct for the bank where 24th stood, about forty yards from me. A brawling cascade separated us, and I was over knees in water in another noisy rapid, so did not hear his remarks, but noticed his gesticulations, and judged from them, he was astonished at the monster I had hold of.

Well, after a rare game of pully-hauly, my scaly enemy took the bottom, and I could not move him. 'Oh! what a weight he must be,' thought I; 'hold on good tackle!' I shook the bait, so as to make his jaws rattle and his teeth ache, when at last he moved with a vengeance, making a violent effort, up and down and all sides, to break away. Then he shewed his massive golden side—glorious sight! I hauled him towards a round hand-net a handy lad held ready in the water—no gaff with me—but too soon yet. Away he sped, bending the rod alarmingly, and making the winch talk loudly. I turned him again, and repeated the attempt to net him—away he rushed again. I then humoured him, and tired him with the rod and short line, until he was bagged, the lad going up to his middle, and when in the net he could not lift him out himself.

He was a regular monster in size, but beautiful to behold—a truly handsome fish, of lustrous golden hues. He was carried off in triumph, suspended from my mountain staff across the shoulders of two well-sized youths, who could but just keep his tail off the ground.

Great was the admiration in camp, and many and various the guesses at his weight. 24th and I each had a 24-lb. weighing hook: putting both together, a weight of 48 lb. was required to bring both indicators flush, which my captive did; so we rated him as a fifty-pounder.

I must not dismiss this sporting incident without recording the excellent qualities of this fish when brought to table. He had hung all night, disembowelled: in the morning was not scaled, but skinned, and being cut in lateral scallops was simply fried, and without any exaggeration was delicious, only inferior to a good salmon. It was firm and rich, of a brown colour, flaked with curd, and though I was prepared with anchovy sauce, that was scouted. I never myself eat any mahseer, or other Indian river fish, anything like it.

My two guests chatted away at dinner, a glass or two of ale being highly appropriate on the occasion of this huge success. We parted at nine, early hours being essential, they intending to proceed onwards at dawn, I to stop and try my luck again.

25th April. Rijaori. I tried the upper pool above the town, a beautiful and most promising-looking pool: but, after trying every persuasive and seducing attitude, failed to move an admirer, and being chilled returned to camp and breakfast, when I regaled upon the morsel I have above described.

I passed the day reading, and anxious for the shades of evening to permit my further attempts on the fishes, but to cut short this evening's proceeding need only say that I fastened to another leviathan in the same pool, after many indecisive offers had been made; but, woe is me! he at once, after feeling himself fast and trying rod and line, bored straight down, and cutting my bottom-line over a stone got clear off with my set of spinning tackle. Let me draw a veil over my misery, nor again awake memory to the bitterness of my disappointment.

26th April. To Thanna. The road still running in company with the river, the courses only being reversed. This day's march was much pleasanter than any previous one, there being but little up and down comparatively, and the pathway in many places lying under shady wooded slopes, its sides fringed with numbers of sweet-smelling shrubs.

The approach to Thanna presents a lovely view of the Rattan Panjal range in front; and on the left-hand is a well-wooded range of hills, beneath which are undulating slopes, whereon is a good deal of cultivation which is in some parts carried in terraces to the tops of the hills. There is an old fort-like building, formerly the habitation of some ruffian of a rajah, I presume. The camp was pitched close to a small village on the road to the Rattan Pir. At this place Suleiman had an attentive audience of some ten or twelve respectable natives, who listened to his account of our religion with pleasure, and were glad to accept some Gospels and tracts, never having, they said, obtained any accurate idea before of what the Christian Faith consisted.

I have omitted to note the effect produced by Suleiman at the different stations, so will retrace my steps for that purpose.

At Rijaori, the first day, he was not only repulsed, but threatened. On the second day, however, he had listeners, and distributed some books.

At Nowshera, favourable results—being listened to calmly and attentively, some enquiries and discussions entered into, and some Gospels and tracts received. There was here a teacher in a school, who had been educated in the mission school of Lahore, and he it was whose influence operated favourably. He took some books for his school.

I forgot to mention an occurrence at Bhimber. I had noticed in the day a man lying near the 'baraduri,' who was apparently suffering, and continually uttered cries and moans from the same spot. I called Suleiman, and with a light proceeded to make enquiries; when it appeared that this unfortunate man had fallen from a mulberry tree close by, and had disabled himself so much that he could not proceed on his way home to Cashmere. So there he was left to shift for himself, dependent on the charity of passers by, wholly unable to raise himself from the ground. I sent for the havildar of the guard, and giving the disabled man five rupees, which I understood to be ample for the purpose, ordered him to be removed to a house, to be cared for, and sent to his home when recovered.

Thinking this a good opportunity, I called the attention of some thirty people, who were looking on, to the fact that the Christian religion thus enjoined its professors to obey their Lord's commands, and that the religion of Jesus Christ was love. Not being sufficiently fluent myself, I requested Suleiman to use this living text, and he addressed the assemblage, who seemed much impressed, and expressed their entire concurrence in the sentiments and principles uttered. But this is often the case without any further consequences.

27th April. From Thanna across the Rattin Pir pass to Byramgullah.

This is a stiff pull, but not precipitous. The path winds about, taking advantage of the slopes of the mountain to gain the summit gradually. There is a faquir's establishment on the top, and the view on either side is very fine. That looking down over the plain past Rijaori and Nowshera—over the several wave-like lines of inferior hills into the plains of the Punjab of limitless extent, lost only in vapour and distance—is grand from its great extent, and beautiful in its varied features as in its colouring.

The other side presents the masses of the Pir Panjal, covered with snow. This range is of bold massive proportions, and affords the traveller a truly sublime picture of mountain scenery.

The descent to Byramgullah is steep and rugged, and altogether wearisome. But, when accomplished, one is amply compensated for one's toils. The road from the foot of the mountain crosses a bridge over a picturesque torrent, clear and rapid, rushing in roaring cascades below. There is here every component part of a beautiful landscape, but space. The valley is confined, there being but just room for the river and a small bit of level on an elevated bank. This is shut in by lofty hills, some entirely clothed with a rich mantle of foliage, others having intervals of grassy slopes. But the whole is singularly beautiful.

There is a fort on an isolated hill, of curious structure, only capable of defence against bows and arrows, I should think; but it is a picturesque object, of a Swiss character as to architectural appearance.

28th April. Along the bed of the torrent to Possianah, crossing some thirty-five bridges (so called), very awkward for riding, but, on the whole, an easy march, the scenery of a romantic character.

Possianah is a singularly built village, on the precipitous side of a mountain which is the vis-a-vis of the redoubtable Pir Panjal; which here, lifting his snowy summit to the clouds, frowns down upon you in all his majesty and grandeur, looking by no means affable to approach, and promising an arduous struggle to get the better of.

The village is at this time more miserable than ever, its ordinary inhabitants having deserted it to escape the rigours of the winter; there remained or had returned only two or three. Many houses, being most inappropriately built with flat roofs, had fallen in, and altogether the place had anything but a cheerful aspect.

Here, however, I must pass two days, the 29th being Sunday. So I had the hovel, used as a baraduri, cleaned out, and there ensconced myself and traps, and had nothing whatever to complain of,—the most magnificent scenery around me, a delightful climate (the wind, perhaps, a little too chill here), and no scarcity of creature comforts.

29th April. Sunday. I halted at Possianah. When at Byramgullah, I heard the Pir was not passable for tattoos, so left mine there to await orders, intending to leave them to come on in a few days, when the road would probably be open. But from a near reconnoitre of the mountain as to snow, and from information acquired, I determined to run the risk, and sent for my ponies.

As I was at breakfast a saheb was announced, and a stout party made his appearance, a M. Olive, a French merchant in the shawl trade, who passes the winter season at Amritsir, returning to Cashmere, when the passes open, for business.

The Maharajah does not permit Europeans to reside in the valley during the winter; perhaps, from jealousy of their becoming permanent residents, and finally annexing the country; perhaps, because the winter is the time for collecting his revenue, when, it is said, the most infamous oppression is practised, and complaints are rife and loud.

I had seen the new comer, but was not acquainted with him, and could do no less than invite him to share my homely fare, and after some polite demur he fell to. He spoke no English, and my French had been lying 'perdue' a couple of years or so; but I assayed to converse, and eking out my French with Hindostani managed to keep up the conversation without difficulty. The stout gent had been carried all the way from Amritsir in a jan-pan—a sort of covered chair on poles—which four or six men at a time carry on their shoulders. How he could ever get up the Pir Panjal, I could not imagine.

Another traveller had also arrived—one, by the bye, I should have previously noted as having arrived at Rijaori the day I halted there—an artillery Vet, who had been suffering from some affection of the head, and irritability of nerves. He dined with me at Rijaori, and highly approved the mahseer, which he pronounced equal to salmon, but far inferior in my opinion.

In the course of the day I found the unfortunate Vet had sent his pony round by the Poonah pass from Baramoolah, and he lamented having done so, groaning over the prospect of the morrow's arduous exertions. I, therefore, placed mine at his disposal, as I prefer footing it, especially when the path is difficult.

30th April. From Possianah to Dupchin. The road from Possianah descends to the torrent roaring at a considerable depth below, from which the ascent recommences, so that you have to descend from a considerable elevation, perhaps a quarter of the height of the Pir, and then again ascend on the other side; which loss of way is provoking. From Possianah to the foot of the Pir is, I imagine, two miles, the latter part of the road very rough and stony.

I started on this occasion without any refreshment, such as tea, thinking I should better husband my breath, and work my lungs more easily: and I think the idea a success, as I ascended with much more ease and comfort than on the former occasion, when I primed myself with tea, hard eggs, &c. It is, undoubtedly, a tremendous pull; and one meets with a provoking deception as to distance. For when about a quarter of the height has been ascended, the first flight, as it were, up to the snow drift, the traveller looking above him, puffing and panting with his violent efforts, sees above him what appears to be the summit close at hand, which is but the top of the lower ridge, from which runs a somewhat level path on the slope to the snow drift—an enormous mass of snow, some half-mile long, and, I suppose, from one to two hundred yards broad, and, I fancy, from fifty to a hundred feet deep, filling a gorge of the mountain which commences quite at the summit. Over this mass we struggled, a violent icy blast in our faces, to a point where the path turns off to the left, and climbs upwards by zigzags to the more gradual slope under the summit. Here I overtook a woman carrying a boy of, perhaps, five years old, who, poor little creature, was crying bitterly from cold, his teeth chattering, and presenting a forlorn appearance. The woman was sitting down disconsolate, unable to proceed. I tried to persuade her to put the lad down, and lead him, to restore circulation, but she did not adopt my suggestion; so, leaving a man to help them on, I continued my ascent, and finally reached the top.

The height is, I believe, some 10,000 feet above the sea. The view, looking back, is magnificent—an endless succession of wave-like lines of hills terminating, as they gradually recede, in the hot vapours of the Punjab.

It was pleasant to look down the steep and rugged path we had won our way up, there beholding others still toiling and struggling upwards, the coolies with their loads in a long-drawn straggling line, here coming into view, and quickly disappearing behind some projection or in some bend of the road, but constantly to be seen resting on their crutches. I watched my ponies with some anxiety. They had been stripped in order to give them every freedom of limb, and several coolies had been told off to assist them. They were more than half-way up when I saw them: it was just at a difficult point, where the snow was deep and soft, and the path hung on the side of the mountain. The old Yarkandi broke through the snow, and was plunging and struggling violently, but after three or four desperate efforts got out of trouble. The other avoided this place. I find the former from his very caution apt to go off the good path, and get himself into difficulties. When the snow gives, he goes down on his knees and so hobbles on.

I did not wait longer, but strode away over the snowy plains, which descend in a very gentle incline to the Alliahabad Serai. The sensation was delightful after the troublesome ascent, and I enjoyed the change of play of muscles amazingly, as did my two little dogs to whom the snow was a novelty. They kept frisking and bounding about, rushing off to a distance, then occasionally taking a roll.

The landscape, as a winter scene, was perfect,—one glittering field of snow, lofty hills on either side also covered with snow, the sun shining cheerily, and the difficult entrance to the valley achieved. But after a time my eyes ached from the glare, and I was glad when a mile or two of descent brought us to patches of brown hillside. There were two very awkward watercourses to cross, the banks high, precipitous, and covered with snow, giving every chance of a tumble.

I got well over, and found the serai, where I had intended to halt, in such a state from snow, melted and unmelted, and the only place for camping in a similar condition that, shrinking from its chill uninviting aspect, I determined to push on; so after my usual breakfast of cold tea and hard eggs I again sped on my way—and a toilsome way it was. The sun was now very hot, and the path running over ridges and down gorges of rock on the slopes of the mountain, and encumbered with snow, in enormous drifts in some of the ravines, made this additional eight miles (I think it was) a formidable addition to the ascent of the Panjal.

I forgot to mention that on the top of the Pir is a faquir's hut, where last year we were supplied with the most delicious draught of milk we had ever tasted. But the faquir had not yet ventured to face the inclement climate, so no milk this time.

There is also a small watch tower of an octagonal form, of which there are several to be seen, here and there, along the route. This forms a very conspicuous object, being so distinctly seen at Possianah as to deceive one as to the distance; and I fancy that an European accustomed to the denser atmosphere of the mountain regions in that quarter of the globe would be astonished at the atmospheric effects here. Rarely, except in case of a thunderstorm, and in the rainy season which lasts about two months, is there any vapour to impede the vision, which roams over snowy peaks of various chains of mountains far on the other side of Cashmere.

The beauties of this scenery, in its magnificence and colossal proportions, its illimitable extent and brilliancy of colouring, is far beyond any description. All around you nature exhibits herself in her most attractive forms, presenting almost every variety of shape and colour, mountain and valley, rock and dell, forests of noble pines and individual giants waving their monstrous arms overhead as you pursue your path, with foaming torrents dashing at the bottom of the precipices below you, gushing rills of purest water trickling from the hills on whose slopes you move, and from the path to the torrent below you stretch undulating grassy slopes, here steep, there gently inclining, occasionally intercepted by a rough ravine through which tumbles a torrent, and the whole surface gay with many flowers which the while perfume the air—the 'tout ensemble' is such as to send the observant traveller, however much his limbs may be taxed, exhilarated and rejoicing on his way. It is a new existence to any one coming from the depressing monotony of the interminable plains of the Punjab.

I had a long time to wait at Dupchin before any of my followers arrived; so I took a snooze under a pine tree adjoining a fine stream, at which I had slaked my thirst. The whole of my effects did not arrive until about five o'clock. There was no village, no house here, it being simply used as a camp ground, for which it offered some facilities—a level surface, wood and water in abundance—food we had brought with us.

The night was bitterly cold, but my servants managed tolerably, four or five sleeping in my smaller tent, as many as it would hold. Others and the coolies coiling themselves up in their warm blankets under a pine-clad bank, screening them from the wind, by the help of rousing fires of dry pine wood kept up through the night, if not perfectly comfortable, did not suffer: for they did not grumble—a good sign.

1st May. To Shupyim. The first part of the road is rough and difficult, through a pine forest. You then cross the river by a bridge, the scenery charming; emerge from the forest, and enter upon level grass lands. We halted at Heerpoor for breakfast, a small village where supplies are to be got: there is an old serai, one small room only habitable, but good ground for camping.

The road from Heerpoor to Shupyim is good, over level grassy elevated land, park-like scenery on either hand, the valley of Cashmere widening before you, and a glorious display of mountains beyond it.

One may consider oneself fairly in the valley here, having left the mountains behind; there remain only slight elevations between Shupyim and Sirinuggur.

2nd May. I followed the path to Sirinuggur which, although one of the principal roads to the capital, was but a bridle path, in some places difficult to find, and leading over rivers and streams, some of which, being without bridges, are awkward to cross.

We halted at a village called Serai, from there being the remains of one there. Ramoo is the usual station, but it does not divide the distance so equally, being too near Shupyim.

We had some difficulty in obtaining supplies, Jamhal Khan being compelled to resort to harsh measures, such as kicking and so forth, to bring the village official to a sense of his duties, and the importance of a 'burra saheb.' This discipline was that best adapted to his rude perceptions: and after some vociferations, and making as though he would apply to me, who cruelly stopped the address with threats of further coercive measures, he roused himself, and set to work with activity to get what was required.

M. Olive came up: he had intended going right on to Sirinuggur, expecting horses out to meet him, with his city man of business. The latter did appear, and informed him that the ponies were sent the other road, it being understood he would enter the valley of Baramoolah. M. O. decided to remain, and readily accepted my invitation 'a gouter:' when with some biscuits and potted bloaters, washed down by a bottle of excellent hock, we contrived to open the sources of our eloquence, and sat out regardless of the sun which, though the air was pleasant and fresh, had a powerful tanning effect, as my face indicated on retiring to my tent. Previous to thus taking 'tiffin,' I proposed to M. Olive that we should unite our provisions and dine together, as I had some claret on which I wished to have his judgment pronounced. He readily assented, remarking that his khansamah should have orders to combine culinary operations with mine.

I strolled out, and went in the direction of Sirinuggur, looking to obtain a view of that city, but could only discern its site, indicated by the fort of Hari-Parbut, conspicuous on a solitary hill, and by the poplar trees, forming avenues round the city.

I returned and sat down to dinner with M. Olive, who, by the bye, added nothing to the repast, apologising as he had intended dining at Sirinuggur. However, I had abundance, and the claret was greatly admired, and fully appreciated, M. Olive declaring it to be 'une veritable acquisition': it had, however, considerable body, so we did not drink more than half the bottle—sufficient again to engage us in uninterrupted conversation.

M. Olive became quite eloquent, and getting on some pet topics connected with France and her glories, Louis Nap. and his genius and policy, he launched out and discussed these matters with great intelligence. He is a very agreeable companion, having all the politeness of manner of the well-educated Frenchman, and being a man of sense and observation I found all he enlarged upon, and his views and opinions, interesting and instructive.

CHAPTER III.

SIRINUGGUR—TO THE WURDWAN.

3rd May. To the city of Sirinuggur—the immediate object and termination of the first part of my journey. The road was indifferent and uninteresting, running through a low level country with undulations, more or less elevated, and water-courses.

We passed some splendid chunar trees, and occasional stretches of verdant turf; and on either side, adjoining the road, were growing large patches of lilies, blue and white, scenting the air with the most delicate perfume. About a mile from the city one enters an avenue of poplars, leading on to a bridge crossing the river Jhelum which flows through the midst of the city; and from this bridge one obtains a general idea of the city itself. The impression is far from favourable, the houses appearing mean and in a state of ruin and neglect, the population squalid and dirty. Nor does a more intimate acquaintance remove this impression. The site of the city is beautiful, the surrounding scenery all that could be wished, but man, in himself and his works, has disfigured and defiled as lovely a spot as could be anywhere selected in the universe.

I was conducted to a small house on the Jhelum, called Colonel Browne's house, from his frequently residing there. It is kept for the senior officer arriving, and I happen at this time to be that important individual. There was no noticeable difference between this and the eight or nine small residences on either side. They are paltry buildings, only calculated for roughing it 'en garçon.' They are, however, pleasantly situated on the right bank of the Jhelum, at considerable intervals, shady groves in rear, and well removed from the smells and sounds of the city and its multitude.

I was waited upon by the Maharajah's Vakeel, the Baboo, Mohur Chunder, a most intelligent, active, and obliging official, affording every information and every assistance possible in one's affairs. He is the 'factotum' as regards Europeans, being, I believe, retained on account of his tact in giving them satisfaction, and keeping things 'serene' between them and the residents. He provided me with a boat, partly thatched, and six men, to pull about and do the lions, the river being the highway.

I had written to the Baboo to engage two shikarries whom I named, and he had despatched a 'purwanah' for their attendance, but had not yet heard of them. This I did not regret, as I wished to look about me a bit before starting upon any fresh excursion.

In the afternoon I took boat, and descended the river, passing amid the city under some half-dozen bridges of, I think, four arches each, if arches they may be called, for the tops are flat. The piers are constructed of large rough timbers in the log, placed in layers transversely, and the roadway is formed of longitudinal and transverse timbers its whole length. The 'tetes-de-pont' are nearly all of wood, with a rough stone pediment.

The Jhelum is very deep, and the stream strong, the water not clear. The city is, undoubtedly, interesting as viewed in this manner, and the buildings decidedly picturesque from the very irregularity of their dilapidations. They are built principally of timber, roofs slightly aslant covered with earth, on which is generally grass or other vegetation. Some buildings are of brick and wood; a few of stone, brick, and wood, the stone forming the foundation, and many of them bearing distinct signs of having been portions of other buildings of a by-gone age.

The banks of the river are high and steep, built up in some places by stone facings. Houses with balconies projecting are supported by wooden props sloping to the wall, and there resting in what appears a very precarious manner—just stayed on an irregular ledge of the stone facing at hazard, and any interstice to make up the measurement filled in with chips. There are a few houses of more pretension and better finish, exhibiting more taste and elegance in their decoration in carved wood. These belong to wealthy merchants, and they have some nondescript sort of glazed windows; but the houses generally have only lattices.

There are no buildings especially to notice, except the Rajah's residence, or fort, as they call it, a long, rambling string of buildings on the left bank, connected with which is the most conspicuous object in the city, a new Hindoo temple, with a gilt pyramido-conical cupola. This is new and glaring, and, therefore, quite out of harmony with the mass of buildings around it. There are also two or three old wooden 'musjeds,' constructed when the professors of Islam were in the ascendant, now in a state of rapid decay, as appears to be the race and religion they represent.

We pulled down beyond the city to the new houses building by the Maharajah for Europeans, an out of the way place, though affording a fine view of the fort of Hari-Parbut and the mountain ranges looking N.E., but too remote from the bazaar to suit most visitors.

I returned up the river, and enjoyed the trip much. The banks of the river and the houses overhanging are prettily diversified by trees, here and there. One sees some odd wooden buildings floating and attached to the shore, used for purposes of cleanliness, washing, &c.; yet is the city abominably dirty, beyond anything I ever saw.

4th May. I took my boat, and, on the representation of Jamhal Khan, gun and shot for wild fowl, and was pulled rapidly down stream. We turned up a canal, and passing under some beautiful trees, the air fresh and pure, lending a charm to everything, we entered a sort of sluice gate by which the waters of the Dal have exit, passing through this channel to the Jhelum.

In this Dal are the far-famed floating gardens, in which vegetables are cultivated. There are also beautiful isles forming groves and gardens, which in the palmy days of the Mahomedan conquerors were places of constant resort for the indulgence of luxury and pleasure, and still attract numerous parties of pleasure, European, of course, and native, the latter adopting quite the pic-nic style. The floating gardens are formed of the weeds dragged up from the bottom, with which the lake is covered, with the exception of large open spaces under the mountains to whose sides sloping downwards it carries its waters. This lake is partly artificial, as it is pent in by embankments with sluice gates, the system of which, however, I am unacquainted with. This piece of water is of great extent, and is one of the most important features of the neighbouring scenery.

I returned to the same outlet by a circuitous route among the weed islands and gardens: and when seated at breakfast in my upper-storied room, from which a beautifully diversified prospect was visible, I quite revelled in the delightful sensations of the delicious climate and surrounding loveliness of scenery.

I called upon the Government Agent, a resident—an anomalous appointment. The individual holding it is a civilian, and his duties are to maintain amiable relations between English visitors and the inhabitants, adjust any disputes, and check irregularities; a duty—from the peculiar position which gives no direct authority over officers—calling for much tact and judgment. Had a long conversation with the present incumbent, Mr. Forde.

I cruised down the river in the evening, and saw some decidedly pretty faces among the young girls washing or drawing water at the river side: but none appear to exhibit themselves but those of mature years and the very young. Probably the Hindoos adopt the custom of the Mahomedans in this respect. It is a mixed population, and it is reasonable to imagine such a fashion to prevail. I was disposed to reject the generally pronounced opinion that there is much female beauty among the Cashmiries, but I now consider it extremely probable there is. The features are of quite a distinct type from the Hindoos of the plains, as is the complexion which is a clear rich olive-brown—eyes dark and fine—mouths rather large, but teeth even and white. The hair, also, appears to be finer in fibre than that of the people of Hindostan. It is generally worn as far as I could see, in a number of small plaits, divided from the centre of the forehead, and falling regularly all round the head, their extremities being lengthened by some artificial hair or wool, which continues the plait. The centre plaits resting on the middle of the back are longest, and extend to the swell: all the points are worked into a sort of finishing plait, from the centre of which depends a large tassel. The effect, were the hair but clean, would, I think, be charming. Of the figures I can say nothing, as they are enveloped in a hideous, shapeless, woollen smock, of no pretension to form or fashion. This appears to be the only article of dress the lower classes wear, and I have seen no other. I have been much struck with the decidedly Jewish caste of countenance repeatedly exhibited. Some faces, I have noticed, would be positively affirmed to belong to that remarkable race, if in Europe.

Another observation I made was, that the expression was quite different from other Asiatic races I am acquainted with, there being an open, frank, and agreeable intelligent look about the Cashmiries quite European, and such as you would expect to meet with only in a highly-civilized people. I should like to unravel the mystery of their origin, but that is lost in the mists of early traditions, not to be relied on: and their country has undergone so many changes of rulers, that the original race, though perhaps still retaining much of its own characteristics, has imbibed those of the races commingling with them.

5th May. I walked through the city to the Jumma Musjed, the principal place of Mahomedan worship, now much dilapidated and rapidly yielding to the desolating inroads of time, without any attempt, apparently, to check or repair its ravages. A complete panorama of the city is presented to the visitor from the top of the 'musjed.' The city, unworthy of the name, is only an irregular collection of wooden hovels, extending over some two hundred acres, its form undefined. The surrounding country is picturesque, presenting a pleasing variety of mountain and water, but deficient in timber. The beauty of the valley consists in what is really out of the valley, in the glorious range of mountains forming it, with their never-ending variety of form and colour. The valley is a dead flat, with uplands also level which, in their remarkable resemblance to shores, with other corresponding features, have given rise to the theory entertained by scientific men, that the valley was once a lake. And there is a tradition generally prevalent and confidently believed by the Cashmiries, that their valley was a lake, and they have legends as numerous as the Irish about it: and connected with every fountain and spring, and almost every remarkable natural feature in the country, is some wondrous fable of goblin, sprite, or fairy.

The fort of Hari-Parbut overlooking the city is a fine object, and should form a part of every sketch of Sirinuggur and its environs. The famous Takt-i-Suleiman also claims especial notice. This is a very ancient Hindoo temple, crowning a hill of considerable height which bounds the eastern side of the Dal lake. I ascended to the Takt this afternoon, and enjoyed a beautiful and extensive panoramic view around, too lovely and varied for description. The ascent was steep, and the sun warm, but the air when on the summit, fresh and pure, soon refreshed me. I descended on the Jhelum side of the hill, and made for the boat which was to meet me, and so returned.

6th May. Sunday. I took a walk round the Jhelum side of the Takt-i-Suleiman to the Dal lake; and then made my way back by its shore.

It appears to me advisable that both a chaplain and a surgeon should be provided by Government during the leave season in Sirinuggur, as so large a number of officers resort there.

Suleiman has not succeeded in hiring a place in the city, as I had directed him; but has been stirring himself, and was waited upon here by some Affghans, who wished to possess the Scriptures, of which they had heard.

7th May. I took boat, and went down the river, and selected a place to sketch—the sun very hot, and the boat constantly in motion. One of the boatmen caught a fish; it was handsome in form and colour, bearing a resemblance to a trout, but without spots. I had him for breakfast—very bony, and not particularly good in flavour.

I determined to make a start somewhere; heard nothing of my shikarries expected, so directed another to attend. I went down river, and got out to visit a shoemaker's shop, who was making some leather socks for me to wear with grass sandals, the best things for climbing slippery hills. They require socks to be divided to admit the great toe separately, as the bands of the sandal pass between that toe and the others; and as the grass thong is apt to chafe one unaccustomed to it, the protection of a leather over a thick worsted sock is desirable.

8th May. I employed the day in dividing my stock of stores, preparing clothes, &c.: had an interview with a shikarry, Subhan, who shewed good certificates from officers who had employed him. He recommended me to go to the Wurdwan, and I decided to do so.

Phuttoo, and another shikarry who was with me last year, arrived; so all goes well. I agreed with Jamhal Khan, who is unfit for mountain work from asthma, to give him his discharge. I take with me Abdoolah, Ali Bucks, the 'bheestie,' and assistant scullion, and Buddoo, 'classee,' who is likewise personal attendant. The bearer and Suleiman remain behind with my effects, as do my ponies and 'syces'; also little Fan, who is about to increase the canine race, and needs quiet and nursing.

I have engaged two large boats, which convey me and my staff and baggage as far as Islamabad, which will take two days to reach by their mode of progression—one man tracking, hauling the boat with a tow-rope, another steering with a paddle. But I am told they keep it up day and night.

I made all arrangements with the invaluable Baboo, with reference to my servants and effects. I propose remaining in the Wurdwan valley above a month, and having my things sent on to meet me on the Ladâk road, to which I propose making my way by an outlet from the Wurdwan. The Wurdwan is reputed to be the best locality for shikar in Cashmere. Ibex are plentiful, bears also, and in the autumn, 'bara sing.'

I went down river, and sent to the shoemaker, who was reported to have gone up to my place: had a pleasant row, and took a farewell view of the beauties of the landscape: had everything packed and ready for an early start in the morning.

9th May. Embarked myself and belongings—servants, shikarries, and baggage in separate boat. My folding bed had just room for it under the thatch. The boats are long, narrow for their length, and flat-bottomed; they are floored, and, barring the necessity of constantly stooping, not incommodious.

We got off at last, after the usual delays, and made slowly up the stream, propelled by one-man power, a heavy prospect: but everything charming around, so I went in for pictorial enjoyment. After half an hour of this tedious confinement, I jumped ashore, and took my way by the river side, making short cuts at some of the bends and turns which are numerous; for, after toiling around them some six hours, we were within a quarter of a mile of the Takt-i-Suleiman, as the crow flies, though no doubt we had navigated twelve or fourteen miles. This did not look encouraging.

Having made good headway, I sat under a noble 'chunar' tree, awaiting the arrival of the boats, when I breakfasted, and embarked, and we pursued our watery way. Again I went ashore, and walked through the country until stopped by a creek, and, the sun being very hot, then took shelter under my thatch, and so on until dusk, when I halted or anchored for dinner, turned in about nine, and roused at daybreak,—

10th May. I went ashore, and walked from half-past five to half-past seven, and having cut off some tremendous 'detours,' as I thought, I sat down to await the boats. Nine o'clock, and no boats—saw two men hurrying: a sepoy, of whom two of the Maharajah's attend me, to assist in procuring supplies, &c., as is usual in this country, and Buddoo came up, and informed me that I had followed the wrong river. Here was a business. I ascertained the direction of the right one, got a boat, and crossing the deceptive stream, made across country to the boats, which we hit upon without difficulty; and without further adventure or mishap, but in dull and prosperous monotony, we punted our way to Islamabad, where we arrived about 4 P.M., and after some delay, procuring coolies, I was safely lodged in the 'baraduri' which Willis and I occupied last autumn.

Everything the same, but now familiar and less interesting; I think some of the larger fishes have been taken out of the tank—my old acquaintance the kotwal officiously civil as usual—the vizier, my friend Ahmet Shah, the kardar, absent in the neighbourhood. I made all arrangements to go on towards the Wurdwan in the morning, and sent on a sepoy to arrange for coolies and supplies—which have to be carried with us—at Shanguz, the village we are to halt at to-morrow.

May 11th. I got well away early, and had a pleasant march over a level grassy tract of country, crossing a deep watercourse now and then, and, passing through a very pretty village, stopped in a delightful spot under some giant chunars on a bank overhanging a rivulet, a village close at hand. Then, having breakfasted, I came on here to Shanguz, also a prettily situated village, with its stream, its irregular garden plats, grassy slopes, and noble chunar trees: under one of which leafy monsters, my humble tent, a little thing just containing my bed, is pitched.

Ahmet Shah and the kotwal came all the way from Islamabad, the former to pay his respects and make his acknowledgments for a turban I sent him from the Punjab, as a recognition of his great civility and attention last year. He brought me a beautiful cock pheasant alive, one of the Meynahl: he had been caught about a month, so I hope he may live. I should like to take some of these birds home and naturalize them; they would be highly prized. They may be called a link between the pea-fowl and the pheasant. They have a delicate top knot, and their colour is the most brilliant deep blue, rifle-green, and bronze, of glossy and metallic sheen. The tail is plain buff; there he falls off in plumage. He is much larger than the English bird. He is to be put in a cage, and kept for me till I return to the Punjab.

There is a thunder-storm, and rain now falling—a bore for my retinue, who have but a leafy canopy over them: but they have lots of covering. I purchased my three servants each a warm Cashmere blanket yesterday, four rupees each, rather a heavy pull as I had, previous to leaving Amritsir, given each of them a warm suit. But, poor chaps, they will have to rough it in the Wurdwan snows, so some additional warm wrapper is necessary.

I am snug in my little canvas nutshell, though without room to turn round. I have now, to my surprise, brought up my diary to this date, and feel as if I could stick to it. To-morrow is my birthday: what a crowd of thoughts arise and connect themselves with it!

12th May. Nah-bugh. We arrived here at a quarter to nine, having in the earlier portion of the journey passed through a beautiful country.

The path led along the slopes of some hills of moderate height, well-wooded and, here and there, opening out into smooth lawns; the woods were full of blossoms, a white clematis very plentiful and full of flower. The trees and shrubs, in their character and distribution, and indeed the whole scene, strongly resembled an extensive shrubbery or wilderness, intended to look wild and natural, such as we see in the domains of the wealthy in Old England. And to strengthen the resemblance, the well-remembered voice of the cuckoo resounded over hill and dale, and one remained perched on a tree near enough to be distinctly observed. Other birds were singing lustily: among them the blackbird's sweet melody was plainly distinguished. It is, I believe, the same bird, and sings the same notes as the English bird. The cuckoo, also, is precisely similar to our welcome spring visitor, and, curious enough, the Cashmiries also call him 'cuckoo.'

How pleasant it was to traverse these lovely glades, lifting the eyes from which, mountain ranges presented themselves, the more distant rugged and bleak, and covered with snow, those nearer displaying their many diverging slopes in multiplied ramifications, some open and grassy, others with nearly all the ridges covered with pine forests, with which other trees mingling agreeably contrasted their diverse colours.

I must not forget to note that this my birth-day was ushered in by a real May morning, much such in temperature as the finest and brightest in England would be; and abundance of May, the thorn being in full blossom, adorned and perfumed the way side. There was also white clover, and a veritable bumble-bee, with the same portly person and drab coloured behind as the common English one. The banks, also, sported their violets, but, alas! without fragrance, and the wild strawberry was peeping out of the bushes and grass all around. Who could fail to exult in exuberance of spirits, thus surrounded by nature's choicest beauties? Certainly not I. Rejoicing, and buoyant with vigorous health, my mind undisturbed, having a long holiday before me, and feeling within me the ability and taste, fresh and capable as ever of old, to appreciate and enjoy the blessings of Providence so amply vouchsafed me, I felt my whole being full to overflowing of joy, admiration, gratitude, and praise. I gave myself up to reflections suitable to the day—

—Was interrupted by the shikarries rushing into my tent, to apprise me of the arrival of another saheb with shikarries and guns. They were in great excitement, in consequence of the probability of the new comer interfering with their plans for my shooting operations, by occupying the localities they desired to hunt. I had, as usual, given notice of my intention to rest here to-morrow, Sunday. The shikarries tried to shake this resolve by pointing out the advantages to be gained by pushing on, and getting first into the Wurdwan valley; but I was proof against such arguments.

The dreaded stranger proved to be an officer of the 79th from Lahore, on two months' leave. I asked him to dinner, and fortunately, in addition to my usual stew, had a rice pudding, to which I added guava jelly; a rich plumcake brought up the rear. These solids, with a glass or two of very fair sherry, was quite a feast in these wild regions, and my luxurious habits astonished my sporting companion; to whom, to save my character, I revealed that it was my birthday, and repeated my friend D— —'s quaint apology for an unusual extravagance, "Sure, and it isn't every day that Shamus kills a bullock."

My guest informed me that he had just missed two shots at bara sing near the village, the coolies having given him information of four or five of those animals having crossed their path. He intended going further to day, but I believe has halted for the night. He told me the spot in the Wurdwan he is making for, which my shikarries tell me is out of our beat; so all is serene, except the weather—a heavy thunder-shower, and more coming—the sky unsettled.

This is a charming bivouac, my camp by a village, on a level spot of turf shaded by walnut trees. Below, in a cultivated valley, runs an inconsiderable river, divided into many channels. The stream runs towards the South, the valley of its formation disappearing in the distance, as shut in gradually by a succession of hills, prolongations of the spurs of the mountains. But a considerable extent of the valley is visible, and forms a lovely landscape. I strolled out after dinner, and remained gazing over its charms, till dusk warned me to return. I then sat outside reading by the light of my lantern, an honest stable utensil, broken in upon by a consultation with my shikarries, who are in good spirits, and anticipate great sport.

An aspiration to heaven, a thought to home, and my birth-day, my forty-second is ended. What may not happen ere I see another—should such be the will of God!

13th May. Sunday. Nah-bugh. Rain continued to pour all day. I was visited, however, by the lumbadar of Eish Mackahm whose acquaintance I made last year, and the jolly, lusty-looking individual, hearing of my arrival at Islamabad, had come three days' journey to see me, bringing as a propitiatory 'nuzzur,' some of his cakes of bread, which I had formerly commended, and two jars of delicious honey. My stout friend is by no means loquacious, and is blind of one eye; but with the other he steadily contemplated me, appearing to receive much inward satisfaction therefrom.

He brought with him, and introduced, a renowned shikarry, a fine-looking middle-aged man, who said he was desirous of an interview, as he had heard so much of my character as a hunter. It is true that in this country it needs but small exploits to win fame, so expansive is rumour, the inhabitants delighting in tattle, and magnifying their consequence by exalting the performances and success of the saheb they attend in the chase. But I suspect my sporting visitor had other views, more interested—perhaps, hoping for employment. I was really pleased to see the 'lumbadar,' who was most civil and obliging last year. He was detained by the continued rain, so I gave orders for the due entertainment of himself and followers, who found suitable accommodation in the village.

14th May. We moved on towards the Wurdwan, the path leading up the Nah-bugh valley, which gradually narrowed, cultivation appearing only at intervals, until it ceased altogether, as the valley became transformed into a wild, rugged ravine, shut in by steep and lofty hills, dotted with firs. We advanced to the foot of the pass, nearly to the snow, and there encamped.

I went out in the afternoon to look for game, and ascended some steep hills, very hard work; having traversed much ground without seeing anything, I sat down, peering from an eminence, down on the slopes below, like an eagle from his eyrie. One of the shikarries went a little further on, and shortly gave notice of game in view: we rapidly closed with him, and learned that a bear with two cubs were in the adjoining ravine.

Away, in pursuit—we sighted the chase, who were moving quickly away, here and there grubbing, routing, and feeding, as is the wont of these creatures. Over very rough ground we climbed, and scrambled; and descended to the bed of the ravine. The Bruin family, still going ahead, were concealed by a projecting ledge of rock, to which we hurried; and from the fall of stones down the hill on the other side the rock, we knew that we were close on our game. We turned the angle, and saw B. junior peeping. He did not see us; but a step or two further and B. major's acute nasal perceptions indicated danger; so, giving office to the young uns, off scuttled the trio at a good round pace up the hill. There was no time to lose, so rapidly aiming at the old bear, I struck her hard somewhere in the back; but, after stumbling and uttering a fierce growl, she went on, but was again descried, when I fired the second barrel ineffectually, then loaded and pursued up hill. The chase was soon in view, labouring heavily. We got to the top of the hill, and a few paces down the declivity was B. major alone, standing. Hearing her pursuers, she shuffled on, when I fired and brought her down, finishing her with another barrel.

Leaving men to take the skin, we went after the Meynahl pheasants, some of which had been seen; and after trying in vain to get within shot of these beautiful birds, we descended the hill, and when near the bottom, the leading shikarry suddenly stopped, and directed me to prepare for action. I, supposing a Meynahl pheasant to be the object, took the double gun, but was told to change, and, following the direction of the shikarry, saw the great ugly head of a large bear, protruding from the bushes—only the head visible. I fired the single Whitworth, but ineffectually. The animal was about fifty yards off only, and I found the sight at two hundred yards, which accounted for the ball passing over his head. He hastened rapidly out of danger. Then we returned to camp.

15th May. Up and away, to mount the pass leading into the Wurdwan. It was laborious climbing, but after some half-dozen pauses, I reached the summit—glorious scenery all around, and a magnificent backward and downward view into the valley of Cashmere, passing over which the eye rested on the Pir Panjal range, which formed a fitting background to so splendid a picture. There was an extensive tract of snow to traverse, leading with a slight downward slope into the Wurdwan, which soon was partly indicated, rather than revealed, by the system of snowy mountains.

I had two shots with the Whitworth at a small animal, the natives call 'drin,' which I suppose from its habits to be the marmot. It is of a dark red-brown, burrows, sits on a stone close to its hole, and chatters. The little animal was about one hundred and twenty yards from me: the first bullet passed about an inch over it. It soon took up the same position again, and the second missile struck the stone close under it; so that the fragments must have struck him. He made a precipitate dive, and we saw no more of him.

I halted to breakfast; then pushed on, the path a tolerable one, following the windings of the hills on whose sides it hung—the scenery wild, and romantic, and full of interest. We crossed many ravines and snowdrifts. We met two coolies who had accompanied my late guest of the 79th, returning: they informed the shikarries that the saheb had not gone down the valley, but up to the ground that we had hoped to secure. Wrath of shikarries excessive—unmeasured abuse heaped upon conflicting party—all sorts of plans of retaliation suggested, and appeals made to me to exercise the authority of my superior rank and order the offender back. I took it all very quietly, and succeeded not only in calming the angry men, but put them in good humour by suggesting various problematical advantages to be derived from the presence of the other party.

We came at length—and really at length, for it was a long stretch—in view of the Wurdwan, the valley opening out many thousand feet below, two or three small villages with their clustering hovels and irregular patches of cultivation shewing themselves. A rapid stream, of dimensions and volume claiming, perhaps, to be styled a river, was brawling and fighting its way against innumerable obstacles and impediments down the vale. A very steep winding path brought us down to its banks, and instead of crossing over to the village of Ainshin, as we should have done, had it not been already in possession of a hostile party, we moved along the right bank upwards.

We went on some two or three miles to a village, where it was proposed to camp, but received information here that the other saheb had taken up position in a village just opposite,—indeed we saw his coolies arrive there—and had gone up the mountain, where four or five shots had been heard in rapid succession. Great jabber among the shikarries.

I thought over the matter, and did not like to submit to be jockeyed and out-manœuvred in such an underhand way; so, although we had already completed a very long and toilsome march, and the baggage must be far in the rear, I determined to make a forward movement, and turning the enemy's flank, take up position in front of him, on his line of march. The shikarries were full of glee at the idea of the long faces of the contending ones, when they should find themselves outwitted.

We procured half-a-dozen fresh hands from the village, sent them to the rear to assist in bringing up the baggage, and then moved onwards; and, having gained some three miles, crossed the river by an ingenious bridge of some forty yards span, a considerable body of water of some depth rushing below, and took post at the village of Ofith, across the enemy's route, and securing possession of the Kuzuznai valley, whose overhanging cliffs are famous for ibex. The village is situated in the very mouth of the valley, the position, therefore, admirable.

Heavy rain coming on, I got to leeward of a big tree, and in the course of two or three hours had the satisfaction of seeing my three personal attendants coming up, along the left side of the river. They had passed through the enemy's camp, their appearance producing consternation and serious enquiries as to where their saheb was, and where he was going to. The enquiring shikarry was informed that their saheb was not going to be done, but they did not know where he would stop, most likely in the best place. Expressions of astonishment at the length of our march, and ill-concealed signs of disappointment and defeat, on the part of shikarry, who threatened to give us the 'go-by' yet. Much merriment at this recital among my forces. Notwithstanding the (I should think) twenty-four miles rough march, I started off to hunt, information of the habitat of bears in the vicinity having been given. There were only about two hours of daylight before us; we recrossed the river, and two 'bara sing' were descried by the keen-sighted Subhan, feeding high up on a hill side. Pursuit was resolved—up a snow drift in a ravine, then up the steep side of the hill, crawling with hands and feet, literally clinging to the side of the hill. We made observations near the crest of this spur—the animals on the 'qui vive,' looking out, standing on a superior ridge. We paused, while a practicable route was sought for: then climbed onwards to more level ground, and saw the game, now three in number on the opposite height, perhaps three hundred yards off, but could not be sure, as there were boughs intervening. We tried for a better position, but our prey, declining nearer intimacy, absconded, and left us looking ruefully at each other, with a nasty descent before us.

I got down safe, and on reaching camp found all my things safely arrived, and dinner ready:—turned in, hopeful for the following day's sport.

CHAPTER IV.

SHIKAR IN THE WURDWAN.

16th May. Off up the Wurdwan, not the Kuzuznai, the shikarries reserving that.

We had a tremendous climb ere we even looked about for game, two hours, I should think, of exhausting efforts. I wore grass sandals, or could not have kept my footing. Subhan, the leader, the younger of my three shikarries, with astonishing acuteness of vision, at last suddenly dropped to game, and pointed out several bara sing feeding together. They were in a spot most difficult of approach without discovery; and these creatures at this season are wonderfully wary. There were no sheltering timbers under which stealthily to steal upon our prey. However, after consultation, leaving three attendants to remain behind in concealment, we climbed upwards, hoping to find covering ground, but had to stop, as we could not but discover ourselves. Here some of the deer were seen to lie down, one only standing, and great hopes were entertained of a successful stalk.

Two other deer came into view higher up the mountain. We remained still, watching about an hour, when a backward movement, and then further ascent was determined on. As we turned about on our sides to move off, two does, that were close upon us in the rear, dashed off and away down hill, but without any sensible effect upon our hopes. It was a most arduous struggle up the hill side, slippery with hoar frost, and fearfully steep. With extreme difficulty we reached a narrow ledge, on which we all four could just cling, some one way, some another—a giddy height—when, to our infinite disgust, we saw the three attendants moving out below. All sorts of signs and gesticulations were made to stay them, but on they blundered. I had yesterday pointed out to the shikarries the folly of having these followers, as, forming with us a long line when ascending or crossing a hill, *we* no sooner pass out of sight, than *they* come into view; so that any animal getting a glimpse of us, and regarding the spot from which we have passed, sees the followers coming across the same place, and, of course, decamps. I had tried to impress the importance of this simple fact upon them; but they are so wedded to their own habits, and trust so entirely to luck, rather than skill, in approaching game that, though acknowledging the force of my observations, they did not act upon them.

At last this blundering train, looking upwards, saw our impatient gestures, and, mistaking their meaning, only quickened their pace. At length they did understand, and lay down.

We now descended, and crossed the face of the hill towards the deer. We discerned them now afoot, leisurely moving upwards, and cropping the fresh grass that came in their way. They were in a favourable place to approach now: but we had to be cautious, and keep out of sight. We moved with studied step, and reached the position from which we expected to open fire—nothing visible: we thought the prey probably behind some of the many inequalities of ground, peered everywhere, and shifted position, till the whole ground was closely scanned; but no game. They might have gently crossed the hill feeding: but no, they were clean gone.

A misgiving now struck me, and, looking back, there were the abominable coolies plodding contentedly on. They had moved, when we descended, and came right out in sight of the deer which, of course, they had completely scared away.

In this unsuccessful chase we crossed some fearful places, the most difficult being sloping masses of snow overlaying precipices, yawning for the unlucky wight whose feet might slip. I gave up the attempt to cross these unaided, after one narrow escape, having slipped and fallen, but fortunately recovered myself. The mode of crossing was by digging holes in the snow for the foot to cling to, as we slowly progressed. It was, without exaggeration, imminently hazardous, and I must own to have been unnerved more than once.

I breakfasted, and lay down to wait until afternoon, when the animals, having reposed in some inaccessible lair during the day, again come forth, out into the grassy slopes, to feed.

Subhan, the ever quick-sighted, espied two bara sing far distant and below us: the spy glass confirmed his vision. The plan of operations decided upon, we made our approaches over easier ground, being now lower down, yet some thousands of feet high, and gained a rising ground overlooking the place in which the animals had been seen feeding. We could not see them now, but saw a large stag high up above us, quite out of hope. We remained long watching, and saw nothing, so descended to move nearer, under the impression that the deer had gone lower down the hollow; making for the edge of which, we became suddenly conscious of the presence of our game, who had been all the time in front of our late position, concealed by the rising ground. One, a fine doe, turned round, pausing, and presenting a broadside, hurriedly I grasped a rifle, put up a sight, and fired, only to miss. The affrighted animal, giving a prodigious bound, hurried after the others up the hill, pausing and turning, now and again, to gaze back upon their intruders. I put the Whitworth up, once or twice, but forbore to fire.

This great disappointment resulted from a mistake on the part of Subhan who, in his eagerness, did not exercise his usual cautious approach, reconnoitring all around, but advanced direct on the point where he thought to find the game. Following them, we came to a deep ravine, forbidding further advance in that direction: the chasm, coming down from the summit of the mountain, widening as it descended, defied, I thought, any efforts of mine.

A violent shower of rain coming on, compelled us to seek shelter, such as we could find. The shikarries, all three, tried to screen themselves behind a large fir: I got capital shelter to leeward of a fallen pine, whose massive roots, upturned with the earth about them, afforded good covert. I was about twenty yards from the shikarries who suddenly all jumped up, calling out to me, "Saheb, Saheb," and rushed, terror stricken, each, gun in hand, to me for refuge, and squatted down, cowering and exclaiming, "Balloo, Balloo,"—the bear, the bear—pointing to the tree from which they had just bolted. I had already ordered them to be quiet and give me a gun, all of which they grasped, and, in their terror, made no effort to uncover; so that had Bruin, who shewed his ugly countenance, come right on, straight at us, he would have found us unprepared. But, catching a sight of my face, he altered his course, and, sheering off, rushed by us some fifty yards below. I hastily fired at him, but without effect.

He was a very large bear. It is quite unaccountable, this attack of his. He was close on the shikarries, before they were aware of him. He came up the hill on the top of which their tree grew: they fled precipitately shouting, as I have said, their countenances exhibiting the utmost terror. The brute, also, gave a fierce roar, which certainly would lead one to think him bent on mischief. But there are few instances of their being the aggressors, I believe: so Bruin's intentions must ever remain a mystery. If, annoyed by the storm, and finding human beings in his way as he rushed blindly on, he instinctively held on his course, and uttered his angry threats, simply to frighten them out of his path, which I think probable, he certainly succeeded to a marvel: for I never saw fellows in a greater funk, helplessly unnerved.

This ended the first day's hunt in the Wurdwan, when although we saw plenty of game, and three shots were expended, we had the misfortune to be unsuccessful.

17th May. Full of pleasing anticipations of success to-day from the favourable reports of game being abundant.

We went up the Kuzuznai, a narrow valley with precipitous, inaccessible cliffs on the right-hand, and grassy slopes of a steep pitch running down from the mountains on the left, abundance of snow on either hand. We met a native, whose replies, when interrogated as to game, I judged from what I could gather to be rather discouraging. After having advanced two or three miles from Ofith, we reached a small farm, a couple of log houses—all the dwellings in this valley are of the same description, rough log houses roofed with slabs of timber—a few patches of ploughed land, but unlimited grazing. It was here thought advisable to send back, and order up camp to be nearer the shooting, which was done accordingly.

A bear was seen in a hollow on the left hand. We went after him, but if there before, he was no where visible, when we had climbed up to greet him; so we descended, and pursued our way up the narrow valley, crossing repeatedly large masses of snow, much of which had accumulated by downward drifts, and some by slips from the overhanging mountains.

It was in this very valley that, some few years ago, Dr. Rae and five native attendants were overwhelmed and swept to destruction by an avalanche; among the number was the brother of my shikarry, Phuttoo who himself, with an officer of the 87th R.I.F., narrowly escaped perishing also, by rushing forward as the great mass swept down with resistless force—thus avoiding the fate of the less fortunate, whose bodies remained buried under the superincumbent mass for many months, in spite of great exertions made by large bodies of labourers to exhume them.

Whilst I am writing in my tent, thundering sounds of falling masses of snow are audible now and then, and, looking out, I see the 'debris' falling down the cliffs opposite. It is grand and imposing.

We wended on our toilsome way, struggling across snow, and gradually ascending. Presently we descried a bear ahead, soon after another, both feeding on the slopes. We endeavoured to get at them, but whether they got wind of us, or what not, is matter for imagination, but we only arrived to see each successively leisurely taking his way up the mountain.

We had now come to the end of our beat in this direction, further progress being forbidden by the snows: so we descended, and took possession of a mass of rock, isolated in an extensive tract of snow, filling the valley from side to side. Here we breakfasted.

Rain came on. I wrapped myself in my 'choga,' warm Cashmere over coat, and lay down, falling into a disturbed and restless sleep, every now and then waking from the rain on my face, rapidly getting wet through, and this in the midst of snow. At length up got Subhan, who with the others had been sitting closely wrapped up in their blankets over a fire they had contrived to light, and proposed that I should remove below the rock. I had previously asked him, if there was no better place to put the guns than on the rock, and he had answered 'No'; so, surprised at this proposal, I followed him, and found a comparatively comfortable habitation formed by the projecting ledge of this massive rock, in which, late in the season, lambs are sheltered. There, in much hampered attitudes, the height being only three or four feet, and the floor formed of large pieces of rock that had fallen down, I endeavoured to make the best of things. A small fire, the space only admitting of a very small one, was lighted, and thereat we tried to warm our chilled limbs, and dry our dripping clothes. I had no idea that I could endure so much smoke: I sat right in the middle of it, there being no help for it. I chatted with the shikarries, who related anecdotes of the sahebs with whom they had hunted before. After a time they went to sleep, some sitting on the snow, others lying on the pieces of stone. The rain poured. I should have been quite dry, had I only come here at first: however, with an occasional shudder, more, I believe, from the knowledge that my outer garment was wet, and the extremely dismal effect of the combination of rain and snow without—dense clouds, too, actually enfolding us at this elevation, probably 15,000 feet—I bore up cheerily.

I was at length left to myself, the shikarries preferring the larger fire outside, on the top of the rock, though exposed to wind and rain, to the small amount of caloric derivable from my few embers. I stirred up my fire occasionally, and sat, thinking and thinking, guiding my thoughts to pleasant subjects and agreeable recollections as much as possible, until I felt not only quite contented, but even disinclined to move. Thus I passed the time from 10 A.M. till 5 P.M.

At that hour Subhan came to me, and said it had cleared up, and I should be better above. I obeyed. The clouds were still heavy and lowering, shifting up and down, breaking and allowing us occasional and most welcome glimpses of the sun, or rather, sunshine. The effect was striking and grand in the extreme. This rugged, wild gorge enveloped in ever-shifting, varying vapours of different degrees of density—now one peak visible, but to be obscured, and another to be ushered on the scene—it appeared as if all above was commotion, silent commotion, the clouds and mountain-summits playing at hide and seek.

We took a final warm at the fire: I threw off my overcoat, and, shivering in my scanty shooting dress, started off over the tract of snow campwards, the shikarries ever looking about for game.

We had advanced within a mile or two of the new site for the bivouac, when Mooktoo, this time, who was in his usual place behind me, exclaimed that animals were in sight. The spyglass was put in request, and sure enough, said Subhan, there were some ten or twelve keyl (ibex) disporting themselves on a distant mountain. It was long ere I caught sight of them, looking at the wrong place. But at last I did see them plainly: two were rearing up on their hind legs, fighting.

Well—we sat there hopelessly gazing, until the snow, on which we were squatting, produced the natural effect, and, penetrating my frame, set my teeth chattering: so on we went, but some way further we came in sight of another flock of ibex, much nearer, though on the same mountain. They were plainly visible to the naked eye, and with the glass their horns and relative proportions were distinctly seen, and commented upon.

This was an exciting sight. "Could nothing be done?" I asked anxiously. "Nothing this evening," was the reply. So, on we trudged, I submitting patiently to the fiat, and casting many a side glance upwards, causing me many a trip and stumble in my rough path. As we came more under the mountain on which the ibex were, a change of position on their part effected a change in the minds of the shikarries who, calling a halt, held a brief consultation together. Then, their eyes sparkling with excitement, they uncovered the guns, and off we started.

I little thought, as I hastily followed the active Subhan, what work I had cut out for me. The place the ibex were in did not appear high up, nor did the ground appear very difficult from the distance; but when I began to breast it, I found out my mistake, both as to incline and altitude. I strove and struggled, scrambled and clawed my upward path, until quite breathless and exhausted, and found I was but at the very commencement of the ascent. Having gained breath, I went through the same severe efforts, to find apparently the same prospects, but with this terrible difference that, by my own exertions, I had now created a precipice below me, fearful to look upon.

Subhan now suggested giving up the attempt: but a sort of infatuated obstinacy seized me. As well as the heaving of my distressed lungs permitted, I articulated, with an upward glance, 'Go on.' Indeed, I felt at the time a sort of necessity to move upwards, in spite of all difficulties, so appalling was the aspect of the descent now necessary; so clinging to the surface, embracing, as it were, as much of the mountain as I could clasp, and helping myself occasionally with my spiked staff, I still struggled upwards, coming to bare smooth places that I thought it impossible to climb over. At times, pausing at such critical spots, I felt my head wavering, my courage waning, and my nerves unstrung, my hold relaxing, my feet slipping, and then a sort of frenzy seized me, and, summoning every energy I possessed, I recklessly dashed on, on all fours, feeling that to hesitate for one moment, to keep hand or foot a second on one spot, would inevitably plunge me into the abyss below.

The shikarries, each carrying a gun in one hand, made their way with extreme difficulty, and, I believe, not without trepidation. But they possess a clutch, and a tenacity, and adhesion of toe, peculiar to this variety of biped, which gives them firmness and confidence anywhere. It was a very different thing for me.

At length, we gained the top of this spur of the mountain, which actually offered no footing, the ridge being sharp, and the other side not only precipitous, but hollowed out. Here lying, holding on tooth and nail, we observed the ibex, which had taken the alarm, and were rapidly moving away; and even had they remained, we could not have got at them. So all our trouble, and the horrible ordeal of fear I had undergone, were utterly thrown away.

"Had we not better remain up?" I asked Phuttoo, as the evening was darkening apace. He shook his head, and said, it would never do: so without more ado, I nerved myself for the trial, and got down by slow degrees, wondering how I ever succeeded in getting up.

I felt thankful for my safe return, and rejoiced at the sight of my tent, and a blazing fire before it, cheerfully lighting up the surrounding gloom: changed my dress—and that reminds me, that I have forgotten to note the presence in the herbage on these mountains of a most disagreeable insect, a species of tick or bug: the vile thing abounds, and seems to be ever on the look out for creatures passing by, for we were quite tormented by them. I have picked off a dozen at a time from my dress. They bite sharp, working their heads into your flesh, and there hooking on with their forceps. I, with much trouble, and no little smarting, detached three thus adhering to my person this evening, and many candidates for the same honours were discovered trespassing on my premises—a murrain on them!

I enjoyed my dinner amazingly, the fright I had been in having, perhaps, stimulated my appetite. I realized the sensation, that to be alive, with a good appetite, and a savoury stew for its gratification, was vastly preferable to being a mangled mass of senseless humanity at the foot of a precipice, with ever so many big horned ibex at top. It was so late that I turned in very soon after dinner, and had some apprehensions of a disagreeable night, perhaps visitations of night-mare, repeating in my dreams the horrors of that terrible ascent, and waking up with that horrid, indescribable feeling experienced when one dreams one is precipitated from a great height, and whirling downwards, awake to find it is all a dream.

However, I slept well, awaking occasionally, when I heard it raining hard, and rejoiced, hoping it would continue, as I felt that a day's rest would be beneficial, my feet having been considerably chafed by all the scratching and clawing they had been put to.

18th May. I lay in bed later than usual, intentionally, not at once obeying the call of the clamorous cock, or the blithely-singing birds, who begin their concert in these parts ere day-light does appear. When, however, day-light unmistakably forced its appearance under my tent, I up and dressed in shooting trim, resolute to tackle the mountain, however steep, and pursue the ibex anywhere and everywhere. Such was the effect of a good night's rest: so, summoning the drowsy classee, Buddoo, to throw open the closely folded entrance, I went outside, and found there a most unpromising morning, the mountains frowning grimly down, when occasionally visible through dense, chill-looking masses of fog, snow all over the heights, damp, slop, and general discomfort everywhere. Nature, however grand in features, looked uninviting and repulsive.

I looked abroad, and shuddered at the prospect of breasting the hill side. Phuttoo came shivering towards me, and, making his salaam, told me we must not attempt the mountain in such weather. Quite satisfied with asking him, if such was really his advice, and being answered in the affirmative, I ordered Buddoo to close the tent, and pulled the blankets over me, really congratulating myself on being prevented fulfilling my desires and intentions.

19th May. The rain having fallen heavily during the night, the atmosphere, at the early hour in which I rose and peeped out of my tent, was laden with dense vapours which, heaving and swelling, moved up and down the valley, now revealing, now concealing portions of its bold features, and altogether creating a strikingly impressive and interesting effect on the beautiful, though rugged, scenery. The clouds of vapour, after an apparently internal struggle, would transform themselves into transparent draperies of varied form and strength of light—the rays of the rising sun struggling with the misty impediments to the general diffusion of his genial beams, here and there penetrating through them, then anon repulsed and excluded—when the curtain, as it were, dropped over the scene, and chill gloom again reigned around. The lower ranges of the mountains, which yesterday were free from snow, were now shrouded in its white mantle, what was rain below, falling as snow above; in consequence of which the ibex haunts were pronounced quite impracticable for the present. So I patiently awaited the favourable time, and rested quite satisfied in gazing on and admiring the ever-changing, and always beautiful, natural effects developing themselves around me, until breakfast; after which the shikarries came, and shouldering the guns, the hour being now propitious, we directed our steps for the mountain on which we had lately discovered the ibex.

This time we ascended by the opposite side to the very summit of the mountain, our path lying nearly the whole distance over a snow-drift filling a ravine, down which, under the snow, rushed a roaring torrent, appearing at intervals of the ascent, where from sudden vertical descents it dashed down in foaming cascades, flashing, sparkling, glittering in open day for a moment, again to go muttering and rumbling under the super-incumbent masses of snow, again to gain partial freedom, until undergoing various similar alternations it emerged into the main torrent that, pursuing its troubled course down this small valley, adds its tributary waters to the Wurdwan river.

Many fissures were crossed, disclosing the dark waters seething and hurtling below; and the whole struggle to the heights above, although perhaps not so arduous or dangerous as that of the previous day, was yet full of peril, and called for a stout heart and firm nerves to achieve. The most difficult and critical times were when, the course of the torrent making a rapid and regular turn and deep fall, it was necessary to leave the snow, ascend the bank, and make one's way along the smooth, wet, precipitous escarpment overhanging the fearful depths below, on which it would not do to look or think. A lesser evil was the terrible, blinding glare, reflected by the intensely white snow through which we ploughed. This, after a time, compelled me to close my eyes, and go floundering on, the best way I could, with an occasional squint to ascertain whether I was following my leader. At length we accomplished the ascent, and glad I was to sit down, and recruit my somewhat exhausted energies.

The shikarries, reconnoitring, discovered ibex far down, below us, among the rifts and gorges into which the mountain, near its base, is severed. They were near the spot where they were first descried. After the usual consultation, the 'bunderbus' was determined, and a descent towards the game commenced. We had to cross patches of snow at a fearful degree of incline, and let ourselves down lying on our sides or backs, scotching ourselves with heels or staves as best we might, until we gained a shelf midway down, whence observations were again made, and plans concocted. A halt was here made, as the animals were not in sight, being, it was supposed, now taking their 'siesta' in some secure retirement. A watch was kept; and at length a shikarry, holding up one finger, indicated one animal having made his appearance, then two, then three, until they numbered five—the very five fine-horned fellows seen the other day, and so much coveted.

Again the stalk was resumed with all guile and subtlety: but, in spite of every precaution, in such extremely difficult and dangerous ground some sounds would arise—a stone loosened, rolling down &c.—though we were well out of sight, nor on the same slope. We at last reached the crest of a slope, on the other side of which were the ibex within easy range, as was supposed. Cautiously, rifles ready, we slowly raised our heads to sight the intended victims—higher and higher, this side and that—but only a blank.

Deep sighs of disappointment were audible. Every height was scrutinized, every hollow peered into, before the sad reality was fully admitted, that our prey had escaped, and without leaving a clue to their mode of exit. We sat disconsolate, and while wistfully gazing about saw a string of nine ibex calmly pursuing their way, taking a bite here and there on a mountain side opposite. Soon after, four or five cross a ravine on the snow far up above us; which I believe to have been the identical animals we were in search of, who had completely outwitted us, and gained an inaccessible refuge without our detecting them stealing away—so closely had we kept our concealment.

It was not the most satisfactory prospect having to return and descend, every step risking life or limb. We had to reclimb the summit, and again descend, the path full of peril as before. When halfway, two young ibex were disturbed, and I ineffectually fired every barrel I had, as they bounded away. The suddenness of their appearance, and the nature of the ground giving me no footing, made my chances 'nil.'

I got back weary, and had unfortunately reproduced an old injury by my slips and strenuous efforts to keep my footing, a large lump from some overtaxed muscle having formed immediately behind my right knee, giving no acute pain, but a sense of diminished strength, and a sensation that it would become worse.

20th May. Sunday. After breakfast, a lad, one of the valley, who accompanied us yesterday, found his way to me when unobserved by the shikarries, and criticised their method of approaching game, of which he disapproved. Having observed him to be active and intelligent, and knowing that he had been hunting with officers, I talked with him, and finally arranged for another attempt on the ibex, he leading and to have the entire control and management of the arrangements. He was much gratified. Anticipating jealousy, and, perhaps, obstruction on the part of my shikarries, I assembled them, and put the matter in such a light that they entered into the plan with perfect good humour.

21st May. Away under the auspices of the ambitious young Kamal to the same mountain, to ascend by the same route. Ere reaching the base, we observed three ibex on a snowy crest, I believe keeping watch and ward. We had not ascended far, when Kamal, all ardour and vigilance, leading the way, stopped suddenly, and announced ibex in sight, and near at hand. We prepared to attack. Leaving one of our number at this place, we set to work to climb, the ordinary difficulties being greatly augmented by a quantity of hail lying on the surface, and by a frost having made the grass, which had been wet with rain or melted snow, terribly slippery.

As I toiled and struggled in agonies of partial suffocation from my exertions up the steep, a bear was reported in sight. I did not take notice of the ignoble beast, being then in hot chase of the much-coveted ibex, but was suddenly startled by a fierce growl, and saw Bruin rushing by, within a few yards. But I would not have fired in the attitude I was in, had the rifle been in my hand. We shortly got sight of an ibex on the look-out, on a prominent point affording a good view around. We lay still some time: the ibex fed, then quietly walked out of sight; when believing it was all as we could wish, we made what speed we could up the mountain to the look-out place of the sentinel. We could thence see nothing: so ascended higher, on to a place where the game must be, had they not taken alarm and fled. Every probable place was examined—but no occupants. At last we saw nine ibex on the summit of an adjoining eminence, far out of reach, and they leisurely making their retreat still further. Whether the beast of a bear had given the alarm, we could not tell.

We descended, and took our former route. A small goat-like deer, called a 'kustoora,' was seen. We stalked up to within eighty yards, the animal up above and looking down. I changed my rifle for one carried by Mooktoo, the right barrel of which he had loaded this morning, so I thought it was sure to go off: the other had been loaded since Saturday. I aimed steadily—the cap only exploded—the animal bounded off, stopped, and gazed: I pulled the other trigger, when the powder went off hissing, fizzing, and smoking like a squib, and the bullet dropped about a yard from the muzzle. I suppose some snow had got into it. This was a dreadful disappointment.

After breakfast we proceeded up among the snowy summits: we saw nothing, lay down, and went to sleep. Then on again to another point, and again stopped for observations: then we began to descend, pausing here and there, but not a vestige of an ibex to be seen: all had vanished, I scanned every possible spot with the glass, but saw none, so gave up all hopes of ibex, and later in the day descended to look for bears on the lower slopes.

Kamal, away on the left, made signs of game, an old and a young bear down in a deep hollow. I got into position, and fired down, wounding the old bear: fired all my remaining barrels as she made off: then loaded, and off in pursuit—rugged ground, and two deep awkward ravines to cross. At last we sighted the chase, slowly crawling ahead, but a difficult ravine between us. We crossed it, and up the hill to intercept Bruin, but paused on the brink of a precipitous and impassable ravine. Subhan's keen eyes detected the bear pausing on a ledge, partially concealed by a bush. She half-turned to look back on her pursuers, when a ball struck her, and she toppled over, rolling down the hill-side. We had to make a considerable detour to get to her:—looked for others in vain, so returned to camp.

It is supposed by the shikarries that a pack of wild dogs, whose tracks we found in the snow following on those of ibex, had driven those animals away.

22nd May. A long march up the Wurdwan. We passed Busman on the left-bank, crossed the river by a bridge at Goombrah—at which village my sporting rival of the 79th had bivouacked—and moved along the bank to a small village. We saw three bears feeding on a hill-side across the river. It was decided to stop here, and try to get these bears: so we halted. But Phuttoo failing to persuade the villagers to rebuild a bridge which had been washed away, and being unable to cross the river at any place nearer, we continued our route to our previous destination, Shugkenuz.

The road lay along the bank of the river which had fallen in, so that we experienced much difficulty in getting on, the steep inaccessible hill precluding all chance of a route higher up: so, hanging on how we might, we scrambled across the face of the landslip, the rapid river rushing roaring below, and luckily without mishap reached and crossed a bridge, and on to the village, which is prettily situated—the bivouac charming.

A mountain path from Palgham enters the Wurdwan here, but is impracticable now for all but mountaineers. We rested some hours; then went off to beat up the quarters of the three bears we had seen from the opposite side when on the march. We sighted our three acquaintances high up on a rock; prepared to meet them on the slope we supposed they would descend to; had a difficult, fatiguing climb. At last we gained a ridge from which the game was visible, all three feeding, distance about one hundred yards. I wished to wait for a chance of their coming nearer; but Subhan urged me to fire at once, and the largest bear, mother of the other two, I suppose, then looking up, I fired and hit her somewhere in front. Great confusion and discomfiture ensued. I fired and hit another, and discharged my other barrels as they slowly retreated; but, not being able to pursue from the difficulty of the ground, saw my wounded prey gradually disappear up the hill, just able to crawl away.

I returned to camp, weary and lame. Regretting much wounding poor brutes thus, to escape only to die in agonies, I made some half-resolutions to give up shooting.

Leg very bad, but not worse, I went to bed lamenting my ill success.

CHAPTER V.

SHIKAR IN THE WURDWAN.

23rd May. Ere thoroughly awakened this morning, I enjoyed pleasing fancies in a confused doze, under the influence of the soft notes of a cuckoo perched on a tree immediately over my head, whence he sweetly serenaded me, or rather treated me to a morning solo; which, though a monotonous performance, touched many a sympathetic and vibrating chord within, creating delicious harmonies, recalling old memories—the open window, dewy mornings, fresh summer-perfumed air, the welcome ringing of old Jonas' sharpening scythe, which operation has a remarkable charm for me, I suppose as essentially characteristic of summer seasons, and associated with the inhaled fragrance of new-mown hay, added to many a mingled note of thrush, linnet, and blackbird and other feathered songsters.

Often, on such mornings, did the dear old man, according to agreement, lightly cast up gravel at my window to arouse me to be up and after my night-lines. Oh, happy memories!—The scythe of time has now done its work upon him, and gathered to the harvest one of the dearest associates of my youthful days: but there is another youth to come, an everlasting youth, to be enjoyed in an eternal spring—Oh! may we be there reunited, this humble follower, and all to whom my heart tenderly yearns!

I made up some accounts, and paid sundry monies, wrote instructions to the Baboo, and despatched a messenger therewith, and, in the afternoon, went forth to hunt. A bear was in sight high up on the mountain which shelters the small cluster of huts constituting the village. He was reported to be a continual visitor to the same green spot. The climb was anything but inviting to a limping cripple; and the place looked so bare and unapproachable, that I felt convinced we should not succeed, and so assured the shikarries. But still we made the attempt, and, after a very fatiguing hour's ascent, had the poor reward of seeing the wary Bruin making off. But, uncertain as to the quarter whence the suspected danger threatened, he paused on the hill opposite to us, and we lay a long time hoping he would again descend to feed; which at last we thought he really had done, and so cautiously crawled to a shooting position. But Bruin had only concealed himself in order to unmask his enemies, as it would appear; for he displayed his person in the same place, and then sat partially concealed by boughs. At last, seeing no probable change in our relative positions, I fired Whitworth, the bolt passing close beneath his stomach, also the other rifle without effect, the distance some three hundred yards. Bruin losing patience at this repeated annoyance, quietly jogged off up hill, and disappeared over the summit.

We descended much more rapidly than we came up. Getting upon a snow drift, we ran and slid down merrily, and continued our hunt along the base of a range; and Subhan and a villager, who had gone to reconnoitre, declaring they saw a bear in a spot indicated, we proceeded to make his acquaintance, and after much toil found no trace of living creature, so concluded our informants to have mistaken a stone for a bear, an error the keenest-sighted are liable to.

24th May. Away in another direction up the valley. We soon saw two bears across the river moving ahead along the slope of the opposite hill. We crossed the river by a natural bridge of snow. One of the bears crossed the snow drift, up which we were pursuing our way to intercept them, about one hundred and fifty yards ahead of us. We lay still, screened by shrubs: followed on, and saw him grubbing among some bushes. I cocked the rifle, at the click of which the cautious beast became suspicious, and looked up, facing me. Thinking him about to abscond, I fired—and away he rushed, disappeared in the bushes, and we saw nothing more of him. I could not account for my failure: the shot was a fair one.

After remaining some time on the look out without seeing any game, we returned to camp to breakfast; and by the advice of the shikarries, and in order to satisfy them, I discharged all my weapons at a mark, making fair practice: but decided on reducing the charge of powder. I cheered up the shikarries, saying we would now consign to oblivion our previous failures, and make a fresh start.

In the afternoon, across the river, retracing the road we came by, we ascended the hill, and all lay down, shikarries together in whispering conversation.

Suddenly I became aware of the presence of a bear in the jungle some distance off. He appeared contemplating an approach in our direction, but, hesitating, turned into the jungle, apparently to seek an open feeding ground just visible beyond, and where we expected him. Subhan went forward to watch him, and soon beckoned us on. We overtook him, and cautiously skirted a patch of jungle, prying into it; when Bruin, suddenly emerging from behind a projecting bank, twigged us, and was off as rapidly as his awkward gait permitted. He was noticed, however, pausing some distance off in the jungle up the hill. Putting up a sight, I fired, and down he came towards us, evidently hit we thought. I fired again at a glimpse of him through a bush: after which he was seen by the shikarries slowly trudging up the hill through the snow and bushes, shaking his head from side to side, as though, at least, highly disapproving our proceedings, if not actually a severe sufferer.

Two shikarries, confident he was hit, entered the bushes to track him. Phuttoo and I remained: and presently we saw another bear a long way up the ravine scoring the mountain on whose side we were. We signalled the others to us, and then proceeded to stalk the new comer, who, however, on our raising our heads to arrange for assault and battery, had wisely disappeared; but in his place was a musk deer, 'kustoora,' which I wounded. The poor creature scrambled off, one hind leg broken. Subhan with a rifle pursued, and overtaking the chase fired both barrels at some ten yards without effect. He then got above the deer, and kept it down the hollow, the poor thing making astonishing efforts to escape; which it would have done down the valley, but for an attendant there stationed, who, being hailed, joined in the chase, and turned the animal up towards me who, by the help of two mountain staves, was descending rapidly to the scene of action, followed by Phuttoo.

At last the persecuted creature came within range, paused, and a well-aimed Whitworth bolt rolled it lifeless down the hill, to the great satisfaction of the shikarries who, shouting triumphantly, dashed down to perform the necessary Mahomedan ceremony of cutting the throat with an invocation to Allah, without which the flesh would be to them unlawful; and they entertained a shrewd idea it would become their perquisite, the rather as I had a sheep slaughtered that morning for my own consumption.

Heavy rain overtook us; but this little success cheered us up, and the prospect of a feast of flesh put the shikarries in high spirits.

25th May. Off in the direction taken the first evening, when I fired with such ill success. We did not catch a glimpse of a bear now, though on that occasion we saw five.

In the evening, we went up the valley, and having met a pedlar merchant, and three coolies with his goods coming down we considered it of no use going on, so returned. I had some talk with these people, the ugliest imaginable. They had come from Ladâk, and described the road to be at present all but impassable from depth of snow, and do not think it will be safe for a month. We saw two bears far up a valley on the left hand, as we neared camp, and resolved to seek them the following morning.

26th May. We started as arranged, crossed the bridge, and as soon as we obtained a view into the vale were gratified by the sight of two bears quietly feeding, and in a favourable position. We made a long and careful stalk to the spot, and looking about found our expected prey had moved out of ken. We saw another bear higher up above us, but went in search of our former acquaintances, giving them the preference.

After a time we spied them as yet free from suspicion; and got near enough to the larger which, however, just as I had gained breath and position to fire, got behind a bush which partially screened it: and the other one, occupying an open spot, whence our every move was conspicuous, I judged it best to wait a bit; and as the latter animal was slowly approaching the former as it fed, I felt secure of one or both, when, to my infinite disgust, the larger of the two suddenly scuttled off, alarmed, as I believe, by the noise of the third bear which was now nearing the others. However that may be, off it went. The other, catching the alarm, turned and fled too, but stopped to look about for the cause of alarm; so, taking advantage of this chance, I levelled Whitworth, and rolled him over, a long shot. Up he got, and hobbled off, his left shoulder apparently broken. I prepared to pursue; but seeing No. 3, confused and frightened, had turned, and was making off in our direction, I tried to intercept him, but he kept a long way off. However, taking aim at about two hundred and fifty yards, I hit him, and then pursued him, sending Subhan after the other with a rifle.

I had three shots at my retreating game, without any apparent effect, and then returned towards camp. Subhan overtaking us, having been equally unsuccessful, gloom and despondency pervaded the party. I half try to dissuade myself from trying the chase again, and take to sketching instead.

In the evening a bear was visible on another portion of the mountain over the village, high up near the summit. It was proposed to try and stalk him. Professing my confirmed opinion we could never get at him, I, however, fell in with the wishes of the shikarries, and with complete indifference as to the result toiled up the hill-side: and with our best tactics and every effort to circumvent Bruin, he was too many for us, and betook himself to a timely retreat, ere we had approached within five hundred yards of him.

I enjoyed a magnificent prospect from the height we had reached, which gave a beautiful view right down the Wurdwan, for I should think, twenty or thirty miles; and the effects of the lengthening shadows of declining day were extremely fine. How I wished I was an artist, to be able to possess myself of that lovely scene.

I was amply repaid for the fatigues I had undergone, and became perfectly reconciled to my ill luck, and felt quite content and thankful for the blessings I enjoy so abundantly.

27th May. Sunday. At daybreak this morning, when in that state of indecision so often felt at that hour, even by practical early risers like myself, as to turning out forthwith to the raw and frosty air, or indulging in the snug comforts of bed and blankets, Mooktoo intruded his head into my canvas sanctum, and, with sparkling eyes, said there was a bear on the hill side close by. I replied, "It matters not; I am not going after him;" on which he retired. I shortly got up and went out. Sure enough, there was Bruin, as if conscious of security, quietly selecting his herbage on the hill opposite my tent. I could, by walking down to the river's bank—he was on the other side—have got within eighty yards of him, but allowed him the enjoyment of his Sabbath privileges, and saw him, ere long, retire into the jungle.

28th May. Off betimes up the Palgham path, a heavy, steady pull, principally over snow, which at this early hour was firm and afforded tolerable footing, but after being subjected to the heat of the sun becomes soft and treacherous, and very slippery.

We came across the tracks of ibex, with those of dogs in pursuit. Several spots renowned for the former animals were closely reconnoitred, but nothing was stirring.

As we ascended, the snow increased, and the chance of game became less. We paused awhile in an open space among lofty mountains, clad in their white wintry drapery, which here and there receding and opening out, and in other parts cleft into deep and rugged ravines, looked the "beau ideal" of an ibex ground. But still all was lifeless. It was an admirable picture of a winter scene, in all its congealed desolation.

Here we turned, and, retracing our steps some distance, entered another narrow valley, and sending Subhan ahead to observe the condition and prospects of the new route as to snow, he returned, shaking his head and saying there was no open ground in that direction. So nothing remained to be done, but to return to the bivouac.

The snow had by this time become difficult to traverse, lying as the path did on the steep slope of the mountain, at the bottom of which foamed a rapid torrent, and though advancing with cautious and measured steps suddenly my foot slipped, and down I went rapidly, sliding on my side over the smooth surface to the depths below. But a projecting fragment of rock, fallen from above, presented just enough irregularity for me to clutch hold of as I reached it, which luckily I got firm hold of; for Subhan, launching himself after me, came down with such an impetus that, had I not been thus fortified, we should both of us have been inevitably precipitated into the river beneath, which would in all probability have put a finale to my excursion.

We picked ourselves up, and our way on, now with our staves forming steps for my footing. I found the grass sandals here, in the slippery soft snow, worse than ordinary boots, as they gave no hold such as the raised heel does.

The shikarries, of course, though they slipped about, and fell too, found no real difficulty in getting on. I have addressed myself to discovering what can be the cause of such a marked difference, giving them such very superior power of adherence to a smooth, slippery, surface. The reason of this difference is, I believe, in the formation and use of the toes. The feet are remarkably short, and spread out at the toes like half a fan. These mountaineers have never cramped their feet by the use of such distorting leathern bondage, as we torture ourselves with; so that the toes, instead of being strained to a point, are spread out, and every one of them becomes practically a finger, affording clutch and support, which enables the possessors to move with confidence on any inclined surface, however smooth and steep, when, if they slip with one foot, they can easily recover themselves with the other: while we, having rendered our toes useless but as a lever 'en masse,' depend upon the ball of the foot for our hold, which gives, indeed, ample support on smooth level ground, but is quite inadequate for safe progress amid the dangerous paths that ibex hunting leads to. The latter part of our way lay over a snow drift inclining rapidly, down which we sped at a smart pace, digging in our heels, occasionally getting too much way on, and having to make considerable exertions to steer clear of danger. The exercise was exhilarating. Arrived in the village, I was met by Abdoolah, khansamah who, much excited, declared that thirteen animals, which he thought to be 'kustoora,' had just passed along the path on the other side the river, and were now in sight. We were much puzzled at this confident statement, and on bringing the spyglass to bear found the visitors to be a pack of wild dogs.

There the destructive rascals were, some standing, some reclining, looking as though quite at home, and ready for anything. They were a bright light-red, with sharp noses and pricked ears and long bushy tails, almost the size, and somewhat resembling, a middle-sized red Irish setter.

I moved towards them, but they were off immediately, though quite leisurely.

There was great consternation and uproar in the village during the day. This troop of marauders, it would appear, crossed the river over the snow, some three or four miles up, and slinking down had audaciously attacked the cattle grazing within a few hundred yards of my tent. They had bitten two severely, and dispersed the others: but, being disturbed by the enraged peasants, had made off.

In the afternoon we went down the river after bears, of which I had myself seen four yesterday, in my evening stroll, on the opposite hill; and my servants reported two to have been feeding a long time just opposite my tent, while I was away on my fruitless expedition. As we wended our way towards a new bridge the villagers were putting up, we saw two bears across the river. We had to wait some time for the completion of the bridge: then crossed, and away up the hill, and had a hard difficult climb to the spot where I shot the 'kustoora,' after the bear that had led me there on that occasion: but the cunning fellow was "up to snuff," and we only saw his hind parts as he retreated in the distance. Much toil for nought. Descending to the river, Subhan, ever keen and vigilant, descried a bear up the hill near by. All dropped. The bear, unconscious of the neighbourhood of enemies, continued to feed. I adjusted Whitworth with much care, and, firing, rolled Bruin headlong down the hills where we despatched him. Leaving the 'melster' to skin him, it being now late and raining hard, we went on to camp.

Soon after we got in, the night closed on us. We heard loud shouts across the river from the 'melster,' to whom assistance was sent. He had been terrified out of his senses by the sudden appearance of the pack of wild dogs come to dispute the possession of the carcase with him, or even to worry him—all one to them.

No wonder he sung out lustily. A fire soon gleamed there and the work was safely accomplished. Great encouragement felt by the shikarries at this small success.

29th May. We had determined to push far up the valley, so started early. We saw an old and a young bear far up out of reach, and again saw the pack of wild dogs, whose presence sufficiently accounts for the small number of animals seen, and their extreme wariness. These brutes have been all over the valley: we find their traces in every direction we go.

The shikarries tell me they hunt most systematically, and in a manner so well planned and carried out as to be nearly always successful. When the presence and position of their prey is ascertained, they divide into couples, and take up their several allotted positions so as to cut off the animal pursued. Some run straight, relieving each other alternately; and whether going up or down fresh relays are at hand, so that the object they pursue has little chance of escape.

We reached the end of the valley, passing most likely spots for game, but all blank. We stopped till 3 P.M.; then retraced our steps, and when nearing camp a bear was perceived some way up the mountain.

The stalk was arranged, and so successfully that we arrived within one hundred and fifty yards of Bruin, unannounced by smell or sound. I waited for breath; then, poising Whitworth, despatched the leaden messenger, which created much confusion in poor Bruin's mind and person. He rushed off: a ball from the Enfield smote him through the snout, and another so bewildered him that he turned and crossed us: two more missiles were discharged at him, but only shrinking he retreated out of sight. Guns loaded, pursuit took place, and the chase was soon seen, evidently in considerable difficulties, pausing at steep pitches of the hill.

Up we pursued through the snow, puffing, gasping, slipping about, but in the ardour of the chase heedless of danger. I got a position, and was aiming as well as my rapidly-heaving lungs permitted, when Phuttoo's staff escaping went rattling down the mountain, and the bear catching the clatter moved on, making for a narrow pass. We, too, pushed on, and, ascending the rock on one side of the pass with difficulty, saw our game resting evidently sick, having made his way across a ravine. He moved upwards, so, though breathless, panting, I was obliged to fire—distance perhaps one hundred and sixty yards or so: but Whitworth was true, and Bruin, struck in the back, retreated downwards, when a well-directed Enfield ball prostrated him lifeless.

There was great rejoicing; for it had been a very exciting and arduous chase, calling for energies and skill. The victim was sent rolling down the mountain side to the bottom, where he was duly despoiled, and a very fine, furry skin he wore.

The shikarries are now in great glee, and general congratulations, fun, and good humour, have replaced long faces, sighs, and melancholy.

30th May. Off to the place where I was so unfortunate the other morning, losing two wounded bears—a lovely, bright, frosty morning, following a bitter cold night. Nature was all smile and sparkle, the freshness of the air, and surrounding beauties of scenery, furnishing an ample stock from which to draw abundant enjoyment without the addition of other stimulus.

But, from the first height on which we stopped to examine the surrounding ground a bear was espied in motion. He stopped in a grassy hollow to feed; so, the mode of approach having been determined, we ascended until in his immediate neighbourhood, and, it being ascertained he was still on that spot, I took up position, and saluted him with a missile from Whitworth. He flinched, and made off: but two successive shots from the Enfield rolled him over stone dead. The first shot had passed through his body. He was rolled down the hill-side to be skinned; and, there leaving him, we continued our search for more victims, but unsuccessfully, so returned to camp.

31st May. Before starting this morning I was informed by the sepoy attending me, who with two coolies had been sent yesterday down the valley to Busman to procure two sheep and other supplies for the onward journey, that he had selected—I suppose, seized on—two sheep, when the villagers collecting set upon him, abused and beat him and the coolies, setting his authority as the Maharajah's servant and my attendant at defiance. This outrage created intense indignation. The shikarries were profuse in their abuse, and suggested all sorts of retaliation. It being necessary that something should be done to vindicate my dignity, and also to prevent a repetition of such misconduct which, if permitted to go unpunished, would prevent Europeans coming into the valley at all, I announced my intention of sending in the sepoy, with coolies and skins, to carry my complaint and make his own statement to the Vizier at Sirinuggur. This was to be carried out after breakfast. The shikarries and other attendants were pacified with this decision.

We then took the same direction as yesterday, and after a mile or two's trudge spied a bear in an open place, difficult of approach. We made a long circuit, and stalked up to his position with great caution and patience, but found his place vacant, and no clue to his retreat.

We pursued our way, and discovered another hairy individual taking his morning meal in a ravine. I got within fifty yards of him, and knelt, awaiting a clear view of his person, now partially eclipsed by bushes. His whole broadside being presented, I fired and over he rolled—got up, made an approach to us, then disappeared up the hill-side. I had not the least doubt he was shot right through behind the shoulder. Subhan, after some little delay, went after him, but returned, not finding blood on the track, which is by no means an incontestible proof, as it is very difficult to detect blood in small quantities on the bare dark soil, and the thickness and length of the woolly coat of bears, at this season of the year, absorbs and staunches the blood which, thus congealing, does not in many cases reach the ground, until the wounded animal has gone some distance.

I returned disconsolate, and wrote an official report to Punnoo, Vizier, of the misconduct of the Busman folk, recommending some check to be administered to them. Whilst writing, my messenger, whom I had despatched to Sirinuggur for lead, returned bringing that indispensable article with him, of which I had now quite run out, having expended so many bullets uselessly, firing all my barrels at wounded bears when at long distances, for the chance of a 'nailer' being administered. He brought me also letters and newspapers, a very seasonable supply; for in this solitary mode of life these links, which connect one with absent friends and keep one 'au fait' of passing occurrences, are invaluable.

In the evening we went down valley and across the river after a bear on the opposite hill. We were cut off from him, when in sight, by a deep hollow which we could not cross without exposing ourselves, and the brute was even now uneasy, looking up, and sticking up his ugly snout in the air to catch any objectionable savour. We drew back, and made a long detour, and arrived to find Bruin's place void.

We went on through some jungle, and suddenly started a bear to the surprise of both parties. He scuttled off in their usual clumsy style, and pulled up on the hill behind a large tree whose branches protected him. With studious care I endeavoured to open his position, and at last got sight of his forehand; he was from one hundred and fifty to two hundred yards off. I rested the Enfield, and, taking steady aim, fired, and evidently hit. He scrambled up the rocks, I firing my other barrels at him, apparently striking him again, but not stopping him.

I sent Subhan after him, and then moved slowly on, much dejected at such repeated failures, the more vexatious from the animals being badly wounded. After some time we heard a shot, and congratulated ourselves on Subhan's having retrieved the bear: but when he, after a long time, rejoined us, we found that he had fired at a 'kustoora,' and had not seen the bear.

Back to camp:—Subhan and Mooktoo remaining unusually late at the fire, I went out, and they told me they had a proposal to make, viz. to leave me and Phuttoo to cast bullets in the morning, while they tried to find the wounded bear. I accepted readily this suggestion.

1st June. We converted all the lead into bullets before breakfast. I was reading the papers, when Subhan popped his head into the tent, and gave me the welcome intelligence, that they had brought back the skin of the bear, having tracked him high up the hill, where he was found under a rock, and he made a charge at them: they, however, killed him. My shot had entered immediately behind the left shoulder, passed through the body, and out behind the right shoulder. Yet he went off as described; and would have been lost, as many others have been, had he not been thus tracked up. It is wonderful what they carry away.

By advice of the shikarries I resolved to move to-morrow down to Goombrah, now evacuated by t'other hunter, who is said to have killed only two or three bears there, and not to have climbed the hills at all; so, as ibex are said to be tolerably numerous among the mountain summits, I may have a chance of getting a shot at those much-prized animals—but I quite dread the work.

2nd June. I was informed by Phuttoo at an early hour, that it was raining and cloudy, so countermanded the move for the present, hoping that the day might clear.

At 1 P.M. the weather mended; the clouds broke, the sun appeared, and we thought we were sure of a fine afternoon. I struck tent, packed up and started all the things, remaining myself behind for an hour or two, for the chance of a meeting with Bruin.

We were miserably deceived in the weather; black clouds rolled up, thunder crashed overhead, and down descended the rain in torrents. We waited some time under shelter for a lull; then set forth, soon to experience a down-pour as heavy as ever. We trudged grimly through it. Having crossed the river, we saw an old and two young bears on the side we had left—soon after, another on the same side. We could not retrace our steps in such weather—all the hunt washed out of us.

We arrived at our new bivouac, draggled and wet—found the tent just up, but nothing yet in it—got under the eaves of a house, and patiently abided the announcement of the tent being ready; then changed clothes, had a roaring fire lit close to my tent, and made a hearty dinner. The night bitterly cold.

3rd June. Sunday. The ground was white with snow, there having been a considerable fall during the night.

I strolled up the narrow valley, which is similar to that of Kuzuznai, leading from the Wurdwan in an easterly direction—a brawling stream dashing down it, the mountains steep, and their lower portions covered with pines on the southern side; more accessible, bare, and open, on the north. I enjoyed a delightful stroll. The sunlit features of the romantic scenery, bright and glowing, though wintry, harmonizing with my feelings, suggested a happy train of meditation which accompanied me back to my tent.

The afternoon was dismal and sloppy, rain continuing on and off till night.

A noisy brawl was occasioned by my people having gone out to procure a sheep, and having, after much trouble and search, succeeded in discovering at a neighbouring hamlet the place where they had been concealed, 'nolens volens,' brought off two fine ewes, the ostensible proprietors following with a 'posse comitatus', clamorous and loudly vociferating remonstrances, and indulging in their choicest abuse.

It certainly goes much against my grain to sanction any forcible appropriation: but what to do? These Wurdwanites are the most impracticable of savages. It is quite useless treating them with the kindness, liberality, and consideration one practises to civilized people. They neither understand nor appreciate it. They refuse to part with their stock or produce, as it would appear, solely to enjoy the unaccustomed luxury of asserting a right, and the privilege of giving a refusal; which they think they may do with impunity in the case of a saheb, but would crouch and fawn in the most abject servility, were it one of the native officials. This is a noticeable trait in the character of this rude people. I am, therefore, compelled to exercise arbitrary authority over them, or I should not be able to procure supplies. Their ungracious denials do not proceed from any wish to retain their property in expectation of higher profit: for I, as do others I understand, pay them nearly double the price the articles are worth, or would realise if disposed of to native dealers in the usual course of sale. So that one can only attribute their rejection of liberal trading offers to churlish brutish perversity. The shikarries affirm this to be the real state of the case, so I feel little compunction in allowing things to take their course, always insisting conscientiously on a liberal rate of payment being actually made.

I do not know either the extent, or the amount of population, of this valley: but the latter must be inconsiderable, as the soil, though extremely fertile, is limited as regards facilities for cultivation. The valley and its ramifications being narrow, with sides steeply shelving, offer few and small level spots for raising grain: and the whole surface is covered with rocks and stones, the 'debris' of the impending mountains, shattered at periods by convulsions of nature; and every winter greatly increases these impediments to husbandry, when the accumulated snows, becoming detached, are precipitated into the valleys, carrying with them countless stones which, gathering as they descend, are scattered below in all directions. The small patches of arable are, therefore, cleared with great labour, the stones being collected in heaps: and some idea may be formed of their quantity by the fact that spaces of only a yard in width, intervening between these heaps, are ploughed and sown. The cultivated lands, viewed from the heights above, may be likened to a piece of cloth on which a child, having spilt ink, has amused itself by tracing it all over, in charming varieties of lineal figures, with its fingers.

Barley is principally, if not altogether, the produce, and its farina, with curds, the staple food of the people. Though agricultural efforts are thus necessarily restricted, ample scope is given for the depasturing of flocks and herds, the mountains up to a great height being well covered with a rich earth yielding an abundant vegetation, suitable in its varieties to all animals, and offering not a few edible productions to man; such for example, as leeks, garlic, carrots, and other roots, and several sorts of substitutes for greens, whose species and names I am ignorant of, but which I daily devour.

The cattle are small, and by the laws of the ruler of these realms, a Hindoo, are strictly forbidden to be killed. The penalty for disobedience was, until recently, death; and many instances of its fulfilment have been related to me, Mussulmen being the victims of this iniquitous system. But since British influence has been brought to bear upon the Prince of this territory, and a wholesome respect for our government, and dread of its displeasure, established, "nous avons changé toute cela." It is not now a life for a life, but the punishment is the next in severity in the penal code.

Cattle are used for carriage, countless droves being employed in the conveyance of salt, and every other article of merchandise between Cashmere and the adjoining countries. As food the milk is eaten when curdled, and some 'ghee' is made, but not for the market.

Sheep are plentiful and large flocks are brought into the valley to depasture from Cashmere. Their fleece is their chief remunerating property. A few goats are reared, and at every village I have met with a score or so of ponies of an indifferent, leggy breed. Fowls are not plentiful, and gardens appear nowhere.

The inhabitants are very low in the scale of civilization, but as they have little acquaintance with things beyond their valley, they have few wants or desires which it does not supply. Their existence is patriarchal and simple. Either sex have but one style of garment, a baggy, shapeless smock of warm woollen homespun, the produce of their own flocks, and the work of their own hands.

Their houses, or hovels, are of wood, the sides of logs, the interstices filled with clay, the roofs of split slabs. No care is taken in their construction to fit them for protection from the extreme rigours of the winter; so I conclude their inmates suffer much at that season, as do their flocks and herds, as their unthrifty, apathetic habits do not allow them to store up sufficient dry fodder to support them, while the deep snows cover the ground. Dirt and filth abound in the villages and their precincts; and the people are martyrs to hydrophobia. The males are stout, hale, and well-looking: the females, as far as my limited opportunities of observation permitted an opinion, are haggard and ugly. They, poor creatures! as in all races where man's nature is least refined, have the greater portion of the labours of life to endure. The males give me the idea of being contented and happy enough in their ignorance. They profess Mahomedanism, and in each hamlet is a small musjed, with either a resident moulvie, or an itinerant one, to officiate.

They complain much, as do all the Maharajah's subjects, of the heavy imposts levied on them, and to this attribute their indifference to bettering their condition, asserting that if they increased their substance, they would be only the marks for the rapacity of the government screws. This is, no doubt, in part true; but I think their natural indisposition to exertion is now the main hindrance to industry and enterprise. These poor peasants have to pay the Maharajah five rupees per annum for every hundred head of sheep, cattle, &c., and three rupees for every measure of ground computed to yield one maund (eighty lbs) of grain. This latter burden they bitterly complain of, as whatever the harvest the full amount is exacted: and when it is considered that the intrinsic value of the maund of grain,—the marketable price—is but one rupee, it does appear abominably rapacious to extort three times the value, and whether the harvest fails or not. Formerly, under a system but lately changed, the cultivators paid in kind, equally dividing the produce, and with this they were, they say, satisfied. At any rate, they now view its abrogation with regret.

As regards the sporting resources and capabilities of the Wurdwan, they no longer exist, but in the traditions and memories of by-gone days. These grounds have been now so constantly hunted, and the animals yet surviving, so harassed and disturbed, that with the exception of a few bears—ignoble game—there remains hardly an animal to reward the toil of the hunter. After my present experience, I would not myself again, nor would I recommend any other sportsman to try his chance in the Wurdwan, unless in the autumn, when the stags bellow; there may be, possibly, good sport then, but I should be disposed to try elsewhere.

CHAPTER VI.

SHIKAR IN THE WURDWAN.

4th June. Up the valley, through some beautiful grassy bottoms along the stream, most likely places for the resort of game. But we got over some miles of ground, ere any glimpse of an animal was obtained: then some ibex were seen up the mountain, which before long, scared by some cause unknown, were seen in rapid career to the inaccessible summits.

We soon moved on: but in the gorge where the ibex were seen a bear was descried, and the ground being favourable we gained his neighbourhood, and a shot from the Enfield smote him in the shoulder. He made off, but after receiving several more shots was brought rolling down.

We continued our course up the valley, still through most promising coverts, far the prettiest shooting ground I had seen; we saw traces of bara sing, and numerous of bears, and halted for the day in a clear space, there to await the evening. Snow fell, and it became bitterly cold. We took shelter under some firs, and after a time had a fire, round which we squatted comfortably chatting.

In due time we moved back towards camp—saw a bear, and were about the right place, when getting our wind he fled amain. Continuing our beat carefully through the jungle, Subhan dropped to game, and, following his indicator, I saw a dark coloured animal raise up its head. I said, "it is a bullock": but no, it was a bear, an unusually large and dark one, and when he looked up, with his ears pricked up, they looking like short horns gave him the momentary appearance of some species of 'bos,' such as the musk ox. But bear, and nothing else, was he.

We stalked, and raising our heads saw him immediately below us, not half a dozen paces off, in a hollow. I aimed to take him between the shoulders—off went the gun, and off went the bear, another shot striking him; then he disappeared. I pursued with Phuttoo—lost all traces, and turned, when we saw Subhan and Mooktoo in hot chase across a snowdrift bridging the stream, on which we soon detected the bloody tracks of the bear. Hopes were raised. The rocky, precipitous mountain side was difficult to surmount, but I had faith in Subhan, especially on a bloody trail.

Phuttoo and I, reconnoitring from below, espied the chase high up, crossing the side of the hill at a slow walk. We hailed the pursuing hunters, encouraging them in their efforts; saw them emerge, and enter faithfully on the trail. Then we moved further on, and again I viewed the chase higher up still, slowly making for a pine-clad crag where, from its appearance, I judged he would pull up. Anxiety now became extreme. The ground presented such difficulties, and I had lost sight of the hunters, who I feared might have given up the chase in despair. I sat in suspense, gazing upwards, and expressing hopes hardly entertained to Phuttoo, when crack! went a rifle, the whereabouts denoted by a small puff of smoke on the top of the crag mentioned. Now all was serene. I felt sure of victory: when another shot, resounding from a more distant spot, dimmed my bright hopes, and doubts again assailed me—another shot, hopes again brightened—an exclamation from an attendant behind, and the bear was seen clearly defined on the snow, in a ravine leading down from the crag, evidently dropping. Suddenly he rolled over, and simultaneously a shot rung out, and smoke appeared from above him. He slid down the snow: the hunters came in view following cautiously, and soon after we saw one discharge two shots at the prostrate, but still formidable brute. Then huge stones were cast at him, and he was pushed and hustled, till, getting way on, he came rolling and sliding on the snow to the bottom of the ravine; to which place we now made our way, and found our prey a monster for these parts, by far the largest bear I have seen here.

He was riddled with bullets; my first shot had entered between the shoulders, at the base of the neck, and came out at the belly: the second struck him well in the middle of the shoulder. Yet he went off as described, and was nearly lost, as many an one has been before. I returned very "koosh"—the shikarries, too, proud of this capture, and their share in it. The bear, they say, turned on them, and put them to flight. They are great cowards these men, as, I believe, all the Cashmiries are. Phuttoo, however, is an exception.

5th June. Again, up the valley some distance beyond yesterday's beat—some most likely places for game. We saw some ibex in an inaccessible place, and halted for the day.

At 2 P.M. we ascended, and gained a view of a fine stretch of open grassy slope beyond our halting place, where the valley makes a bend to the left. Here we stopped a couple of hours: nothing seen but a bear out of reach. We descended, and wended our way down valley.

A bear was seen: we went after him, and disturbed two bara sing hinds which were too knowing for us, so to our first attraction, whom we saw disporting himself on the snow which he cantered across. We were after him, when Subhan recoiled, saying there was another bear in the same spot just quitted by the first.

True enough—so after him; and I was crawling to a position about one hundred and twenty yards from him, when he twigged something wrong, and looked up. He cocked his ears, when I cocked the rifle, and fearing his flight I fired hurriedly, but hit him, I believe, well behind the shoulder. He started, and staggered—then came straight for us. I waited, prepared to give him second barrel. Passing a few paces above us on the side of the hill, he gave an angry roar as he cast a passing glance at us, and I gave him No. 2 somewhere in the ribs, whereat he winced, but rolled on his course and vanished, Mooktoo on his tracks, then the rest of us. But, sending Subhan to assist the former, Phuttoo and I went after the first bear on our homeward route, but saw nothing of him.

When a couple of miles or so from camp, a breathless villager met us, and said there was a bara sing down by the river, not far from camp. Much excited, he started off at a run. I made him walk, but talk, and that loudly, he would; and when he suddenly pointed out the bara sing in the valley below, he loudly proclaimed its presence. The animal was evidently attentive and alarmed; so an attempt we made to approach it was unsuccessful.

We made the bivouac; and from the prolonged absence of the two hunters we entertained delusive hopes that they had secured the wounded bear. But not so: they came in presently, having failed to get near the brute, which had betaken itself to a steep craggy height. I regret this loss much: he was a very large bear, of an unusually light colour, hair very long.

6th June. Off in a direction towards my late bivouac, a sharp frost and very cold. By the way, the frost was so severe on Monday, that the water just poured out in a pewter cup to clean my teeth was frozen over by the time I had washed my hands and face—pretty well for the 4th of June.

I saw nothing at all; went nearly as far as the bridge, and then returned to breakfast. Bear skins were laid out to dry—a sudden thought striking me, I told Mooktoo I would give five rupees 'backsheesh' for the skin of the wounded bear, escaped yesterday. He and Subhan have accordingly gone to try their luck, and I mean to go with Phuttoo in the evening to look for the bara sing in the willow bottom.

We went a short distance, but it did not put in an appearance this time when wanted. The two hunters returned in the evening reporting the bear to have gone miles away; but they had killed a female ibex, of which feat they were very proud, and the camp and the village rejoiced in the prospect of a feast of flesh; which, however, looked so uninviting that I declined it, and my servants, Hindoo fashion, would not eat it, because I would not; so the villagers had the more. I tipped the shikarries one rupee each; but doubt much if they took up the trail of the bear.

7th June. Remained in camp: resolved on an attempt on the ibex to-morrow.

8th June. An early start, and a stiff job climbing the mountain, which took us nearly two hours, and our toil was unrewarded by the sight of a single ibex. The hunters carefully reconnoitred the whole neighbourhood ineffectually.

Whilst at breakfast, they came and reported a bear in view, asleep under a tree. I descended to the assault over difficult ground; and Bruin, asleep with one eye open, was distrustful, and hearing the click of my rifle, when cocking, made off. I fired three shots, all striking him, and quite disabling him; two shikarries after him, who fired three shots close by, and after some time I saw the wounded bear crawling along, a considerable way off: after some time, three or four shots more, then silence—again, a shot or two. Phuttoo and I remained on the look out, wondering what the issue was; and thus for two hours, I think, we waited, once getting a glimpse of the hunters far below us in some jungle. They did, at length, return, bringing the bear's skin, upon which some ten bullets were expended, and reporting that they had wounded a female bara sing.

We remained up all day, though all hopes of ibex had been destroyed by the noise of the repeated discharges: descended in the afternoon, and going through some jungle I espied a deer, but could not get Subhan, who was leading, to acknowledge my low signal which a brawling stream close by drowned the sound of. I seized a rifle from Mooktoo, and fired: the animal bounded out of sight. Subhan followed to see the effect, and stopped, beckoning me on, so I knew the shot had told. Hurrying to him, he pointed to the animal stretched on the ground, and advised another shot which hitting the back, traversed the body, coming out at the left shoulder. It was but a kustoora after all, but a fine specimen, with long teeth protruding from the upper jaw.

9th June. Phuttoo and Mooktoo complaining of head aches, &c., Subhan came at dawn to my tent, suggesting remaining in camp till evening. I readily acquiesced, having had a hard day's work yesterday.

I started in the afternoon in a new direction; climbing the steep fir-clad hill opposite the village, we reached the crest where we hoped to meet with bara sing, but only saw their fresh tracks, so sat down to watch.

Subhan ascended higher with the telescope, and returned after some time reporting a bear as big as a bullock in sight, so we addressed ourselves to approach him. Descending the hill-side, a splendid and extensive grassy slope presented itself, along which we wended our way, and after about a mile's walk came upon the bear, truly a very large one, and justifying Subhan's comparison. I took my time to gain breath, and as we were well placed as regards covert and wind did not hurry; but, shifting position once or twice till satisfied, let drive Enfield, upon which Bruin turned bewildered, and dashed down hill, partly in our direction. I discharged the other barrel, also rifle, as he crossed a snow drift filling the bottom of a ravine. He still held on, and was commencing the ascent of the opposite hill, when I levelled Whitworth, and down he came spinning, rolling over and over, to the snow, and then slipping and sprawling down that, until he lay still, breathing his last.

The whole party was triumphant: the shikarries got down to him: his sides still heaved: the coolies came up, and, Subhan having by my order cut the animal's throat to extinguish the remaining sparks of life, they proceeded to take off the skin, and had opened it down the belly, when, to their terror and my horror, the poor beast came to life again, as it were, and with a violent movement uttered such a growl as sent his tormenters flying in all directions. I put an end to him by a ball in the head. This is another proof of their surprising tenacity of life.

He was truly a monstrous bear with huge limbs. This formidable beast, it was stated, was the terror of the villagers, having devoured many of their sheep, and put to flight some score of them, who with dogs, &c. attempted his destruction. There was great rejoicing over his destruction.

10th June. Sunday. Remained in camp as usual.

11th June. We moved camp this morning, as previously arranged to Busman, the opposite side of the valley, and I pitched my tent in a very picturesque spot, overlooking the village.

In the afternoon I went down valley, and killed a large doe bara sing, which unfortunately was heavy with young. I much regretted this, but the shikarries had no such scruples. They were delighted at possession of so much meat, and set to work 'con amore' to break up the carcase, a messenger being despatched to bring men from camp to carry in the flesh. I did not feel at all elated at this success; but general satisfaction pervaded my party.

One of the coolies, who accompanied the sepoy to Sirinuggur, arrived, bringing nothing whatever with him. He said the sepoy would be detained some days, until the Maharajah's arrival in the city, to whom he would make his statement personally. The Baboo, too prudent would not trust my letters to this coolie, by which I am much inconvenienced and vexed. The Kardar of Palgham would not either trust him with the rice, &c., which had been ordered; and further said he could not supply it, as there were five sahebs there to provide for. We, therefore, made arrangements for a man to start early to-morrow to Shanguz, to procure supplies there.

12th June. Up the valley leading to Bodicote in expectation of finding ibex. We had a tremendous climb which, though very toilsome, was not dangerous, but saw not a single ibex; we halted in a suitable spot to wait until evening, in hopes of game appearing. There was a bear in sight feeding below us, which, after some discussion, it was decided ought to be left unmolested, for fear the report of the guns might disturb ibex within hearing. Subhan went off to reconnoitre.

After breakfast I sat watching the bear which, having finished his meal, came in our direction, and on to the snow in the ravine below us, where, to my astonishment, he stretched himself out composedly to snooze, apparently approving of cool applications to a distended stomach. Subhan returned, and reported that he could see no ibex in any direction, but had seen their tracks with those of dogs in pursuit; so, auguring ill for our chance of those animals, we resolved to attack our unconscious neighbour below, and descended for that purpose, but could not get within a hundred yards of him; at which distance, aiming at his head, I despatched an Enfield, which just missed him, and off he went down the snow in the utmost amazement, and came nigh to breaking his neck, but pulled up, ploughing deep into the snow with his long claws, and sliding some distance—a most ridiculous object.

Having gained some three hundred yards thus, he stopped and looked all round. We remained quite still, concealed by a rock. He then slowly descended the rocks on our side, and, choosing a good site, there he seated himself, looking anxiously from side to side. We waited, hoping for an opportunity of quitting our position undiscovered: and so we remained for half an hour at least, when Subhan, thinking we could withdraw backwards out of sight, tried if it would do, and beckoning us we stealthily followed, and, having gained a screen, turned and again tried to renew our acquaintance with Bruin, who from the nature of the ground could not now be seen.

We continued to descend the rocks towards his supposed position, and had got close upon it without discovering him. Mooktoo, from behind, made signals of seeing him, but Subhan and I could not catch a glimpse of him, until we gained the projecting rock under which he was sleeping, again thinking himself secure. The wind lifting his long hair betrayed him. He was lying with his head towards us, not four yards off, his head concealed by the rock, so I struck him between the shoulders, when he dropped backwards, and away he rolled over and over, in a most surprising manner. I saw him at one time high in mid air, as he bounded from a projecting rock, as though he had been discharged from a mortar: and he went rolling down the precipitous ravine for, I should think, three quarters of a mile, much to the disgust of those who had to descend and skin him,—a very fine large skin, with long yellowish fur. We saw other bears as we descended in the evening, but out of reach, so we got nothing more. It was a very hard day's work. We had to cross a snowdrift over the river, in which was a large fissure, which, however, only required nerve to cross safely.

13th June. Off to the place where I killed the doe bara sing. After some time we saw a bear apparently in retreat up hill. Thinking it useless pursuing, I turned towards camp; but Subhan pointed out the bear stopping on the precise spot on which the bara sing had been cut up, probably picking up the refuse. I resolved to try for him, so we ascended, and, having gained our point, thought him clean gone, when I saw something move in the bushes—again thought I was deceived, when the shikarries twigged him in some bushes across the ravine—a long shot. I struck him with an Enfield, evidently a severe wound, bringing him down, and fired other guns at him, as after deceiving us, making as though he were going to die on the spot, he went off in the jungle. I sent the shikarries in pursuit, and ere long they appeared with the dead bear, drawing him down the snow—a small brute riddled with bullets.

On our way to camp we saw a fox with a splendid brush. I got within some eighty yards of him, and levelled Whitworth, steadying him on a rock—bang! and away went renard. Asking where the ball struck, the shikarries said, high up above the fox. I thought this very odd, and accused Phuttoo of putting in too much powder, who declared he had only put in the regular charge. Meantime, the fox was running up and down, and round and round, in an absurd manner, Mooktoo laughing at him, who sung out he had dropped dead, and ran off to secure him. Phuttoo and I, looking on, saw, as we thought, the animal betaking himself to the hills at a good pace, and called out to Mooktoo to come back, saying it was of no use. But on he went, not heeding us, and was soon seen striking something, and then held up the dead fox, another having run off, and deceived Phuttoo and me. The victim was shot right through behind the shoulders.

14th June. A rainy morning, with every appearance of a continuance—so, not unwillingly, I betook myself again to the comfortable warmth of my blankets.

In the afternoon I went in the same direction as yesterday, and seeing a bear high up on a hill, attempted to get at him—but in vain; scrambled about the heights, but, seeing nothing more, gave up and returned to bivouac.

15th June. Up ere dawn, a long day in prospect, it having been determined to shift camp to a village on the opposite side of the valley, and we hunters to climb a mountain, from which we should descend to the bridge leading to our new quarters in the afternoon.

When rather more than half-way up a bear was descried, to which we approached with due caution, but owing to the formation of the ground could not get nearer than some hundred and fifty yards; so that I fired at that distance, and struck him well in the middle of the shoulder. Recoiling from the blow, he then made straight for our position, and gained a rising ground just over us, when seeing us he paused, looking very ugly, then turned, when trying my other barrel, it missed fire, the cap being bad. We pursued and soon sighted the chase, in pursuit of which Subhan and Mooktoo continued, Phuttoo and I looking on—the mountain side, up which Bruin held his limping course, being spread out plainly before us; and we had the unsatisfactory view of the abortive efforts made to secure the wounded animal. The two hunters, not being able to see the wounded bear as we did, made slow progress, expecting to meet their foe at every step behind some rock; so Bruin, though slowly dragging along, and occasionally pausing to look back, made two paces to their one, and so disappeared over the crest of the mountain. Whereupon, Phuttoo and I set off to climb up and rejoin the others. And sharp work we had; but finally reached our two companions who, not sighting the game, had given up the chase in despair.

We again set forward to gain a favourable spot to pass the day in, where I proceeded to breakfast, the others retiring somewhere out of sight. Rain and sleet driven by a furious wind now set in, with thunder roaring majestically immediately above us. I screened myself as well as I could under a fir tree, and passed the chill hours, some two or three, reading.

A hind is seen coming forth to graze down below us; and the rain now ceasing we descended in chase, but could not get near the wary creature which, winding us, I imagine, from afar, was seen cantering smartly away, ere we were within long shot of it.

On reaching camp we found the man, despatched on the 12th for provisions, returned, having made a rapid journey. He had met the sepoy who had been detained at Sirinuggur, and they had made arrangements for the supplies required, now difficult to obtain from some unexplained cause. They had, therefore, to be collected from different villages, and the sepoy remained to convoy the bulk, Kamal, a trusty quiet-mannered fellow, bringing three coolies laden with him, also a complimentary note and presents from Ahmet Shah—some cherries and cakes—and from my stout friend of Eish Mackahm some of his bread cakes, before commended. By the way, he sent me a pair of gloves and socks by the coolie last coming.

16th June. Much rain during the night, but a fair fresh morning which I enjoyed much, reading. In the afternoon, forth to hunt.

Two hinds, young ones apparently, were seen descending the mountain. We tried to intercept them; but a ravine divided us. Lying concealed, we watched them gamboling beyond our savage hand's reach. They finally ascended the hill, and gradually retired from our sight. A plan was then formed to follow them, which took us up the mountain in a direction to cut their route. A stiff and smart climb landed us on the top; Subhan and Mooktoo went off to scout, Phuttoo and I lying in wait.

Two bears came in sight. Phuttoo and I, taking the rifles, moved towards them. The others joined us, having seen nothing: but not having yet examined the ground where the two deer must have passed, or might yet be, I ordered it to be reconnoitred 'en route' after the bears, and there was seen one deer lying down, its head and ridge of back only shewing—distance about eighty yards. I paused for breath behind a rise, the deer looking towards me; prepared rifle, and advanced a little on my knees to get a firmer footing: the deer rose, and standing erect presented its dun side full before me. Taking deadly aim I pulled trigger, when—horror and disgust—the cap only exploded. Away bounded the deer, and also the other—till now unseen, but lying still nearer to us. I fired the other barrel as they gently moved up hill, but ineffectually I believe. Away they went.

The guns had been kept all night in the covers which they were in during yesterday's rain. I had directed the shikarries always to take the leathern covers in the day time, and to put the woollen ones on at night, and had for some time enforced compliance. But of late they had departed from this rule. Finding the woollen covers more easily disposed about their persons, they had carried them in the day, and left them on at night. I think a strong impression was made upon them by to-day's mishap, as thereby they lose a good supply of meat, which is to them a great disappointment.

The two bears of course fled. And other game, both deer and bears, on the side from which we had come up, seen while in the ascent, had also vanished.

I determined to try another entire day on the same mountain on Monday, and then to move forward by the Sooroo Pass towards Ladâk, supposing the sepoy to arrive to-morrow. With him I expect a bullet mould for the Whitworth, having sent in one of the smooth cylindrical bolts as a pattern, the easiest of the two to manufacture, and which Phuttoo and the others assure me can be easily made in the city; so I left the matter in their hands. I did not bring a mould, thinking I had bolts enough with me for that weapon, but had not calculated on the astonishing vitality of the bears.

17th June. Sunday. A walk in the morning; and a delightful one it proved. On returning, the long absent sepoy and some coolies were in sight on the opposite side of the river, and in due time arrived with letters, newspapers, supplies, &c.

18th June. We made a very early start to carry out a plan arranged on Saturday night, to hunt a mountain on which we had seen bara sing. But, from some whimsical notion or other, the shikarries had altered their minds, and, passing by this spot, went on to where we stalked the deer on Saturday, attended by such bad luck. They are queer fellows, possessed of remarkably odd notions on hunting, quite at variance with the true science of the chase. They trust so much to luck, to 'kizmet.' I suppose, being Mahomedans, and hence fatalists, influences them on these points. I cannot say there is any charm in the character of these men, such as one might, perhaps, be disposed to attribute to the hunters of the Cashmere mountains. They are too strongly imbued with the duplicity and covetousness of their race, and they are deficient in those characteristics one loves to ascribe to the mountaineer and hunter—courage, truth, and candour. They do not ever like to exert themselves over much, and have a great regard for the comforts of a house, so that it is difficult to get them well away from the inhabited districts. They are, moreover, constantly begging for something; and, though one may give them double what they are entitled to, they will scheme to dupe you into giving them more, quoting fabulous experiences of the generosity and munificence of saheb so and so. Nor do I consider them by any means good hunters, their talents being confined to a knowledge of the country, and a quick sharp eye. They possess none of that pertinacity and resource which enable hunters to find game when scarce and wild, and to capture it with certainty when severely wounded. They are but poor trackers, and quickly give up all efforts at the pursuit of a wounded animal, if they think it may have gone far. How often I have longed for one or two of my old Australian native hunters! *They* were the fellows to run a tangled trail through bush or over bare rock, like hounds with the chase in view. Of my three shikarries, Phuttoo, Mooktoo, and Subhan, the latter is far the best and more attractive in character. He is young and willing, and is not yet spoiled, not having hitherto acquired all the wiles and tricks of such men as the other two, who are old allies, and work together for their mutual advantage. It is a great drawback to my pleasure in this excursion, not being able to repose confidence in these associates.

We went over a deal of ground, but arrived at the end of our beat without seeing anything; then pulled up for the day. Just as I was finishing breakfast, the hunters came, and informed me there was a bear in sight. I got up and accompanied them a short way up hill. Puffing and blowing, distended with tea and dough cakes, I made heavy way, and, having ascertained the bear to be a long way off in rough and difficult ground, I declined going after him, but sanctioned the attempt on the part of Subhan and Mooktoo, Phuttoo and I taking up a good position to see the fun. After a time we heard three shots in rapid succession; then saw the bear coming towards us. He sheered off, and went best pace up hill, evidently unscathed. Soon after, the hunters appeared, Mooktoo as usual shirking the hard work, and Subhan climbing the heights manfully, as though he intended to catch Bruin. At last they rejoined us.

In the evening we retraced our steps, and at length saw an old and a young bear far ahead of us. Having reached their whereabouts at dusk, I doubted whether to go after them; but, Subhan catching sight of them, I buckled to, and climbed the steep. We found our game, the young one only being visible at first, right under us: then the old one was detected also, and I fired down on her, aiming at and striking her between the shoulders, knocking her over: then, aiming at the young one, the gun did not go off, the cap, I fancy, having fallen off. The old bear scrambled up close to us, uttering fierce growls; then turned and made off. I fired two shots, one breaking a hind leg. Subhan pursued. The young one, a queer looking little brute, sat eyeing us from a height opposite, and I would not allow Mooktoo to fire at him. We followed the chase, and found the bear had fallen down hill into the jungle close by the river. It was too late and too dark to look for her then, so we took the route to camp, all feeling sure of finding her dead in the morning.

19th June. Off to retrieve the wounded bear. We got on its tracks, there being much blood on the trail, and tracked through a bit of jungle into some wet bushy ground, where the shikarries, no longer finding blood to guide them, gave up the chase, and, without examining the neighbouring bushes, turned back towards camp. Aware of the utter uselessness, from former experience, of endeavouring to incline them to continue the search, I went silently back.

20th June. We made an early start towards Shugkenuz. Mooktoo espied two bears in the old place where three were seen on our first coming this way, and on that evening I wounded two. We resolved to try for them, and, continuing our route on towards the bridge, I discovered another high up on our right. We started up, a long and tiresome climb before us; when, getting near the place where we had seen the bear, we found it had moved to the opposite side of the ravine. Our side was very difficult to move on, having a very steep and smooth surface, but bushes to screen us. The bear was wonderfully 'cute of hearing, turning at every snap of a dry twig. I made sure it would be off, but advanced with every caution to a spot where some slight noise was unavoidable, and could not get nearer without being exposed to view. Here Bruin, having looked up and reconnoitred repeatedly, moved upwards; then across the ravine, heading towards us. Mooktoo, excited, declared it to be coming towards us, so I took up as comfortable a position as I could, and prepared rifle. Sure enough Bruin's head appeared over a ridge, coming right for us. He halted, and scrutinized our locality, then advanced and paused; when—crack!—and over and over it rolled down the ravine.

It was a female. And the hunters account for its strange approach to us, by its having from the sound imagined its male friend to be at hand, which individual I had the honour to represent, so little to the satisfaction of the expectant fair one.

Leaving Phuttoo and Kamal to take the spoils, we continued our way, and, crossing the ridge, went in search of the bears first seen. Their place was vacant: no signs of them. But Subhan, having gone ahead, signalled us, and we found he had discovered a bear on the other side the stream which tumbled down this valley. Its movements were eccentric, and again ascribed to its being under the influence of the tender passion. However that may be, the lone one came down to the edge of the stream, there pausing awhile amid the bushes; when an Enfield ball took effect on its shoulder, and ere it recovered its surprise another followed. It was then discovered lying apparently dying under some bushes. Mooktoo went in pursuit, and shortly fired two shots. I then sent Subhan across to help, knowing Mr. Mooktoo to entertain the utmost reverence for a wounded bear, always preserving a respectful distance. Subhan crossed the stream, disappearing in the bushes, which were seen much agitated, bending to and fro, here and there,—a rush and the thwack of sticks being audible even above the roar of the torrent. Then all was still. Next, Subhan appeared at my side; he had settled the bear, with the result of which he was much pleased. It was but a small animal, but a very vicious young female.

We proceeded on to Shugkenuz: in the evening visited the same spot, but saw nothing.

21st June. I had determined yesterday to remain a day here, in order to make complete arrangements for coolies and supplies, as no village is met with between this and Sooroo; and we propose stopping to hunt midway some days, there being good ground for ibex there. I also expect the coolies back from Sirinuggur, a matter of consequence as lead is again running short, those tough bears causing such a consumption of that precious metal.

I started in the morning to hunt a valley across the river, and had proceeded far up the valley, when I perceived the back of a bear shewing above some high rank herbage up the hill-side. Up we went, and came on our prey, and a shot, entering just behind the shoulder, sent him rolling head over heels down hill: but I had to put a ball through his head to finish him.

Mooktoo had not accompanied us, having been lame the last two days from a boil. It is surprising how absurdly ignorant they are of the simplest principles of curative measures and remedies. His were wet gunpowder—because it was an European production, I imagine—and a bandage of woollen stuff. All ready for a move on the morrow.

CHAPTER VII.

SOOROO PASS TO LADÂK.

22nd June. A march, and a long and fatiguing one to the northern extremity of the Wurdwan valley proper, where it narrows to a mere gorge, the mountains closing in and overhanging the pent up torrent, frowning down in savage grandeur—the scenery very wild and striking. We had to cross the river on the snow, and to move over extensive snow drifts covering the steep slope of the bank: the very precarious footing, and the torrent roaring below, made this part of the journey exciting. I was troubled with a badly-fitting sandal which much impeded my movements, and increased the danger of falling, at the same time fatiguing me greatly. Subhan did what he could for me, but was unable altogether to remedy the evil. The river made a sudden turn, coming from due east at right angles into the valley, (which runs, I imagine, pretty direct north and south) up which we continued our course, now very rugged, and at length, to my relief and comfort, halted in a small, irregular, up and down opening, by a large piece of rock which afforded us some protection from the sun, now become excessively hot after ten o'clock. A great but gradual change has taken place as the season has advanced. The mornings and evenings are now cool, not cold, and the days very hot, the sun so powerful as to render my small shuldary tent quite an oven. I try to diminish the temperature by putting my double blanket on the top; but still I suffer much, and find a tree, where there is one at hand, better protection by far.

My followers were very long in appearing, and I felt some anxiety for my servants' safety in so hazardous a path, but was gratified by the simultaneous presence of all three, as I awoke from a troubled doze. The coolies also arrived without accident of any sort.

I went in the afternoon up river to reconnoitre, and had the pleasure of seeing some half-dozen ibex, venerable fellows, with long horns and beards, but on the opposite side of the river, and in a place the approach to which made me shudder to look at. But the attempt must be made to-morrow.

One coolie arrived from Sirinuggur, bringing lead; the other, the duly deputed one, remaining behind to see the Baboo, and deliver his credentials, that individual being absent at some devotional gathering of the pundits at some sacred shrine, most likely devising roguery—therefore, no letters, papers, or bullet mould. Ibex had been seen from camp.

23rd June. Off in pursuit of the ibex seen yesterday. We descended to the river which we crossed on the snow, and up the opposite side,—ibex seen above us.

We lay down to reconnoitre. Two ibex, male and female, were coming in our direction from the heights in the rear. Their intention becoming apparent to continue in our direction, we climbed up to intercept them, and a rough scramble it was. After raising our hopes to the utmost, they turned aside and disappeared. On again—crossing a remarkable place of semicircular form, where the earth appeared to have parted from the mountain, and slipped sheer down into the river, so that an extensive indent of semicircular form remained, its surface loose and smooth, with a harder gravelly ridge forming a ledge, from which it descended sheer to the river. The mountains were of bare rock, rearing sharp peaks of every form high into the heavens. In the further angle, however, of this crescent of desolation, was a knoll covered with gnarled dwarf birch trees and rough underwood. To this we directed our course, and, when gained, it was as nice a spot as could be desired for a hunter's watch stand.

In the course of the day several ibex were seen crossing the slope, having been alarmed by the fall of some pieces of rock which, detached from above, came rattling down near them. We watched them anxiously, hoping they might come our way. But no: they chose the crags. A bear and two 'wee' cubs also came seeking more secure quarters, and evidently bound for our trees; but, winding us some five hundred yards distant, the anxious dam turned about, after several long sniffs, and went off in a different direction.

But one ibex, a buck, remained on the slope where he employed himself, I believe, in licking salt, of which the shikarries tell me there is much in the earth, and which attracts the ibex to this remarkable spot in numbers. After watching his movements for a long time, and it appearing pretty sure that he meant to remain there some time, Subhan and I started on the forlorn hope of stalking him; a feat of great difficulty, as, though the wind was in our favour, the quantity of stones and detritus we had to pass over to get to him—there being in fact no other footing—rendered it impossible to move without sending some detached fragments from this huge loose mass rattling below. Then, the difficulty of moving at all on this steep surface was great. We took advantage of the stunted brushwood to screen our approach, moving on only when the animal, ever looking around after a bite or two, put down his head.

This tedious mode of advance under a broiling sun continued some time; when the animal, being satiated, suddenly descended behind the low ridge on the top of which he had hitherto held post. Then we pushed on, Subhan too impetuous, the loose stones talking loudly. However, we got to fifty yards of the spot, Subhan still going ahead, head down, when I saw the horns, then the head, of the suspicious chase appear above the ridge. Checking Subhan, down we lay, the forepart of our bodies only screened by some dry twigs of brushwood. I took the rifle, and, raising it, found the ramrod hanging out. Putting my hand to the muzzle, I drew it in—the ibex now in full view, shewing his breast, a fine mark. But from the attitude I was in, lying on my right side, with nothing but loose stones to scratch at, I could not, for the life of me, find means to poise the gun and take aim. Subhan lying in front of me on his side, I tried to rest the gun on him, but could only bring it to bear by pressing on the slope of his shoulder as he lay, which afforded no rest. The animal's quick eye now detected the convulsive twitchings of my limbs, and, giving a shrill whistle, he presented his side at which I pulled trigger as he bounded away. A smack was heard, which we hoped was the ball telling, and away we went, but saw the ibex slowly bounding away. He paused at the foot of a rock, wagged his tail rapidly, and vanished with a dive into a gulley.

Subhan, thinking him wounded, pursued. I had also great hopes from the sound, notwithstanding the difficulty of my position; but, on examining the ground whereon the animal stood, I found the spot where the ball struck at his feet, the rifle having slipped down the slope of Subhan's shoulder as I hastily pulled trigger on the startled animal. Subhan returned, discomforted exceedingly. And, repining at the extreme ill luck at being surprised in such an impracticable position, we rejoined our equally disappointed comrades who had been eagerly following our every movement through the telescope. We gained the ground on which the fine old patriarchal long-beards had been seen yesterday—now, alas! where? Far beyond our ken. We returned on our steps; had terrific hard climbing up and down; and I arrived at the bivouac thoroughly done up, with a pain in the back from straining up hill, which may necessitate rest.

While lying waiting on the mountain side, I observed a spot on the river below us, where from the contiguity of certain rocks dividing the stream, it appeared feasible to throw a bridge over, plenty of wood being within reach. But I observe that almost close to this spot the pines and firs cease, and nothing but the dwarf birch appears; and a mile or two further on even this wood ceases, and only bare rock is visible. The shikarries promise to have a bridge made, which will then afford us easy access to some good ibex grounds, now very difficult to get to.

24th June. Sunday. I was very well inclined to enjoy the repose this day brings with it: my back stiff, and an occasional sharp twinge in the lumbar regions, painfully reminded me of my fruitless exertions yesterday. I took a stroll in the afternoon. The shikarries and coolies went to build the bridge.

25th June. I started off to the place where the bridge had been commenced yesterday, but could not be completed owing to the quantity of water, from the melted snows. It was to be finished this morning, the coolies first bringing my things here. We saw some fine ibex on the very crest of the mountain opposite, and resolved to try and get at them in the evening.

The things arrived, and the coolies set to work at the bridge. I made a hearty breakfast, and afterwards went to watch the operations. The rough poles were now across, and the shikarries proposed starting at once. I did not much relish the thoughts of the climb just after breakfast, and the sun exceedingly warm, but acquiesced; so off we went, and crossing this apology for a bridge over the furious torrent was no easy matter. I had to collect my nerves for the attempt. The poles were laid first from one bank to a large, high piece of rock, and from that down to another much lower, and then from that to the other bank: they were very crooked and loose, and moved about and sprung under the pressure of the foot. But I crossed safely, and then breasted the mountain. It was dreadful hard work. After many halts we reached the upper regions, where we found it quite cold, a strong sharp wind blowing. The shikarries went to scout, and returned with the provoking information, that they had watched the ibex which had betaken themselves to a distant and inaccessible portion of the mountain.

Something must be attempted after such an arduous ascent. I determined not to go down without an effort at any rate, so proposed to sleep up on the mountain, sending a coolie to bring some clothes and eatables. This was decided on. Then, looking for a place to wait in till evening, I descended a short way towards a tremendous ravine which cleft the mountain from crest to base, running nearly in a direct line for a couple of miles, its sides of bare rock, precipitous, and rugged. Above this I lay down in no very agreeable state of mind at the prospects before me.

About 3 P.M. I saw the identical five fine ibex emerge, and file slowly across the opposite hill-side. I watched them eagerly without a movement, lying on my back, till they disappeared over the ridge. One was a splendid old fellow, with huge horns, and moved very leisurely behind the others. How I longed to be within reach of him! The shikarries, who had occupied other places to watch, soon joined me, excited by the same sight. We were preparing to move, when two more ibex were seen following in the track of the others. We had to wait till they were out of sight: then, off we went, and had hard work to cross the ravine, and ascend the opposite hill of slate and snow, steeply scarped. We gained the crest, and found the ibex were down on a level open slope, far out of reach, and hardly possible to approach. Here was a disappointment. After a long consultation a plan was formed, we hunters to make a 'detour,' and then the coolies to descend towards the game, and let them be aware of his presence.

It being so arranged, up and away: and after further violent exertions we reached the part of the mountain under which the ibex had been seen feeding—most difficult ground, being very steep, and either of smooth slate, or fragments affording no footing. We gained the top of the ridge. Subhan unfortunately did not reconnoitre, but made a turn to the left to gain a passage through the much-broken rock, when suddenly he shrunk to the ground, as the horns and heads of two magnificent ibex came into view, emerging from a narrow cleft and coming towards us. They, of course, saw us. We were not thirty-five yards apart. Now, to record what took place I can hardly undertake, nor do I exactly know how it happened. The heads, and necks, and ridge of back, of the ibex were alone visible, a piece of rock screening their bodies. No doubt, I was discomposed and flurried by their unexpected appearance so near, and under some unaccountable influence did not at once take aim, from some undefined notion that they would offer a better mark immediately, and for fear of frightening them by any movement. I was, moreover, in a most uncomfortable squatting position on a steep slope. After a second or two one moved forward, and, unfortunately, instead of the movement bringing him better into view, it had the opposite effect, for the ground dipped so that the animal was instantly out of sight; the other moving on, I fired and missed. I was then obliged to rise up to see him. He had not dashed off at the discharge, but moved on at a slow pace, as though quite unconcerned. His whole side was presented as I rose in much agitation to aim, and just as I raised the rifle he dashed down hill, my bullet passing harmlessly over his back. I rushed after him, risking neck or limbs, heedless of every thing but the chase, my second gun in hand: sighted him—on again, when I was brought up by a fearful precipice, a huge abrupt chasm severing the mountain: leaning and peering over, I saw the two ibex below, but was so blown I vainly tried to take aim, so, as the distance was great, gave it up.

I was still looking after the retreating game, when Subhan signalled something exciting, and we found he had spied other four ibex in sight, far off. We assayed to get at them. Our coolie was in sight, and the ibex, taking fright, after a turn or two, made off in our direction, but far away below us. Down we dashed in chase to cut them off. But, ignorant of their point, we failed—with our utmost efforts, and after many slips and escapes, arriving to see them, having crossed the lower end of this chasm, canter off up the opposite hill-side. The shikarries urged me to fire, so putting up sights, hopeless myself, I sent two or three bullets very close to them—that was all.

It was no use to remain up now, so I decided to return to camp, a long and difficult step. We saw coolies down below with the things, descended to them, and found the long absent messenger from Sirinuggur there.

He had letters, newspapers, and the bullet mould for me. This somewhat allayed the unpleasant reflections I was a prey to, and broke in upon my brooding over my mishap; and, on Subhan expressing an intention to move camp onwards in the morning, I suggested that he and Mooktoo should instead try and get at these ibex. They did not appear half inclined for the job, I thought. And no wonder, considering the amount of work we had done.

All the camp was out in evident expectation of our success, hoping for meat. Long faces, when the result was known. My mishap did not prevent my eating my dinner; but it was interrupted oft-times by melancholy ejaculations, and sighs, and groans. I had confessed all to the sympathising Abdoolah, and told him my heart was pained at losing such fine ibex. My Hindostani was not equal to the requisite idiomatic phraseology, I suppose; for, on my shortly retiring to my tent, he followed me, and put his head into my tent. On enquiring what he wanted, "he had come," he said, "to offer to rub my stomach to relieve the pain I complained of." I know I said 'heart,' and not 'stomach.' But this circumstance operated beneficially, and I retired to bed thoroughly knocked up, but mentally serene.

26th June. I was disturbed at an early hour by a rumbling under my bed: the two hunters were getting out the guns. "Mind you bring back the big horned one," I said, and again relapsed into peaceful, strength-restoring slumbers. When up, I set to work to cast bullets, and found the mould for the Whitworth most ingeniously constructed, but with a great deal more art than was actually necessary. The bolt was not true, however, the base of the cylinder being larger than the upper part; but I thought that this could be remedied by the use of the knife and file, though at considerable expense of time and trouble. And so it turned out.

There were letters from Punnoo, Vizier, assuring me the offending villagers should be punished, and from the Baboo on matters of business, and lots of newspapers which were most acceptable.

About 2 P.M. I saw Mooktoo returning alone. He immediately beckoned me. I guessed his object, and called out to the coolies to bustle up and be off to help the shikarries—that they would now find lots of meat. There was a general stir and excitement in the bivouac, all turning out to gaze upon the approaching Mooktoo, still a long way off on the other side the river. He carried something evidently; and, on one of the coolies reaching him, he threw down his load which we then perceived to be the head of an ibex, with fine horns.

He shortly joined us, and proclaimed the welcome news of four fine ibex being the result of their chase. All the coolies were despatched to help Subhan who, in the course of three or four hours, made his appearance with a long train of followers bearing heads and limbs. There were great rejoicings at this great success, and the prospect of a general feast of flesh. I looked mournfully on the unfortunate victims, taking little pleasure in their destruction, as I had not enjoyed the excitement of the chase which was, by the hunters' accounts, a most arduous and perilous one. They had been long traversing the mountains without a sign of game, and were returning, when an ibex was viewed, and following him they had to climb terrific crags; to do which they had even to take off their sandals, and, slinging their guns, climb up on all fours. They became separated, and were in much apprehension for each other's safety. But all turned out most happily for their sport; for Subhan was surprised by a fine buck coming out of a ravine, and presenting him a fair broadside. He knocked him over; when another took his place. He then disposed of that one, and others were thus turned down to Mooktoo who floored his brace, and wounded another. Two or three fell down the precipitous crags, and were consequently much knocked about, but the horns were luckily uninjured. I decided to halt tomorrow to prepare the heads, &c.

27th June. All remained busy in camp, stretching skins, and preparing heads. Rain fell during the day. In the afternoon, it having cleared up, leaving Phuttoo working at the heads, the other two and I went off on the chance of seeing something; but heavy rain again set in, and we returned drenched to camp.

28th June. We struck camp, and set off to next ground. The morning was heavy and cloudy, and it was an uninteresting march along the river bed, here very shallow, and broken into many streams. The mountains, on either hand, were steep and craggy, and their lower slopes, on the southern side, clothed with underwood, dwarf birch, &c., but, on the north side, covered with grass, not a tree or shrub to be seen there. The slopes came right down to the river banks, affording hardly a spot, here or there, on which to pitch a tent. The valley, running east and west, is narrow and wild. We arrived at the camp ground, a rough spot, completely covered with wild leeks or onions, like a cultivated bed. Rain came on, and we hunters were in a poor plight—no shelter whatever, and all the wood and herbage so wet we could not raise a fire for an hour, though every dodge was resorted to: my feet, being saturated, were miserably cold.

The tent and other things were late arriving: the rain turned to snow, and it became bitterly cold; and in the afternoon the snow lay three or four inches deep, even on the low ground.

29th June. I awoke after a bitter cold night, which much interfered with my sleep and comfort. The snow still lay on the ground; but the clouds breaking, giving an occasional gleam of sunshine, every thing was put out to dry.

My dog Sara had been very busy yesterday working, scratching, and digging, at a marmot's burrow. There are numbers of these quaint creatures here constantly seen sitting upright, and uttering a shrill whistle, like the sound of a dog whistle. He continued his operations in the most indefatigable manner to-day; and, having nothing else to do, all set to work to help him unearth the 'varmint'—no easy job, as his earth was under a huge piece of rock. However, at last the poor little beast was assailed in his citadel, and he fought viciously, tooth and claw, but was finally secured by nooses passed over his hind feet, and then dragged ignominiously out to the public gaze. Sara made a rush on him, and tackled him, but not relishing his teeth withdrew from the contest, and I put the poor thing out of further pain by two or three blows on the head.

30th June. We moved on to new ground reported to be frequented by ibex. Several parties, coming down this path, profess to have seen them. Phuttoo, who has been ailing some days, I think from rheumatism, remained to accompany the main body. We, of the light division, came on ahead, and found the carcase of an ibex fresh killed, and partly devoured by wild dogs. This is a terrible blow to our hopes, as in all probability the ibex have been harassed and frightened away from this place. From the camp ground nothing whatever can be seen in the way of game, though the hills look very likely.

In the course of the day some excitement was created by Ali Bucks asserting he saw an ibex. After enquiry and much useless reconnoitring, it was decided to have been a marmot. Soon afterwards I was examining the features of the mountains, and laying out plans for our route in the afternoon with Mooktoo, when we both became aware of real ibex being visible in the very spot I was pointing out as that we should make for. The ibex were numerous, and some large horns among them. They appeared to be excited by something, supposed to be a fight among them. They soon disappeared. But the knowledge that they were actually on the mountain was a great relief, as we feared those rascally dogs had driven them away.

About 2 P.M. we prepared for the chase, and, moving up the valley, reached the glacier from under and out of which the main Wurdwan river flows. This enormous mass of ice and snow fills the upper end of the valley, extending many miles right through the Sooroo Pass, the path running over it. It was awkward work crossing the chasms and rents in it; but it was our only means of getting to the other side of the river. Rain set in, making our anticipated hard labour in ascending the mountain still more formidable and disagreeable.

We paused at the base of the hill to reconnoitre with the glass, and after some time had the satisfaction of seeing the ibex emerge from a hollow, quietly feeding. We counted thirteen. Thus cheered, a plan of attack was considered and fixed. We had as usual a tremendously heavy pull up hill, crossing a place in a ravine much frequented by the ibex; indeed, in smell and appearance like a place where sheep had been folded. Everything tended to raise our hopes.

We worked steadily on, until we reached a good elevation, when Subhan went ahead to scout, and returned with the pleasing intelligence that the ibex were in sight, and undisturbed.

We mounted higher with great caution. Subhan, again scouting, made signs to us—the game was lying down. On, again—excitement becoming great, as we neared our intended prey. Subhan peeped over the crest of the sharp rocky ridge, under shelter of which we were stealthily advancing, and made unmistakable signs of something unexpected and exciting. He beckoned me to bring a rifle; so I climbed to his look-out place, and was gratified by the sight of a single ibex, a large buck, with a magnificent pair of horns. Taking time for breath—the animal evidently unconscious of danger—I fired, the ball apparently striking the shoulder, and breaking the off leg. The animal—wonderful to relate—hardly noticed the wound or the noise, and, to our infinite astonishment, began to eat again. I fired another shot, again striking the shoulder—the animal again shewing little signs of concern, but shortly, with great deliberation, lay down. Not knowing what to make of such strange conduct, I fired another shot, which effectually did the business.

The guns being reloaded, we looked about, and saw a large flock of ibex startled at the reports, but puzzled to know their meaning. Following Subhan, I advanced to intercept them, and gained an eminence overlooking their position which was in a grassy hollow. It was a stirring sight. I suppose there were thirty or forty of them. And leading the way was the master of the herd, a very large buck, with splendid horns.

This one I singled out, but was some time ere I could adjust my rifle, and get a steady aim, as he moved on, here and there, over the uneven ground. I was lying down; but, as he was increasing his distance, there was no time to lose, and I fired, the missile apparently striking him well behind the shoulder. He started, and recoiled, and made off down hill; and at the discharge a regular hurry-skurry took place among the others who, crowding together, took downwards. Two shots brought down one, and wounded others, and away they all went. I loaded and pursued; but they had got across a huge ravine, and were about six hundred yards off. I tried the Enfield; but the bullets struck close to them, and that was all.

I loaded, and turned back to the victims, and found the first a very old animal with only one tooth in his head, his horns very long, but somewhat worn and dilapidated. He was as thin as could be. The other was a young buck.

I now bethought me of the fine fellow I had taken such pains about, and had wounded. We found his bloody trail, and sighted him a long way off, slowly moving on up the mountain. I sent Subhan and a coolie in pursuit, and returned with Mooktoo to skin the others. Heavy rain descended, then snow, with loud peals of thunder over head. A coolie descended the mountain to hail the encampment for assistance. We were in sight of our tents, though miles away, far above them.

A shot was heard in the direction Subhan had taken; and, just as the second animal was skinned, he returned, saying he had killed the wounded ibex, but it was not the big one. This I could not understand, being sure *that* we saw was the identical leader of the herd.

We now descended, again crossed the glacier, and were welcomed in camp, where universal glee prevailed at our success. Poor old Phuttoo was much delighted, and chattering away gaily, calling to mind how he had told me that some day I should have great sport with the ibex.

When the ibex that Subhan had finished was brought in—it was brought in bodily—I exclaimed at once that it was not the one we had seen retreating, not a doubt of it. Subhan declared it was wounded, however. That is probable enough: but the animal we saw was the big buck, the size and colour quite unmistakable—nothing like this little bit of a creature. Subhan acknowledged that owing to the snow, rain, and dense clouds, he could not follow the trail; and, seeing this wounded ibex before him, thought that must be the one he was following, so finished it, and came back.

This was very unsatisfactory, as I gave up a capital chance at the main body to try for this big fellow. I told Subhan that I thought it ought to be retrieved; so he and Mooktoo are going to try and find him to-morrow. I distributed 'backsheesh,' and this being the Mahomedan great day, the 'Eed,' I had in the morning given the shikarries a leg of mutton, tea and sugar, &c.; and now they are singing away merrily.

1st July. Sunday. Much rain fell during the night. Subhan went off to try and discover the wounded ibex.

Heavy rain set in, in the afternoon, and continued without intermission until dark. It was very cold.

Subhan returned quite unsuccessful, the rain having obliterated the tracks. I regret this loss much. It was such a splendid animal, the pick of the herd.

2nd July. On turning out of my tent, dressed and ready to march, I found that a hard frost had come on in the night, and much snow had fallen on the mountains; in consequence of which the glacier was declared to be too dangerous to attempt to cross, as the numerous rents and fissures would be thinly coated over with frozen snow, rendering it impossible to detect and avoid them. I submitted the more patiently to this delay, as the swelling behind my knee was considerably enlarged by my struggles over the slippery ground on Saturday; and I, somehow or other, clung to the forlorn hope of there being a chance of retrieving the lost ibex, if we remained here; that a flight of vultures, buzzards, or crows might point out the carcase.

But no such good fortune appears to await me, as I have been scanning the mountain side till almost blind, but no favourable augury in the skies. The ibex must now be given up as irretrievable.

3rd July. Although rain had fallen, and at early dawn the weather was very unsettled, the shikarries roused me up. I had made up my mind that they would not think it advisable to move, so had composed myself to another allowance of sleep; but was soon dressed, and on the march.

The glacier, which we now had to cross, has all the disagreeables of that peculiarity without its redeeming features, its varied and brilliant tints, such as are renowned in Alpine scenery. This was an ugly, dull, dirty, stony mass of ice and snow filling up the gorge in the chain of mountains, forming the pass through its ridge from the Wurdwan to Sooroo. The ascent was not difficult, except from the cumbering rocks and stones which, brought down from the heights, the accumulation of centuries, lie in heaps and masses, huge and unsightly, nothing picturesque about them. Even their colours are dull and repulsive. And here and there is a yawning chasm, descending into depths unknown, very hideous when looked into.

We had barely reached the general level, when a violent snow-storm burst upon us. The heavens were black, the wind howled in furious gusts, the weather and accompaniments enabling one to realise one's fancies and ideas of a mountain pass in a storm. We battled manfully against it, diverging here and there to avoid danger; and so toiling on reached the most elevated part, the ascent gradual. Here we were free from the rocks and stones, there being only the ice and snow, a layer of fresh-fallen snow having re-carpeted the surface. We crossed many a gaping fissure, and proved that the precaution of the shikarries in not starting the other day was reasonable; for our guide, a Wurdwan peasant, suddenly plunged down, but recovered himself. He had fallen through a crust of drifted snow concealing one of those ugly rents which stretch across from side to side of the gorge.

Our path led to the left. The snow-storm had subsided, and the sun was now shining. The direct course of the pass, hitherto followed, appeared to be obstructed by insurmountable obstacles in the shape of ice and snow, ranged in tiers and ridges to a great height. The mountains, on either side, had been throughout precipitous and extremely rugged—huge crags without a vestige of vegetation. We had now to ascend, and laborious work it was, the snow being soft, and the sun now hot; in addition to which, one's power of breathing was much affected by the extremely rarefied air at this great elevation. The summit gained, the descent was tolerably easy to us more practised mountaineers; but the glare of the snow was terrible. Mooktoo was attacked by severe pains in the head, and lagged behind. I, after stopping to rest a few minutes, and watching four ibex which shewed on the left, when I got up, was almost blind. Luckily we had nearly passed over the snow, and I recovered immediately on quitting it; and about two miles on we reached our destined bivouac, when I was glad to breakfast.

We were now in a narrow valley with the usual mountain torrent, fed by tributaries joining from other like valleys. The mountains were rugged and almost bare, yielding only patches of brushwood here and there, and some scanty herbage, but looked likely for ibex, were it not that a number of tattoos had been brought here to pick up a hard-earned subsistence. The sun now poured down its vertical rays upon us with tremendous effect, and I took up a position alongside a piece of rock to screen myself as well as I could. Of my party the three servants first appeared. Long afterwards the coolies came straggling in; they had a hard day's work.

I arranged to hunt in the morning, though predicting a total failure, tattoos being in all directions.

4th July. A sharp frost during the night, and lots of ice in the morning. I was only informed, when starting, that three coolies were missing, supposed to have been obliged to remain on the glacier from snow-blindness. I ascertained that they had provisions with them, and assistance had gone. Buddoo, classee, and most of the coolies were more or less blind from inflamed eyes.

We went up a valley westward, and before we had gone above four miles found the tracks of numerous dogs—hateful sight—then those of ibex, also numerous. I despaired of seeing any, but still pushed on to a decided bend in the valley, whence a scout could obtain a view of the whole ground. Here we stopped, and the country being reconnoitred without a sign of animals we retraced our steps to camp. The shikarries were much put out, as they had been confident of finding much game in this spot, and had predicted great success. I was the sooner reconciled to the disappointment from learning that the ibex of this region are a short horned breed, as are those of Thibet and Ladâk generally, they tell me.

I found Abdoolah doctoring all the bad eyes, and a most forlorn spectacle the sufferers presented, their eyes smeared with some ochre-coloured mixture, groping their way about as in the dark.

5th July. Up early, and off down the valley in an easterly direction, the valley very narrow, the slopes running down sharp to the river. The heights after a few miles, gradually receding, opened into a transverse valley in which is situated Sooroo and its fort. A few hamlets are scattered here and there on the lower and level slopes nearer the river.

The fort is a square with four small corner turrets. Some half-dozen sepoys hold watch and ward there, I believe.

The sun was very powerful. It was a new atmosphere, country, and people. The country—but that it is mountains, and mountains only, except the divisions of the mountains which form the valleys—is bare and uninteresting, the denizens thereof of small stout frame, and strongly marked Tartar physiognomy—pukka Thibetans.

I paid off the Wurdwan coolies, and proceed to-morrow on the ordinary 'bunderbus' of coolies from stage to stage, except the five entertained for the campaign.

6th July. We were off soon after daylight, following so followers, scaled the mountain, and so commanded the fortress below. Then, a few musket shots being fired, the valiant Bhooties fled manfully.

Under the young trees on an island, gained by stepping stones, I halted to breakfast. Pleased with the picturesque aspect, the cool shade, and fresh moist air, I determined to rest till the sun's abated heat rendered trudging less disagreeable. In the course of the day my attendants passed on; and in due time we also toiled up the zigzag path to the old fort, and travelling over a very stony valley, with a patch of cultivation here and there, reached our quarters, a charming spot for these barbarous regions, a considerable expanse of richly cultivated land, the crops now forward and high.

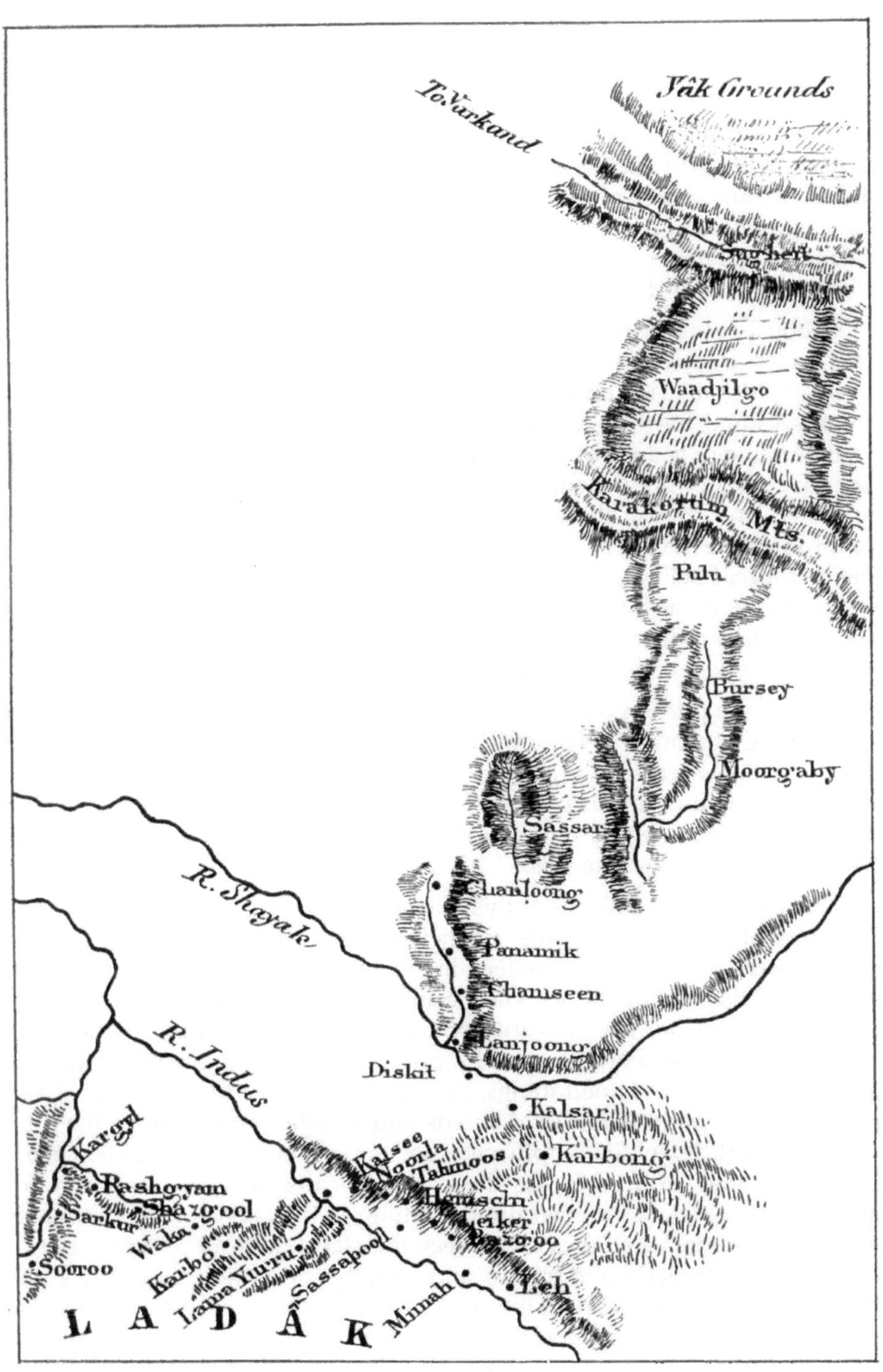

Browne. Lith. Norwich.

The mountains here receding yield a large space for cultivation, of which the inhabitants have availed themselves to the utmost, running their fields and terraces high up the steep slopes, and by means of conduits, ingeniously and laboriously constructed, contrive to compel reluctant nature to bring forth abundant vegetation. The whole landscape is dotted with fine willow trees of large growth, and lines of them flourish thickly planted along the watercourses. And, greatly adding to the beauty and charm of these attractive hamlets, are found a profusion of wild roses, single-blossomed like our red dog-rose, but of powerful perfume. These delicious shrubs line many of the channels for irrigation, reminding one of many a village lane in a far distant land.

The houses of these rude people—rude only in their condition, otherwise personally civil—are rough solid structures of stone, flat-roofed, with a mere hole for a window which, like the door, is closed by a wattled shutter. On the roof is stored the highly-valued, hard-to-be-got supply of fuel, some few fagots, the clippings of the willows, the only species of tree affording anything like timber, and of which their entire stock of implements of husbandry and utensils are formed. Well may they protect and cherish these invaluable trees. They must have some stringent laws for their preservation, and rules for their lopping and felling; the latter extreme measure, I believe, being rarely resorted to, as the branches being lopped, and the very vitals, as it were, of the trunk pared and scooped out, the frame, just the cuticle, clings to life, and again does good service, recovering from its hacking, and putting forth shoots, and putting on branches, times unreckoned.

My tent was pitched on a patch of beautiful greensward, adjoining a square stone building of some pretensions in these parts, a sort of stronghold in days past, and uniting that character with that of a store for grain in the present day, the Maharajah's dues in the various produce being gathered in here from the neighbouring districts. There was but one sepoy here, and a remarkably handsome pleasing-looking young fellow he was.

If the aspect of the villages at this season is charming, that of the inhabitants is, and must at all times be, repulsive. Their features are hideous, excepting an occasional good open forehead, a redeeming feature, giving a look of intelligence to otherwise brutish countenances. Their want of attraction is increased by the state of filth they wallow in. The men are clothed in a sort of loose tunic of dark brown woollen, felt leggings wound round by garters, and felt boots with leathern feet. These are large canoe-shaped things, having no reference to the size or shape of the foot, but are wadded with old shreds and woollen rags to make them fit. A close-fitting skullcap, with an upturned rim, crowns their greasy heads. Then, the females—can they be the fair sex, these hideous specimens of creation human? They wear, also, a dark woollen tunic reaching to the knees, with continuations of the same materials. As far as I have seen they have no head covering, but wear their greasy hair in plaits and tresses, and actually adorn their chevelure with the wild flowers, roses, &c., with all the vanity that might an European beauty. These ill-placed ornaments are disposed over either temple. They also wear felt boots; theirs, as the men's, being wide at top, and reaching above the ancle, giving to both sexes a clumsiness about the feet, which adds to their uncouth, ungraceful appearance. Both sexes wear a goat skin with the hair on, as a cloak. They have some rude gewgaws by way of jewellery; and where are the females found who have not? The Australian aboriginal ladies, who may be quoted as in the most humble circumstances, wear a white bone thrust through the cartilage of the nose-bones, shells, or stones in their ears—and a dab of raw meat fat, by preference, in their locks, and think it the 'ne plus ultra' of feminine adornment. It remains only to note, that so valued and valuable are these creatures here, that one individual is allotted to two or three husbands—one wife to a family of brothers—which of itself sufficiently establishes their utter barbarism.

A young official, a Cashmiri, the moonshi of the Sooroo kardar, had come on with us to make the necessary arrangements for coolies and tattoos. One of the latter had been provided for me to-day, but looked such a woe-begone thing that I did not like to entrust it with my person, somewhat too weighty for such a bit of a steed; so I trudged it out. But, feeling considerable fatigue and soreness of foot from the long rough journey, I assented to a tattoo being provided for the morrow, and several were now paraded for choice, mostly mares with foals beside them. By the bye, I must note that a mile from Sooroo we had to cross a torrent—all torrents here—by one of those ingenious and curious suspension bridges, doubtless the originals from which our magnificent structures were conceived and framed, made of twigs of willow woven into ropes, and the ropes into large cables. They are thus constructed. A pier of stones is built up without mortar, on either side, close to the water: within the pier are planted two upright stems of trees about two feet apart, and a transverse one secured on the top, over which the suspension cables are hauled and strained, and fastened down by large stones piled on them: the footway is a plait of this twig work about ten inches wide, suspended from the two side cables by numerous connecting ropes of like manufacture, of about three feet depth. One ascends the pile of stones, stooping low, creeps through the two uprights, and with a hand on each side-cable performs a sort of acrobatic 'pas' on the slack rope, swinging about uncomfortably. However, I relished the novelty of the thing, this being the first of these bridges I had come across. My little dog, Sara, did not relish it at all, but, having assayed a step or two, retreated in a very ridiculous, nervous manner, and was then ignominiously carried over, enveloped in a cloth, on the sepoy's shoulders, whence he anxiously watched the passage. And how he did skip and jump, when he was safe over!

I must also remember to note that many birds of European kinds were met with, some of which I had not found before, as magpies, and the pretty little goldfinch. There are larks too, which are common enough, and enliven these regions with their merry notes, warbling until quite dark at evening, and again, ere coming day, cheering one with their quick trilling chirp and song. The homely sparrow, too, was present, and also the solemn old crow. A couple of the former quaint, pert, little birds attended most familiarly at my dinner, coming fearlessly close to the table to receive fragments, only temporarily routed by the sudden desperate onslaughts of Sara at them, who pursued them with relentless animosity, they just keeping beyond his reach, and again returning when he, out of breath, was busily occupied with his bone. They were merely birds attached to the village, quite at large, yet wonderfully tame, and treating me as an old acquaintance, jumping to catch bits thrown to them, their bright, little, black eyes glittering and rolling, as they appeared as though they were saucily winking at me—the jolly old birds!

The name of this village was Sarkur, as near as I can define the sound.

CHAPTER VIII.

LADÂK.

7th July. Up at the earliest dawn, and off, with a string of tattoos and foals following. I did not understand the meaning of this, but ere the journey had well commenced discovered that the shikarries had craftily schemed to save their shoe leather, and through the influence of my 'purwanah' had persuaded the moonshi to press these animals into our service. Poor Subhan, however, had as leader to march before me who had resolved not to ride before breakfast at any rate.

The road was very fair, always accompanying the river, and leading through hamlets such as have been already described, some of much interest, with their narrow lanes of rose bushes which were one mass of blossom, and delightfully fragrant. In one place, was a hedge of yellow roses covered with blossoms which were, unlike the red, double and well-formed, but of inferior perfume. The red rose hedge on one side, and yellow on the other, had a pretty effect; and I imagine their being thus placed to be purely accidental.

We tramped on manfully, Subhan and I, the other fellows riding with the moonshi in the rear, for some three or four hours, when arriving at a thriving village where we were to change coolies, not horses, I stopped to breakfast, and on the arrival of attendants started afresh about noon, it being cloudy and tolerably cool. I mounted the moonshi's tattoo, a well-bred, nice looking mare; and oh! the bother of regulating the stirrups, or trying to do so, for I had to ride, after all, with one some eight or nine inches longer than the other; and such a hard scrimpy, little bit of a saddle—I should have been better off, had I walked the whole distance, long though it was, I believe.

Soon after leaving this village we passed through another, and left a large cultivated valley on our right, entering upon a track of rocky desolation.

From the base of the mountains to the river's brink was nothing but heaps of stones, apparently water-worn stones, a very wilderness of stones—ten thousand Londons might have been paved from them, and they would not have been missed. The mountains, big, brown, and ugly, towered behind them; the sun came out fiercely, the saddle pinched, the stirrup leather galled, the little mare, weary, fumbled drearily along through the loose stones, and I did not altogether feel as though I liked it. However, I was charitable to the poor little nag, and, barring an occasional impatient jerk of the bridle and a mild jog of the heel, took no steps to urge her to greater exertions. So, on we slowly wended our weary way, the country after a while improving, and again presenting verdant stretches of cultivation with the usual accompaniment of willow trees, and now, not unfrequently, poplars, most of which, like Greenwich pensioners, had lost a limb or two, or been otherwise maimed. Hedgerows of roses became more abundant, and one or two small villages were lovely with them, and their rich crops of grain—beans, peas, and lucerne, all in bloom—adding beauty and fragrance to the scene. Bright sparkling water, too, in plenty trickled across and down our path.

But, though I tried hard, I could not properly enjoy all these charms: I was so weary and uncomfortable. Some five or six miles beyond where I looked for our halting-place, Kargyl, we at length reached it—an irregular basin, into which flows the river I have been following, and another from the east, both united flowing out in a northerly direction as a large rapid river. A square fort with corner turrets is the principle feature, glaring with whitewash. The crops all around are fresh and green, the whole surrounded by massive mountains of varied form, but of one hue of sombre brown.

8th July. Sunday. A delightful fresh morning, which induced me to take a stroll before breakfast, feeling now perfectly recovered from yesterday's fatigues. I had pitched my tent in a small tope of young poplars, in the midst of which some clear water, escaped from a channel in the hill above, had found its way moistening the ground and producing fine green turf, but leaving a dry sandy space for a tent. Sand-flies were numerous and pertinacious. During the night I was suddenly roused with a sensation of something in my hair; raising my hand I clutched something of peculiar substance, but felt it had legs. I threw it on one side shuddering, and was amused this morning at seeing the object of my fright on the canvas over my head—a large, fat, green caterpillar, with a pair of tweezers at his tail, with which he held on.

My stroll led through the small fields hanging on the hill-side, supported by rough stone walls in terraces, the crops rich and beautifully green. My path was agreeably lined by rose bushes. Many flowers and sweet scented herbs were also on either hand, and some poplars and a fine mulberry tree or two were a great addition to the general features of the landscape. I turned here or there, following the windings, and ups and downs, of the borders of the field, until I had gained an eminence overhanging the valley down which the river rushed and foamed, fields lining its banks. It was a very beautiful view, the lofty mountains exhibiting their massive proportions well-defined at this early hour of the day, a haze in the distance improving the effect. The air was cool, balmy, and delicious, fragrant with the perfume of flowers. Long I gazed around, and much I mused. There was much in the scene before me, and its fresh, sweet, mild atmosphere, that reminded me strongly of other lands that I had visited—Madeira, Malta, the Cape. There appeared to me a decided blending of similarity with the two former, and also a trait or two undefinable of the latter.

I was amused by the manœuvres of a startled child, too small to run away, who had been deserted by his companions, in alarm at my approach. The 'wee' chap was squatted amid some tussocks, and clumps of flag, the blue Iris, I think; and, as I advanced, he turned himself round one, believing that he was effectually concealing himself from the formidable monster approaching. But my sharp hunter's eye had at once detected him, and without stopping, lest he might be too much terrified, I spoke to him caressingly—at least, I tried to. This was before I paused and mused, as above. When I returned, he was still beside his fancied screen, but no longer performed his evolutions. He gazed on me still with evident wonder and awe, though at the same time somewhat reassured, so I did not approach too near. This slight incident, somehow or other, had a pleasing influence on me, and sent me back cheerful to camp.

The sky became overcast, and in the afternoon there was a violent wind, and at last rain, so I kept my covering.

9th July. A very cloudy morning saw me under-weigh at 5 A.M. We crossed the river by a good wooden bridge on rough stone piers, situated just below my tent. Then, ascending the other side, and mounting a stiffish hill, we found ourselves on a table land—open undulating downs—closed in, of course, by mountains. These downs had but a tinge of green, as from the sandy soil and want of water there was but a very light, sparse herbage on them. The air was delicious, cool, and fresh, the rain of yesterday having purified the atmosphere, and brought out all the latent perfume of the plants around.

I tramped gaily on, chatting with Subhan, the other shikarries keeping in the rear on tattoos. I had given no permission or authority for engaging these ponies, and was rather puzzled to know how they were provided. However, I said nothing, intending to ascertain in the evening, as I had no notion of paying for ponies for these lazy scamps. Knowing the parties, I suspected some underhand tricks.

The path for some miles led up a stream bordered by fields interspersed with roses, a few houses here and there; then, leaving the village of Pashgyam, it entered upon a barren ravine, running along the hill-side; and so on, until we came upon more cultivation and a pretty village, where in a charming spot under some willows, by a clear brawling brook, I stopped for breakfast, having been on the march four hours.

My food was not altogether satisfactory; half my tea had oozed out of the bottle; one egg was all yellow, instead of that colour being confined to the yolk. This was pitched into the stream. Another with a slight touch of the jaundice I devoured reluctantly, and repented having done so afterwards. And from the condition of my dough cakes I think Ali Bucks must be moulting, the black hairs are so numerous, and being long they cannot be extracted. Small matters these to an old campaigner. I got some good fresh milk, and the fine air was 'edibles.' After a while, I noticed the arrival of a sepoy with a native who remained discussing something with the shikarries, Mr. Phuttoo being principal. This lasted some time, and they, perceiving that I noticed what was going on, moved away. I called Subhan, and asked him what the sepoy wanted, and what they discussed. Nothing at all, he assured me. Shortly after, a Thibetan came rushing down to me, vociferating and claiming protection; and it turned out that these rascally shikarries had pressed his tattoos by some connivance of the moonshi at Kargyl. I directed them to be given up at once, and turned away in disgust from these lying knaves. It is no use saying any thing. They tell you that it is the 'dustoor,' the custom of the country; and they all practise oppression over each other, whenever they possibly can.

I forgot to record before, that the shikarries told me on the morning I left the camp before reaching Sooroo, a place where they had assured me we should have two or three days' good sport with ibex, that a man, a friend of Subhan's, tending ponies pasturing there, had confided to him the previous night, that the Sooroo kardar, hearing that a 'burra saheb' was coming to 'shikar,' and apprehending that if he found sport he would stop some days and would be troublesome to him for supplies, had sent men with guns and dogs to hunt and scare away the game; that they had killed one ibex, and only left the place the evening we arrived. On first hearing this, I scouted the idea; it was so very improbable. But Subhan and the others repeated the story with such asseverations, and so many plausible corroborations, that I partly believed them. On arriving at Sooroo these knaves assumed a high tone, and frightened the poor old kardar who did not come near me for some time; but having appeased the shikarries by a 'douceur,' as I suppose, they told him I would receive him, and forgive him on apologising. Now I believe the whole story to have been false from beginning to end, and actually plotted and devised to extort something from the kardar. Verily, in these parts, all men are liars.

We continued our route, and plodded on, the sun now hot, finally arriving at our camping place, the village of Shazgool, a Buddhist place, with the lama's house curiously built into the face of a perpendicular rock looking down on the village, a shabby tumble-down place, and some tombs or shrines tawdrily painted with clumsy devices of hideous demons on them. These are paltry looking constructions, of mud principally.

This was a small village of some nine or ten houses in a dilapidated condition; but they are all apparently in like bad case, the inhabitants miserably poor, judging from their appearance and surrounding indications. But they seem to be stout, healthy, and cheerful. The women, I fancy, do most of the work, as with all barbarians. A large wicker basket seems to be a fixture on their backs, and with this appendage they are seen busy in the fields, weeding, putting every shred of herbage so gathered into the said basket which by evening is filled, when they return, and the produce of their industry serves for fodder for cow, sheep, or goat, every blade of vegetation being of value in these barren regions, where nothing grows but what is actually extorted from reluctant nature. How different from the adjoining country of Cashmere, where, on the other hand, nature is profuse in her gifts, covering mountain and valley with the richest herbage, and yielding heavy crops of cereals to the merest scratches of the plough. Both are wonderful countries: Cashmere, for its beauty and fertility; Thibet, for its savage desolation and sterility. The natives of each land, too, partake strongly of the relative characteristics of their native land: the Cashmiries, famous for personal beauty,—the Thibetans, as notorious for ugliness. Strange, though, they possess some taste; for almost every individual of the numbers met travelling yesterday and to-day had a bunch of yellow roses, or other bright flowers stuck in his greasy cap.

10th July. On the march at 5 A.M.—the path as ever in these mountainous regions running by a stream threading the narrow valley. Here and there was a strip of green cultivation, with brown mountains, mounts, huge hillocks, all barren, some craggy, others smoothly rounded, heap on heap, pile on pile, here falling sloping back, allowing the eye to range over many successive wave-like summits, there rising up abruptly with crags, and clefts, and dark ravines, closing in upon and overshadowing the narrow valley. I tried to find some mode of description by which one might give a person verbally some tolerable idea of the combined desolation and grandeur of these scenes; but all in vain.

We had a long and fatiguing ascent, prior to which we passed through the village of Waka, near which abutting on the path, is a sculptured rock standing alone, representing a Hindoo deity. The figure is carved on the face of the rock which is of granite, I think, the height about thirty feet, and the workmanship the average of what one sees in Hindostan. A small mud building closes in the lower extremities of this idol, in which is a shrine; and I found within garlands, and signs of recent worship, some few professors of Hindooism residing close by. The natives call this idol, Mohir Chamba, and say it is of great antiquity; but to me the chiselling appeared fresh and sharp. This, however, from the hard quality of the stone would be the case for a length of time, especially in this dry climate. There are few Hindoos now in Thibet, Buddhism being the prevailing creed. Many mussulmans are scattered among them.

Men are now met with wearing pig-tails, Chinese fashion. They have a different cap, too—a long bag of black woollen stuff which is turned over, covering the top and one side of the head. The Maltese, if I recollect right, wear one precisely similar.

Finding no shelter from the sun after breakfast, having halted an hour we continued our route, now downwards, until we descried one or two willows in a hamlet; for which we made, and glad enough we were to escape the sun's scorching rays, and rest ourselves. We moved on again about two o'clock—much too soon; and, after two or three miles, further grilling, we stopped at Karbo, our halt.

There are many Buddhist monuments here, rude tombs of mud and loose stones. The principal feature is a thing like a great sugared cake, perhaps intended to represent an urn: adjoining and connected with this is a raised oblong, varying in length—some are ten feet, some twenty, others fifty—built up of stones, about four feet high, the top flattish, and covered all over with loose flat stones, all sculptured, both in figures and letters. These tombs contain the bones of sainted lamas, I believe. They are very inferior to the tombs and pagodas met with in Burmah, some of which are beautiful specimens of architecture, and extremely picturesque. All I have seen here as yet are mean and paltry. These monuments are whitewashed, the wash remarkable for its lustrous quality. I questioned Phuttoo as to the composition. He said it was a substance dug out of the earth. I observed that it differed much from that in use in India. He said, it was not 'chunani.' I imagine it to be a kind of chalky pigment.

11th July. Away, with the dawn, though we had not so long a march in prospect as those of the two previous days, which must have been over twenty miles. But it is well to start early to enjoy the freshness of morn, and avoid the excessive heat of the sun which I really think I endure better than the shikarries. The scenery of to-day was similar to that of yesterday, which is, I imagine, the type of the entire region, unless the banks of the Indus present any variety: if so, it will only be in the height and formation of the mountains. There was a gradual ascent, with a sharp pitch at the end, to the summit of the hill on which was a stone Buddhist monument, and in its shade I stopped to breakfast. From this eminence the view was extensive and interesting, the adjacent mountains possessing peculiar features, and being so distributed as to afford good distances.

I stopped till the small building no longer protected me from the sun; then, perforce, braved his potent rays, and pursued my route on to Lama Yurru, our intended bivouac.

As we descended to the level of the valley, opening a bend I detected some wild looking animals moving from among some cattle. Subhan, after a while, declared them to be shâpu, wild sheep; so guns were got ready, and with small prospect of success, the ground being level and bare, we prepared to stalk them. The game, numbering some twenty-five head, rufous coloured animals, of deer-like form and action, with two small upright horns curving backwards, were gambolling, moving here and there; nor did they become aware of dangerous neighbours, until we were about a hundred yards from them, when they stood gazing for some seconds, presenting a fair mark. But, alas! my lungs were heaving so that I could not take aim, Subhan, in spite of my oft-repeated lectures and warnings, hurrying on 'ventre a terre,' so that with the attitude I was quite distressed, and only looked and longed at the inviting target before me, entertaining a sort of hope that they would give me time. But not so; a few seconds only to gaze, and away they cantered in a string across us. Rising, I aimed at the line; the ball struck true in direction but low, I think, the scared animals dashing aside right and left. A thud, however, was heard, and we all thought that one was hit; when looking some little distance beyond, there stood an unfortunate bullock, one hind leg slightly raised from the ground, and blood trickling down. There was only time for an exclamation or two as we followed the herd now making for a hill, when they were on which I fired my battery at them, the distance three or four hundred yards, the balls striking right amongst them—wonderful how they all missed!

Now came full upon me the sense of my misfortune and ill luck. There stood the hapless bullock patiently and silently enduring his wrongs, his poor wounded leg still shrinking from the ground on which the oozing blood was frothing. I was much annoyed and grieved at this mishap. The poor wounded creature looked so melancholy in its patient, silent attitude, and I feared the wound was mortal. The ball from Whitworth, striking the ground, had doubtless glanced, and so struck the wrong animal. I loudly deplored my ill luck: the shikarries dumbfounded muttered together, attributing such a strange accident to the undue influence of evil spirits; and we pursued our way down the dusty path, until the green vale of Lama Yurru greeted our aching eyes—a remarkable place, a stronghold of Buddhism, a monastery and other dwellings of lamas being perched on the top of a singular ridge of rocks of some hundred and fifty feet perpendicular, scooped and hollowed out here and there, divided into buttresses over which were laid the floors of these curious buildings which themselves appear well constructed of sun-dried brick, of two or three stories in height—one the principal mansion of four. Some have little balconies projecting; all have windows, some good-sized and regularly placed, while a number of small loopholes are scattered about the walls. These buildings slope inwards from the base slightly, on the pyramid principle, as I believe all the houses of this country do. Many monuments and tombs are here. Long rows of them stretch along parallel with the path, looking just like a line of huge chess pawns with square pedestals.

A considerable extent of terraced fields along the stream attest the comfortable circumstances of this community. Clumps of yellow and common roses are numerous; but sad havoc has been played with the willows, the stump of many a fine tree recently felled being conspicuous: but about half-a-dozen remain standing. I have not ascertained for what purpose this unusual cutting has taken place: perhaps, some new building or extensive repairs are in contemplation. My tent is pitched on a nice bit of turf, a stream of clear water close at hand, guided to turn a small mill which rumbles away beside me.

On reaching this place I threw myself down disconsolate beneath a shady willow, the shikarries endeavouring to divert me from my gloomy mood by anecdotes of accidents and mishaps of a far more melancholy colour than mine;—how a shikarry had shot a man in his own field for a bear, this very man having indicated that identical spot as the place the bear would be found in, then by fate being led thither himself, and, concealed by the high grain, there slain. Several similar instances were narrated. Phuttoo, the most eloquent and storied of the trio, winding up with an astounding accident that befell his father who, when with Golab Sing and his army, in some unaccountable manner shot a bear; the ball, passing clean through the bear, killed outright six sepoys, all in a lump, and wounded a seventh in the arm. The Maharajah conducted an inquest personally on this lamentable slaughter of his warriors, and found the circumstances so marvellous, and Phuttoo senior's 'kizmet' so wonderful in effecting such destruction with one ball, that he over-looked the loss of his men, and presented him with two hundred rupees, backsheesh;—a nice, veracious, little narrative this. The other shikarries, of course, vouched for its accuracy.

On arrival I despatched a man to ascertain the nature of the wound of the bullock, and to whom it belonged, in order to compensate the owner. Resolved not to hunt to-morrow, needing some repose after these long marches, I arranged to send out two villagers to scout. After dinner the messenger returned, bringing intelligence of the wounded beast which turned out to be a cow, less valuable in these parts than a bullock; which latter, being used for carriage of merchandise, are more highly prized. The wound he seemed to think not mortal. I differ: a Whitworth bolt is no trifle, and the frothing blood a bad symptom.

All the natives of the place came to look at us, and visit the shikarries, Phuttoo being known to some of them. One of the group had in his waist-belt a double flageolet, or rather whistle, which I requested him to play. He made an attempt or two, but failed except to produce some unsatisfactory notes, excusing himself on the plea of nervousness and alarm at performing before so great a dignitary. The two pipes are in unison, I think.

I am going to remain here three or four days; certainly over Sunday, whether sport is found or not, as I want my servants and things from Sirinuggur to join me. My original plan was for them to meet me at Kargyl; but the shikarries made such a bad bunderbus, dissuading me from sending orders from Shugkenuz, as I proposed, that they could only have started from Sirinuggur on the 6th, and we reached Kargyl on the 8th, to which place it is ordinarily eight days' march from the former place. A longer delay is likely to take place owing to a deficiency of coolies, as the messenger of a saheb 'en route' to Ladâk informed us. He said, the Maharajah was sending his whole army to subdue the Gylghit tribes who were in open revolt against his authority, and that all available means of transport had been taken up to accompany the force. He told me there were fears entertained that my baggage could not be sent on at present. This would be unfortunate as I am out of powder nearly, and should have to send in and wait the return of the messenger ere proceeding further. But the Baboo would have written in such an extremity: so I hope, four or five days hence, to welcome my belongings. This messenger overtook us on the march from Kargyl: he is in the employment of Lieut. Brinckman, 94th, who has gone into Chan-than, beyond Ladâk, on a shooting expedition; where I had thought of going but for the strong dissuasions of Phuttoo who represented that country as a most sterile, dusty, and difficult region to traverse, everything—even to grass—having to be carried, and the wild yâk, the only object worth the trouble and risk, even if seen, which was exceedingly doubtful, a most difficult creature to approach.

On these and other similar representations, I abandoned the idea, limiting my travels eastward to Leh and its environs, where I propose remaining a few days, giving Suleiman an opportunity of offering his Scriptures, &c.; thence to make my way to Iskardo, returning to Cashmere through the Tilyl valley, by which time the bara sing will be in season.

12th July. I took a saunter along under the lamas' dwellings, then down into the barley fields—very pleasant this leisurely stroll after my three days' hard, broiling work. The two villagers, sent out at dawn to scout, returned with the unsatisfactory information that they had searched far and wide, but seen nothing. However, we did not place much dependence on them.

In the evening, taking my glass, I went off myself in the direction in which it was stated the game would be found, if anywhere. But not a vestige of shikar could I discover. I saw Subhan go by on the same errand, and returned to dinner. On coming back he reported a barren country without a trace of game.

I had great doubt about trying to-morrow, but after some consultation determined to convince myself on the question of game or no game; and, if none should be found, to shift camp on Saturday across the Indus to Kalsee, reported by the shikarries to be a nice village, with many trees, and undoubted shikar in the neighbourhood; so that will be a pleasanter locale in which to await my things, and it is but eight or nine miles off.

The owner of the wounded cow came to report on the health of that unfortunate quadruped which by his statement is alive, but in a bad way, lying down and eating nothing. I fancy something definite will be known to-morrow.

13th July. I started at dawn with not very pleasant anticipations of my day's work, expecting very hard walking in a barren stony country, with hardly a chance of sport. And so it turned out. We ascended hills, and traversed table lands, and peered into gullies right and left, but saw not a glimpse of game: so, after some three hours and a half of this unsatisfactory toil, we descended to a stream on the road, hard by where I shot the cow; there breakfasted, and returned to camp.

We again passed some of those curious Buddhist erections—long, oblong, tomb-shaped piles. There were two about fifty yards long each, with an interval of some thirty yards. The tops were slightly slanted from the centre, and covered with the smooth, flat, water-worn stones, except a few yards left to be filled in by them. These stones were all inscribed with figures, or Thibetan characters; and I endeavoured to ascertain from the two native attendants, through the interpretation of the shikarries, the meaning of the inscriptions, and the object with which they were so placed. But my gleanings were very scanty, the shikarries having but a limited stock of Hindostani phrases, not a general knowledge of the language, and only a few words of Thibetan. But thus much I made out; that every stone was similar in its inscription, bearing the words—as well as I can letter the sounds—Mâni, Pâni, Pudma-hoo—which I understood to be one of the titles of their divinity, and that these engraved stones were thus presented as an oblation and offering acceptable to their god—being an act of faith and devotion from which as a consequence prosperity is looked for. More I could not discover, the shikarries being very obtuse in apprehending an idea on such subjects. These are not tombs, then, but rather altars.

On return I announced my intention to move to-morrow. The lumbadar came to see me. He had just returned from Leh, had a decided Thibetan face, and wore some ornaments, necklace, ear-rings &c., of red coral and turquoise. These appear to be the fashionable jewels here, nearly all—the poorest even, in rags and tatters—having a bit or two stuck about them. He showed me a card written by poor Moorcroft who perished so sadly in Bokhara, bearing date June 16th, 1822, stating that he had presented a coral to the monastery, as a token of his visit. This lumbadar was an interesting fellow, evidently very bashful and sensitive, but quick in apprehension and intelligent.

The cow case came up for final adjudication, the animal in the same condition; so after some discussion I gave the owner the full price of the cow, as stated, *viz*: six Maharajah rupees—only five shillings English—and, if it recovered, so much the better, he would be a lucky fellow. So ends this sporting episode. It has not been without its good results in establishing the European character for justice.

14th July. We got away at 5 A.M., and took the path onwards to Kalsee. It threads a narrow gorge giving exit to the waters of a torrent, the scenery grand and savage—towering cliffs, beetling crags, shutting out the sky. The path was conducted in the most irregular evolutions and zigzags, and occasionally running almost into the river; so much so that I was reduced to mounting Subhan at two places to keep dry. We crossed several well-constructed bridges, and came upon a much larger stream, which we followed through its devious windings to the Indus. In one place it rushed along a channel cut in the solid rock, each side level and scarped as though by man, the depth being some twelve feet, and the width about six.

At length this ravine, opening out a little, debouched upon the valley of the Indus running at right angles to our course, and here a dirty, shabby-looking river, of some twenty or thirty yards in width, in a narrow and sterile valley, the mountains on either side shelving down so close to the river as to leave little more than a few yards of level on which was the path. We saw on the opposite side men working at a hole, and on our own met others with gold-washing implements,—a wooden, flat, boat-shaped affair, with a cane-work frame, and ladles of gourd. I believe the yield is very scanty.

On, about a mile, to a bridge over the Indus, on this side of which is a Buddhist shrine; on the Ladâk side is a small fort of sun-dried brick, very insignificant—a three-pounder would knock it into 'smithereens' in half a dozen rounds. There are three or four sepoys here. All goods are weighed here, and pay duty before crossing.

It was about half a mile further to Kalsee: and pleasant, indeed, it was to see the green trees and fields. The place appeared quite civilised after the savage country we had traversed. There were large gardens and fields fenced in by stone walls, fruit trees thickly interspersed amid the grain, principally standard peaches, the fruit now at about half its size. The whole wore a charming aspect of industry and improvement. Passing along the walls, we came under the village which, built on the side of a rocky hill, overlooks its smiling terraced fields and orchards, now beautifully green. The path now led under some fine spreading walnuts, affording delicious shade, a most grateful relief to my aching eyes, parched and bloodshot from the burning glare of the barren rocky regions I have been crossing.

No level spot of sufficient space, devoid of grain, being available for my tent, I resolved to purchase the crop under a walnut tree, so ordered the attendance of the Zemindar, with whom the shikarries and sepoy bargained, the price being fixed at a pukka rupee. While this was going on, an alarming attack was made upon the intruders from above. The proprietor's better half, having got tidings from some busy-body of what was going on, descending took up a position above us, and began to wag her tongue violently, as some of the dear creatures can do. Not relishing this music, and fearing that, if she was not satisfied, we should have a constant repetition of it, I offered an additional half-rupee, explaining my reason for this excessive liberality. This being interpreted to the Zemindar caused him and the bystanders much merriment, for I fancy that I made a hit in attributing a voluble tongue to this howling harridan. All was now serene, and I was installed in my barley field under the fine walnut tree; and much did I relish my homely meal, reposing under its pleasant shade.

We had some talk on the prospect of sport here. There are ibex and shâpu a few miles off, but not in any numbers, and the ground very difficult: the latter information I regard little, feeling now equal to anything. I despatched a villager, professing to know the haunts of the animals, to procure accurate information; and on Monday mean to try my fortunes in the chase again. I fancy myself now inured to disappointment and ill-luck.

My tree did not effectually protect me from the sun when declining from its meridian height; so about 2 P.M. it was oppressively hot, and continued so long after sunset. I had not calculated on so sudden a change of temperature, and was really unwell from its effects. Lama Yurru always afforded a cool refreshing breeze; and there is a considerable difference in the altitude of the two places, which gives that place the advantage of the cooling influence of the snows on the neighbouring mountain heights, from which Kalsee is too distant to benefit at this season.

I turned into my little oven of a tent, the heat very great, and innumerable sandflies adding their torments to its discomforts.

15th July. Sunday. After a restless night I arose not feeling much refreshed, but taking a stroll, and ascending a hill, the fresh morning air and fine bold scenery gradually had its beneficial effect on mind and body. I mounted some distance, expecting a prospect in the direction we should proceed to-morrow, where, by the way, Subhan and Mooktoo have gone on their own suggestion to look about and make enquiries. I found the view intercepted by an elevation too considerable to encounter as I felt, so sat down amid the boulders, still having a splendid prospect up the Indus, not seeing much of the river but the adjacent mountains which were more varied in form and broken up than usual here; and the colouring was this morning rich, and yet subdued and toned down under the effects of a delicious haze, the soft morning light sobering the too glaring browns of these naked rocks, leading them away from the foreground by imperceptible variations of shade—here and there a suspicion of olive green—until they were lost in the pervading blues and greys of distance. The tone was soft and mellow yet cool. I was charmed; and my mind soon took that devotional phase which such influences are so apt to produce.

I returned in mind serene and cheerful to camp. I had directed my tent to be shifted a few feet, by which move it was in shade all day, and consequently I felt the heat less. Indeed, I did not experience any discomfort from it, as a strong breeze from northward was blowing, rustling among the leaves overhead, and sweeping with pleasant music over the green crops bending and waving to its pressure, which would have imparted an idea, if not a reality, of coolness to one, had it been actually hotter. The shikarries returned, reporting the ground to be entirely devoid of even the tracks of game. They had extended their search over an extensive range, and had interrogated some native shikarries shooting partridges, but the result ever the same—nothing. We agreed, therefore, to shift camp to-morrow some eight miles further towards Leh, and there try our luck. This country, however, is so barren and desolate that I despair of sport here.

After dinner the shikarries came for a chat. I was interested in their account of the brothers Schlagentweit who were some time in Cashmere, prosecuting their explorations in natural science. Subhan had been in their employ for some months, collecting specimens for them; and his account thereof, and his amazement at such, to him, worthless rubbish being thus treasured and sent to Europe, was very droll. It escaped in the course of his narrative, that these talented naturalists were, from their mysterious experiments, more than suspected of connection with the Evil One, and of practising sorceries, &c.

Subhan, trying to put on an air of unconcern and incredulity, evident uncertainty and suspicion evincing themselves in his tone and manner, described how these 'savans' mysteriously and with cautious secrecy dug holes in a garden at night, covering them over, and leaving a candle or lamp burning near, he and others being ordered to watch and see that no one meddled. "Nobody," said Subhan, "was ever allowed to see what was put into these holes, and, when questioned, the sahebs told them the matter was beyond their comprehension," But, he added, it got about, and was confidently asserted, that these strange operators had purchased a slave to whom they administered doses of 'shrâb' (spirits) till he was insensible: they then buried him in the ground, in order to make a good specimen to add to their collection. The shikarries all eyed me in that peculiar manner denoting a partial belief in a wonder, with a certain sense of its improbability. I burst out laughing, of course, at this extraordinary misconception of some scientific experiments, and believe I removed this lurking suspicion of black deeds on the part of the innocent philosophers from their deluded minds.

I understand that search is still being made after the effects of the unfortunate one of these three, whose death in the wild regions north-east of Simla is yet enveloped in obscurity. I heard just before leaving the Punjab, that some tidings had been received, and there were hopes of recovering the poor fellow's effects and papers, the latter of which would, doubtless, prove valuable to science.

All arranged for a move to-morrow.

CHAPTER IX.

LEH.

16th July. We got off early as usual on such occasions: without making any effort to start at a fixed time, we are always punctual to 5 A.M. within a minute or two. It was a cloudy morning, such as in any other country would indicate rain. Our route lay along the Indus, the surrounding scenery mountainous and barren, with no redeeming features, until we had completed some six miles, which brought us to the considerable village of Noorla, looking nice and flourishing with its green fields and abundant fruit trees, apple and peach, scattered about. We passed through this village, and then turned up a watercourse to the left—north-east—and a mile or two further on arrived at the village of Tahmoos, exhibiting a long stretch of corn fields along the stream, with numbers of apple and peach trees generally interspersed, also some fine flourishing walnuts. Houses were grouped here and there, some on the hill-sides on whose summits are visible what appear to be remains of an extensive fort, but may only be the appurtenances of the Buddhist monasteries and shrines which stand out conspicuously amongst them.

The lamas are evidently strong in this neighbourhood. They, like the monks of old in our native land, are to be found congregated in the most fertile and richest spots in the country. The mode of life and habits of these Buddhist recluses assimilate very much also to those of the monks. They live in sloth and idleness on the labours of an ignorant and superstitious population, in requital for their maintenance and comfort performing such religious rites as their formulary directs, and repeating prayers. But their principle occupation, I am told, is blowing copper horns—from which I have experience of their producing awful sounds—and drinking tea, which they render a substantial article of food by mixing it with butter to the consistency of batter. They wear a monastic dress of a dull red colour. I saw one of the fraternity to-day—and a very ugly specimen he was—pass by, two or three times, with a bright copper concern in his hand about the size and shape of a cook's flour-dredging tin, to which a string and tassel were attached which he kept twirling round as he went. This was probably some devotional act.

We took up a narrow strip of ground shaded by walnut and peach trees—not bad quarters—and here I breakfasted; which meal did not pass over so pleasantly as usual. My milk brought with me was sour: it was carried as usual in a soda-water bottle. I directed fresh to be brought, and when it arrived it was very dirty, as is everything here. Mooktoo and Subhan set to work to prepare it for my use, the process as follows:—Subhan's turban was taken off and two end folds used as a strainer, a portion being depressed into the neck of the soda-water bottle; but as the milk did not run through freely Mooktoo expedited its progress by stirring it up with his finger. This not answering their expectations, the milk was strained into an utensil belonging to them, and then poured into the bottle, Mooktoo's fist encircling the neck answering the purpose of a funnel. All this was openly operated before me, and the bottle, thus 'nicely' replenished, presented to me with a satisfied smile of successful ingenuity. Well, it was as good as usual. Believing that such modes of remedying difficulties are constantly in use with our servants, I determined not to be squeamish,—but must confess that my dog, Sara, had most of the milk.

This spot is surrounded by rocky mountains, huge, bare, and rugged. Little prospect of shikar, I think: so I declined Subhan's suggestion to go forth and try my luck to-morrow, not relishing the thoughts of the tremendous exertions with so little hope to cheer me up, but preferring that Subhan and Mooktoo should experimentalise alone, and on their report I go or not. I expect nothing from their explorations.

17th July. I enjoyed a pleasant stroll before breakfast, descending to the stream and following its course upwards some little distance, then turning and passing through the verdant crops, so fresh and pleasant, with their many willow trees and numerous rose-bushes scattered about in the divisions or fences. The fields were full of people industriously engaged weeding, &c., all of whom saluted me respectfully.

Mooktoo, pleading illness, had not accompanied Subhan in the exploration; following whose direction in the afternoon I thought I might meet him on return, but having gone two or three miles I returned and found him at camp, he having come back by a different route. He had seen neither animals nor their traces throughout the wide tract he had examined.

There was no use remaining here, so I gave directions for moving on to-morrow to Hemschi, a place reported to be good for shikar. But we have information of a saheb being there, who has come from Simla by the Roopschoo road.

After dinner Subhan and Mooktoo came to chat; and as we discussed the demerits of this miserable country, Subhan hinted the advantage of a trip to the Karakorum mountains on the road from Leh to Yarkand, provided we could procure authentic information of the shikar being as abundant there as travellers reported. A friend of Mooktoo, a merchant whom he met in the Wurdwan, had recommended him to take me there, assuring him that animals of several kinds were not only very abundant but tame. I readily entertained this project; and we remained considering and planning a long time, all three quite elated by the glowing pictures of successful sport we conjured up. We set down Phuttoo as too old and unsound for this arduous enterprise, strengthening this disqualification by a strong suspicion we all held of his bad luck, as, somehow or other, my failures always take place when he is present, my successes during his absence—strong presumptive evidence of his kizmet not being prosperous.

I turned in, excited by the visions of the mighty yâks I should encounter in this field unexplored by European hunter.

18th July. A long, tedious ascent of some six or seven miles, and then a moderate descent brought us to Hemschi, a straggling village in a wilderness of stones covering a valley through which a stream wanders to the Indus. The fields have been cleared with immense labour, and are fenced in by the rounded stones simply placed one on the other to the height of three feet. Just as we arrive at the cultivation, are found surrounding a small rocky eminence a number of strange looking trees of the fir species, which at first I conceived to be cedars, but on a close examination in the evening believe them to be junipers of unusual proportions and of an antiquity dating centuries back. These are the first trees of the sort I have seen in the country, and there are none others to be heard of. This would induce the belief that they are not indigenous.

I fixed the site of my bivouac on a barren rocky hill, the best the place afforded, and breakfasted beneath the shade of a spreading rose bush, bearing an abundance of fine blossoms of a large, full, double kind, but wanting in fragrance—still a most agreeable canopy.

My effects to day, as yesterday, were in part borne on the shoulders, not delicate, of women, they always bearing their share of like burdens, their share by far the largest. They appeared quite at home at the labour, and seemed rather to like it, laughing and chatting cheerfully—the hideous, good-humoured wretches. They, one and all, here wear a remarkable coiffure:—a black leather or cloth flap or lappet being worn under the hair so as to protect the ears, to this a fringe is appended, and the frowzy locks in plaits are brought over it in loops, and are tucked up behind, having much the appearance our own dames might have, if after adjusting their chevelure they rubbed their heads for a considerable time in the coal skuttle, and then were dragged through a furze bush. Still there was a sort of resemblance to the style. In every individual the hair is parted in the centre, and over this central division is placed an ornament, a black band on which are fastened pieces of turquoise, some very large—the biggest often as large as a walnut—in front over the forehead, from which they are continued in regular order to the nape of the neck, where further observation is cut short by the goat skin cloak from beneath which a tuft appears, which is to all appearance the tail appendage of the hair and said band which, I fancy, are in some measure connected and twisted together, hanging down the back, like that of the Cashmiries.

No prospect of sport here, the saheb we had heard of having, as we were informed, unsuccessfully hunted the neighbourhood.

19th July. The early part of to-day's march was very trying and fatiguing. The road, crossing two or three minor ranges of the system of mountains, was nothing but climbing steep hills—again, after descending, to repeat the same monotonous toil; all around barren and desolate as usual. We passed two small cultivated patches, and reached Leiker, a good-sized village with one or two quite imposing looking houses, well-built of sun-dried brick, with rows of small windows. Subhan reported this to be Bazgoo, the place we designed to halt at. But after breakfast it was discovered to be Leiker, and Bazgoo some distance on.

About half-past ten we again set out, and endured a dreadful scorching over some arid sandy plains. A village, seen far in the distance, seemed to fly from us. I supposed it to be Bazgoo, and was surprised to find on reaching the top of a gentle rise a sudden deep declivity descending into an extensive valley, and immediately below us a large thriving village. This was Bazgoo. But we had to proceed, passing along by houses and many Buddhist structures of more than ordinary size and dignity, until gaining the end of the village we halted under a fine large apple tree, offering the only shade in an uncultivated spot. We were huddled up close together, which was not satisfactory, and led to my having to enforce silence after enduring the annoyance of much jabber passively, long after I had retired to bed.

20th July. We got away this morning at half-past four, having a long and difficult march to accomplish. About four miles of level sandy plain, passing some Buddhist monuments of very great length, some three or four hundred yards long, the extremities finished by large urnlike masses of masonry on step-formed pedestals, the sides of the latter ornamented with figures in plaister—many of these structures were met with during the day, all being covered with the sculptured stones already described—to a large and flourishing village, that seen from the distance yesterday, Mimah. We then ascended through a ravine twisting and winding, ploughing our way through heavy sand and grit—three-quarters of an hour's most tiresome labour—when, reaching the top, a more open, level country presented itself; which gradually widening opened out into extensive plains of barren sand gradually dipping the Indus, and what looked like a swampy country in the distance, with many snow-capped mountains filling in the background.

We passed a lama fort-like building perched on a hill in the middle of cultivation, on the left, and a small village, on the right (Piang); then descended to the very brink of the Indus which here, instead of rushing violently between high precipitous banks, meanders in divided waters through an expanse of flat meadows covered with grassy turf, a small village dotting the surface here and there. An enormous bank, of miles in length apparently, and one or two in breadth, slopes down in one unbroken line from the mountains to the river's brink on the other (the southern) side; producing a singular effect, looking like an enormous mud bank solidified—brown, barren, and stony. Turning the spur of a range coming right down to the river, an expanse of green turf opens before one, a fort-like building on a high rock in front, and an enclosed garden near it. For this I made, now rather knocked up, my right foot being sore from chafing, causing me to limp heavily. I forced open the door of the garden which only contained willows and poplars, and, finding a tolerable house in the middle empty, took possession of the same, well satisfied with such good shelter, and anxious for refreshment after five hours' most fatiguing tramp.

I sent out to find some messenger to send in to Leh with orders to the thanadar, Basti Ram, to send me a tattoo on which to complete my journey in the afternoon. Coolies under the sepoy made their appearance, and were ordered on, but exchanged at a village close by—this was the third change to day—and, soon after, Subhan trotted up with four tattoos which he had engaged for our party.

I remained under shelter till 4 P.M.; then mounted and took the route to Leh; which place we soon sighted on crossing an elevation, its remarkable fort, formerly the palace of the Rajahs of Ladâk, standing out conspicuous, looking out from the top of a rocky hill under which the city appears to repose.

There was now a dreary plain of gritty sand to be traversed which was unspeakably tiresome, being four or five miles in extent, the sun and glare cruelly strong. This passed, we reached rugged, irregular, cultivated ground, where a good strong nag, of the Bokhara breed, I fancy, sent by Basti Ram, met me; on which I was glad to mount, having with difficulty urged the little mare I was on to a smart walk, she constantly stopping to look after the safety of a small foal, following whinnying behind.

Some way further on a 'posse' appeared, comprising the two sons of Basti Ram in gay attire, with some sepoys in dirty ditto, waiting to receive and welcome me to the city of Leh. We exchanged courteous greeting; and I pursued my way thus escorted to the outskirts of the city (so called), over an infamous path of stones, ditches, and drains, running over the partitions of the fields, when I accorded 'congée' to the gentlemen attending me, and, preceded by an official, made my way to a garden, or enclosure, containing poplars and willow trees, where I found my tent and belongings awaiting me, and was heartily glad of a good wash, nor at all disinclined for dinner afterwards. This was a very long day. I have now reached another prominent point in my travels, where I must, perforce, remain some days, until my effects from Sirinuggur arrive, of which I have no tidings.

Leh is certainly picturesque, but further than that I can say nothing at present in its favour: but imagine it to be a dirty, insignificant place, the fitting capital of a miserable country, and a low degraded population. We shall see.

By the way, I must not omit that, in the narrow ravine on this side Mimah, whose sandy depths caused us so much exertion to traverse, we overtook a party of villagers proceeding with asses laden with firewood to Leh. This being distant some fourteen miles was pretty strong testimony to the nakedness of the environs of Leh. With this party was one in ordinary attire as themselves, but of the clergy—in fact, a lama; and in his hand he carried one of those bright copper affairs I had noticed at Tahmoos. This article was in shape like a child's rattle of large size, the upper or box portion revolving on its axis, the handle. To the box was attached a string some two or three inches long, with a tassel at the end. I now had a good opportunity of ascertaining the use of this singular instrument; and the lama without more ado sat down by the way, and commenced revolving the box, at the same time rolling his eyes about, and mumbling uncouth sounds, stated to be sentences of prayer and adoration, the number of which were calculated by the revolutions of the instrument, indicated by the swinging tassel.

21st July. I arose vigorous and fresh, the night having been cool and pleasant, and just loitered about this enclosure in which I find a tent, horse, and dogs, and attendants of Major Tryon, 7th R.F., who, they tell me, has been in these parts some twenty days, and is now across the Indus shooting, having been away eight days.

About eleven o'clock a saheb rode into the enclosure with many attendants. He turned out to be a Mr. Johnstone, of the Survey, at work in this vicinity. I asked him up to my tent, where we had a long chat; to me a great treat, as I have not seen an European since I left Sirinuggur, now nearly ten weeks. I asked my new acquaintance to share my humble fare at 6 P.M.

I was visited by a nephew of my friend Ahmet Shah of Islamabad, who is in a similar position here to his uncle at that place, being kardar of a large pergunnah, adding to this office the important duties of government moonshi. This rencontre is fortunate as he can give me reliable information of the Karakorum road and country, and also aid me in my purchases and arrangements. As yet the caravan of merchants from Yarkand has not arrived; but they are within five or six stages of Leh. On their arrival he will make searching enquiries as to the chance of success in those regions.

The shikarries, it strikes me, are not so keen now the time approaches to carry out our project, as they were when it was only in embryo. I notice a perceptible lengthening of visage and a melancholy tone in discussing the question, which I attribute to rumours afloat of the Yarkand road being frequented by robbers. It is certain that a merchant of this place was, not long since, plundered of all his property somewhere between here and Yarkand. But that they are afraid of my reproaches, and aware of the uselessness of such a course, I verily believe they would attempt to dissuade me from going now, and I must be careful not to let them humbug me with false reports. I know them to be capable of any amount of falsehoods, of any calibre. Phuttoo wears a particularly suspicious sneaking look to-day, from which I surmise him to be plotting some deceitful trick or other.

I strolled just outside the enclosure in the afternoon, and find Leh to be situated within an arc, almost a complete circle, formed by rugged, naked hills, spurs of a lofty range of mountains—running to all appearance north and south, or thereabouts, in the rear of Leh—from which these spurs stretch down to the Indus, embracing the plain of Leh, leaving open the space debouching on the Indus, up which I came. Leh itself is built upon a ridge which projects from the centre of this arc some short distance into the plain, occupying its extremity—that is, the large building before-mentioned does; but the town is placed on the southern face of the ridge. With the exception of the comparatively small extent of irrigated fields, all around is bare and desolate. Looking from Leh across the Indus, is seen a tract of cultivation of considerable extent, running up into a valley, clusters of houses here and there giving it a cheerful, prosperous aspect. This, I am told, is the village of the rightful owner of Ladâk, where he resides in humble obscurity.

22nd July. Sunday. I find no place to walk to out of this enclosure, all outside being either fields or rough barren ground with difficult paths. The town looks uninviting, so I remained in my tent.

The jemadar, a civil, obliging, intelligent man, in the afternoon informed me that Basti Ram, the thanadar, was waiting in his house, prepared to pay me a visit, if I could receive him. I, of course, assented; and ere long, preceded by a dirty band of soldiery, he made his appearance, seated in a janpan, which being halted at the requisite respectful distance, the old gentleman was assisted forward, and I requested him to be seated on a 'rizai' which had been spread for him. He is a pleasing-looking old man, of mild aspect, bodily infirm, but with a voice still strong.

We chatted a long time; and I hinted at the Karakorum with regard to shikar, but he evidently disapproves of my going in that direction, saying, that the road was bad, the country barren, and no shikar, but that in the Chan-than and Roopschoo country game abounded. He politely assured me of his desire to furnish me with all I required, to any extent, in money, horses, or men.

I questioned him about the sad fate of the poor Schlagentweit brother; and he gave me a long narrative, from which I gather that the unfortunate traveller was plundered on the way to Yarkand; that he reached that place, and thence proceeded on to the Kokand country, where he rode into the presence of a chief, Walli Khan, who, feeling or pretending to feel insulted, ordered his attendants to cut him down, which was instantly done; and thus the unfortunate M. Schlagentweit was murdered, and all his effects plundered. But these had been previously seized, and probably he was then in search of justice, and the restoration of his property. Walli Khan has since denied all share in the death of the saheb; and as he is a powerful chief, with a strong fortress on a steep hill, the thanadar said, "What can be done?" Several men have been sent to try and recover the effects, and procure unmistakable testimony to the circumstances of the murder; but they state all the property to have been scattered here and there in remote parts of Turkistan, and have discovered nothing further as to the foul deed. I am in hopes of yet ascertaining more, when the Yarkand merchants arrive, but it must be acquired through tact and judgment, all enquiries being regarded suspiciously, as perhaps connected with ulterior designs. After a satisfactory interview Basti Ram took leave, the jemadar remaining behind, and giving some interesting particulars of the country north of Leh, through part of which the road to Yarkand runs. The district is called the Lobrah pergunnah; and the jemadar, who once travelled there with a saheb, Dr. Thomson, declares it to abound with game. It is a fertile country, he says, highly cultivated, with abundance of everything. It is reached in three days; in three more a place, called Gopoor, where are upland plains abounding with wild animals; but the yâk is not there met with. Four or five days further travelling in an uninhabited tract will bring one to grassy plains, called Moorgaby: there are yâk, and kyang, and other animals. I requested the jemadar to try and find a resident of Lobrah, who could give me precise information as to the best shooting grounds. This he promised to do.

23rd July. I sent the shikarries and Abdoolah into the town to try and get good reliable information about the Lobrah country, roads, &c. They still bring only vague reports; but all unite in describing the country as possessing much game. There is an evident disinclination to supply information of this part of the country; but through Ahmet Shah's relative, and the jemadar, his friend and subordinate, I believe that I shall succeed in extracting it.

A cloudy day, and a heavy thunderstorm across the Indus, which in time found its way here, describing a semicircular sweep, and coming down upon us with violent gusts of wind, making the poplars and willows bend double. After a time there were heavy drops; then an undecided rain keeping on and off, ever threatening to come down in torrents.

After dinner the jemadar came to report progress; but, further than that the thanadar was willing to further my views in that direction, he merely repeated what he had said before as to game in the Lobrah country. But the bridge over a large river on the way having been broken down, the thanadar had sent his son to have it repaired, and to give orders for my reception, as also to get ready some men acquainted with the haunts of game. So all goes well—if my things would but arrive, of which as yet no tidings. A rainy evening keeping me in till bed-time, I took refuge early in my blankets.

24th July. There was much rain during the night, and a cloudy morning of which I took advantage to visit the town, with a view to select a site for a sketch. The air was cool and fresh, and the roads cleansed by the rain. There are some curious buildings in the town which is very small—a mere village: but there is a good wide street in which is the bazaar,—the shops, small dens in an uniform row on either side. This street is about three hundred yards long, and opens into the serai, a yard surrounded by other dens in which were some dirty travellers. Through this we went, and, passing by the burial ground, ascended a small isolated hill on the top of which is a nondescript building. From the side of this hill is a good view of the town, with the Rajah's residence towering over it; and higher again than that, some way removed up the same ridge, is a lama monastery. Others are on the side of the hill. The whole scene is extremely curious and picturesque. I peeped into some of the little shops, and saw there, of course, Manchester cottons of the most brilliant hues. But nearly every shop was empty, this place being really but an 'entrepôt' affording accommodation to the traffic between Yarkand, Cashmere, and the plains. By all accounts Yarkand is a place of much importance, and a great mart, merchants from all the surrounding regions meeting there for trade and exchange of commodities.

I visited Bella Shah, the principal merchant, who has a comfortable house in the Eastern style—an intelligent-looking man. I had an interesting conversation with him. By the way, had I not applied myself to the study of Hindostani, how much I should have lost. He had been to Yarkand, and described the country as most fertile, the town as a grand place, rich and populous. He further told me that, eight days' journey from Yarkand, on this side, large herds of yâk are met with, and that the country generally abounds with game; that the road is not so very difficult; wood scarce certainly in places, but always something, sticks, weeds, or horsedung to be got for a fire large enough to cook with. This is the information I was wanting; and my mind is now settled to cross the Karakorum range, the pass over which, he assures me, is a very easy one.

After a long and profitable visit I departed, the shikarries, who had attended me, greatly elated at the news. I returned to breakfast very 'koosh,' my domestics listening with glistening eyes to Bella Shah's 'kubbur,' evidently sharing the pleasure I experienced. I was busy writing after breakfast, preparing letters, and bringing up journal to this point, when consciousness of some one near me caused me to look up, and there stood Suleiman, Catechist. I was delighted to see him. He had preceded my baggage, being mounted. He was well, and reported well of my other people, animals and property. He had distributed nearly all the books in Sirinuggur, both to Cashmiries and others: he had once been all but involved in a serious disturbance, some bigoted mussulman, with whom he was disputing, having denounced him as an enemy of the faith, worthy of death. But a pundit, whose friendship he had happily acquired, interfered, and peace was restored.

There was heavy rain in the afternoon; such a down-pour is very rare here. My things did not arrive until five; my two tattoos in fair condition, considering the journey and privations endured in such a country. Little Fan, thin and amazed, did not recognise me: her three pups are thriving. I received some letters, and lots of papers; favourable reports of all my property from the sirdar.

About dinner time Bella Shah was announced, and with him a propitiatory 'nuzzur' of sugar candy and dried fruit. We had a long conversation, in the course of which he confirmed the account given by Basti Ram of the fate of poor Schlagentweit; and again gave me glowing accounts of the abundance of yâk on the other side the Karakorum range. Most exciting were his reminiscences. He laughed at the idea of danger from the Yarkandies; who, he said, came constantly to hunt the yâk, taking the flesh back to Yarkand for sale. He declared that, far from interfering with me, if I offered them a rupee or so, they would shew me the best grounds, and assist me in my hunting. He said that the Yarkand people would never attack an European, though close to the town, or even in the streets; but if he entered a house, then they would set upon him.

The shikarries, who were listening attentively to all that was said, and occasionally joining in, became very merry at this welcome intelligence; and after Bella Shah's departure were vehement in their desire and determination to go over the Karakorum. Before leaving, Bella Shah promised to find me a man well acquainted with the road, and the places where the yâk are to be found; though he assures me there is no difficulty about that, as they abound everywhere. We are all very 'koosh,' every thing promising auspiciously, and so much unexpected aid offering in furtherance of my project.

25th July. I set to work casting bullets before breakfast. It is strange, but these shikarries cannot be trusted to cast any but ordinary spherical bullets. They are too indolent to learn anything, and too careless to be depended upon. I had to dismiss Phuttoo from even attending the ladle to clear away the dross, and install Buddoo in his place, so negligent was he. I continued at this tedious work till breakfast time, by which time I was quite baked, the fire blazing in front of me, and the sun equally hot on my back. Buddoo and my bearer continued the operation, and, to my relief and satisfaction, succeeded capitally.

Suleiman and my servants being urgent for me to send off letters, including theirs, I set to work and wrote for six hours at a stretch, which, as I wrote with paper on knee, stooping over it, gave me a headache; but I managed to finish nine letters in all, including one to General Windham urgently soliciting a month's extension of leave, to enable me to carry out my schemes comfortably. I continued very dizzy; talked over arrangements, and decided to settle and pack up to-morrow, and start the day following.

26th July. An awful night, never to be forgotten! Having read till I was sleepy, I gave way to nature, glad enough to feel the inclination; but awoke after an hour or two with a racking head-ache—terrible agony—such as I remember to have experienced only twice before, and then was driven nearly mad. I tried in vain to find alleviation, or to court repose. Hours passed in agony indescribable; when, as a last resource, hoping to obtain relief in sleep, I got up, and in the dark helped myself to brandy and water. Had I had laudanum, I should have swallowed it readily. This remedy seemed only to increase the malady; but, after a time, its influence threw me into a slumber, and I awoke at daylight—and how thankful to find on collecting myself that the acute pains had subsided, and but an ordinary head-ache remained! I had a cup of tea, and strolled about inspecting my property. Having had everything unpacked for selection, I set aside as few things as possible, wishing to avoid the necessity of many coolies in the inhospitable deserts we should traverse.

I was looking at my tattoo, when two respectable-looking natives approached, and divining their purpose I entered into conversation with them. They were merchants from Kokand, now five years from their native country, having been impeded in their trade and movements by the late rebellion. They described their country as a delightful region, abounding in the most delicious fruits, &c.

After breakfast I called Suleiman, and, taking with me some physic and Holloway's ointment, went to see a servant of Major Tryon's, who, they told me, had some days since run a nail into his hand, which had caused him much suffering. We found the unfortunate man in a dreadful state—I fear hopeless—the flesh having sloughed away, &c. We thoroughly cleaned the sores, spread ointment on linen covering them, then bound the arm up with a layer of cotton to prevent harsh contact, and placed the limb in a sling. The poor suffering creature said he enjoyed great relief, when all this was concluded. I left medicine and ointment with Suleiman to continue the applications; he, good soul! evincing here how thoroughly the religion of our Saviour has converted his heart; for this man was a sweeper, an outcast, not to be approached without defilement. Suleiman promised (and I fully confide in him) to take every care of the miserable being, whose case I look upon as hopeless. His master being absent shooting, I ordered him to be furnished with anything necessary.

Bella Shah again came to visit me, and with him some friends, desirous of a talk I presume, a considerable attendance around. He told me that one man he was engaging to accompany me, when he heard that I was going to shoot wild cattle, refused to go, being a Hindoo; but he had engaged another, a man of even higher qualifications, both in point of familiarity with the localities, and acquaintance with the language required. His name is Abdool. He again assured me of meeting with the yâk in numbers, and we parted promising ourselves an interview on my return.

I had felt wrong in the head all day, but could discover no other symptoms of sickness. All ready for a start in the morning.

CHAPTER X.

TO THE SHAYAK.

27th July. There was considerable delay occasioned by the coolies coming late, and the jemadar not appearing. Neither did the expected guide from Bella Shah appear; and the tattoo provided for me was such a feeble animal that I scorned to bestride him. Having decided to leave my own nags to be fresh for my return, I had been led to expect better things by the jemadar, he having declared that the thanadar would furnish me with horses like my own.

Without waiting for the jemadar, I gave the word to be off, not disliking being compelled to resort to my usual means of locomotion, my legs; and hardly had we left the enclosure than we were entangled in fields, amid the partitions of which the path was lost. An unwilling guide, in the person of a villager whom we appropriated 'sans ceremonie,' conducted us out of the fields to a plain much-worn track, when, concluding that our way was straight before us, I permitted him to abscond. On we trudged, and had made some way, when shouts behind us attracted our notice, and, stopping, we saw a man pursuing. He was one I have omitted to mention as having been provided by the jemadar as agreed, being competent to shew the shooting grounds in the Lobrah district. He fully corroborated the jemadar's statement of the quantities of game to be there met with, ibex, shâpu, and nâpu; and he seemed delighted at the idea of taking service, enforcing upon the shikarries the necessity of taking lots of powder, lead, and the moulds. This looked well. He now overtook us, and told us we were in the wrong path, and must cross a rough hill to get to the right one.

This done, we pursued our way, and had again to look back to ascertain why we were assailed behind by shouts. It was my sepoy with a horse, the one sent by the thanadar on the first day. Putting Mooktoo up, I walked on. We stopped to examine some of the singular altar-like buildings so numerous in this country, around the urnlike top of which were piled a number of the horns of the wild sheep—why, is beyond me; unless they were offerings of successful hunters. Here we were again overtaken by a queer-looking individual who announced himself as Abdool, the man engaged as guide by Bella Shah. He looks a likely chap; quietly sent the other man, whose name is Tar-gness, to the rear, and took upon himself the duties of guide.

A gradual, but rough and fatiguing, ascent brought us to our halting place on the mountain-side, whence we were to climb the summit on the morrow. It is a melancholy spot—only a few stones heaped on one another, as a shelter for travellers or shepherds—distinguishing it from the surrounding waste of rocks and stones. But there is a beautiful clear stream at hand.

I was just at the end of my breakfast, when a stir took place, and, looking about, a score or so of laden horses appeared descending from a slope close by, headed by their owner, a Yarkand merchant, whom we hastened to greet, and to overwhelm with questions. He was a jolly, good-humoured old man, of a ruddy countenance, and readily entered at large into conversation, detailing his journey, the obstacles met with, &c. First of all, the yâk were met with in great herds two or three days' journey beyond the Karakorum. Of this there was no doubt. But there was a band of freebooters, some two hundred strong, somewhere on the Yarkand road, lying in wait for merchants. He had evaded them; but he did not know what had befallen other merchants who were to leave Yarkand about the same time: of them he had heard nothing. He gave us most valuable information of the road to follow, the places to halt at, and certain spots where the yâk would certainly be found; in describing which he mentioned one at the ziarat, or shrine, erected where the marble and alabaster were quarried, with which Shah Jehan, and other of the Mogul emperors, constructed the magnificent edifices, palatial and sepulchral, which still adorn Delhi and Agra, to the astonishment and admiration of all. This was news to me, as I had fancied that the place whence this material had been procured was quite unknown. It is an interesting spot to visit, let alone the yâk there frequenting. The old gentleman told me he had some gold coins bearing the stamp, and date corresponding, of Alexander the Great. These he had got at great expense, and I understood him expressly for some saheb in the Punjab where he is going.

I bought some felt nambas of him to serve as blankets for my servants and shikarries, and for myself, paying 1. 8 rupees Cos. each, and two rupees for a red one of superior fabrique, but damaged. I endeavoured to deal with him for a couple of his ill-conditioned, raw-backed, galled tattoos, intending to send them to Leh to pick up and gain condition by my return, and take on my own with me. The unconscionable old chap, on my pointing out two, asked two hundred rupees for one, and three hundred for the other. I said, a deal was out of the question. After a time I offered him one hundred rupees for the two, through the shikarries. No; he wouldn't think of it. Well, his team went on, he having to remain till my servants came, to be paid for the nambas. Thinking how pleasant it would be to have my own hard-conditioned nags with me—perchance, to pursue thereon some wounded yâks—I called Subhan, and directed him to offer one hundred and fifty rupees for the two; but the obstinate old man would not accept the offer. This was an outside price for the animals, if in condition for work; so I made no further attempt to persuade the reluctant proprietor to part with his quads. He had long to wait for his rupees: but on the arrival of my servants, having paid him, I offered him a rupee, 'backsheesh,' he having given me some dried fruit. At this he demurred, and actually needed remonstrance to make him accept. Then, with many polite salaams, he went on his way.

My khansamah and the shikarries had blundered sadly about arrangements; for, although they knew that there was no village, no supplies or wood here, they had not taken care to ascertain that due provision had been made for our necessities, trusting all to the jemadar without enquiring at starting. Messengers had been despatched, but night approached without their returning; and Abdoolah was warming me some food by the scanty fire some horse-dung, chips, and bits of matting afforded, when a portion of wood arrived, and in the course of an hour the other things. The night was very cold, a violent hailstorm having burst upon us in the afternoon.

28th July. We got off by 5 A.M., Phuttoo on the horse, and Mooktoo, who complained of severe headache, on a tattoo ridden yesterday by Abdoolah. The ascent of the mountain was most arduous, the natural difficulties being much increased by the difficulty of respiration. All suffered much from this. The mountain being extremely steep and rugged, the path necessarily running into innumerable zigzags to render the ascent at all practicable was cumbered with sharp stones, as was the entire mountain-side. Indeed, this is the characteristic of the range. From summit to base these mountains are thickly covered with fragments crumbled from their massive bodies, which by the action of the weather, intense frosts, &c. are splintered up and strewn with the débris, as though the stone breakers had been busily at work all over the surface, not leaving a square yard vacant. Many a time had I to pause for breath ere the summit was reached; and we had some snow hard-frozen to cross, covering the whole northern face of the mountain, at the base of which was a small lake, formed by the melted snow filling a basin. The descent was more abrupt than the ascent, but except that the snow was hard and slippery, it was much easier to accomplish. Heavy rain set in below, which was hail and sleet above. I was glad to be out of that.

We met a train of laden yâks, the property of my merchant friend of yesterday, whose name, by the way, is Nassir Khan. A jolly, ruddy, round-faced young man, quite plebeian-English in appearance, was in charge of them; and, in reply to queries from Abdool and myself, he assured us that the yâk and other game abounded where Nassir Khan had told us. Joyfully commenting on the coincidence of testimony we jogged on, and halted at a stone shed, where by a fire smoking was a Yarkandi, left behind to tend two of Nassir Khan's disabled horses. This man also gave us, and others who followed, similar glowing accounts of the quantities of yâk met with near the Karakorum, himself getting quite excited by the recollection of them.

The sun now shone out, and finding our destination, Karbong, still some miles off, I determined to breakfast; after which I mounted the nag, preceded by Abdool and Phuttoo, leaving poor Subhan, just come up and quite knocked up, to repose, and Kamal to attend him. I rode slowly on, the road execrable, and passed herds of yâk and flocks of sheep. The sun came out, and seemed to take vengeance on us for having hitherto escaped him; the rays, reflected from the white sandy soil and stones, not only roasted, but blinded one. We passed a horrid idol, the head of some deity, rudely moulded in clay, of hideous features painted red, occupying a niche in one of those altar-buildings, the tops of which were piled with wild sheeps-horns; and the bushy tails of the yâk were waving thereon, suspended from poles. Some fresh flowers were deposited in the niche before this ugly demon—a recent devotional offering.

At last we reached Karbong, a few scattered stone houses in irrigated fields in a valley of stones, or rather on the slopes of the mountain, the valley lying apparently further on, where huge mountains, rounded and abrupt, not in a range, but individual masses, presented their curved outlines rapidly inclining downwards to depths shut out from view. I had hoped for a somewhat level country, but as yet it is, if possible, more mountainous, and of huger masses than ever.

On arrival I took especial care of my horse, getting him lots of grain and grass of which he stood much in need. I could find no shelter from the sun, but a namba spread on sticks, which was better than nothing. Subhan came in after some time, better after his repose: he could give no intelligence of Mooktoo and the others. My three servants next came, all right, Abdoolah telling me with a grin, that he had left Mooktoo and the Cashmere coolies, five of them, on the top of the mountain, blubbering. This afforded him much amusement. These Cashmiries are certainly wretched cowardly creatures—no energy about them, once in difficulties.

All came in towards evening, when Abdoolah quizzed them unmercifully. Mooktoo complaining much, I determined to physic him, and gave him three Peake's pills at night. Abdoolah, the hard-hearted, scouts the idea of fever, asserting his ailment to be the result of eight days' idleness and good living; and this is my opinion too. To-morrow being Sunday offers an acceptable day of rest to all parties.

I sent off a messenger with an order written by the village gyalpo, at the dictation of Phuttoo, assisted by Abdool, the guide, to the thanadar's son, directing him to provide everything requisite in tattoos, food, &c., for a month's excursion to the Karakorum. He is at present two stages off, at Diskit. I desired the stock to be gathered at Chanloong, five stages off, and the last village on our route. Here I paid off and dismissed the Leh coolies who tendered their salaam, apparently thankful for their payment and release.

I have now the satisfaction of having accomplished one of the greatest difficulties in my way. Abdool says there is another awkward mountain to cross at Sassar, but that the Karakorum pass is not difficult, though long and tedious. We ought to reach the pass in twelve days now: it generally occupies fifteen with laden animals to or from Leh.

29th July. Sunday. I allowed the day to open fully ere I turned out, after having enjoyed a good night's rest. The mountains are truly grand and majestic, as viewed from this spot; and during the changing effects of a humid atmosphere they presented some magnificent pictures. Again I longed to be able truly to depict them.

The three Peake's pills having had no effect on Mooktoo, I gave him two more; nor did this additional motive power produce any result, yet he says he feels much better. A messenger passed through, bearing instructions from the thanadar to his son to take care that my wishes were attended to, and no trouble given me—very civil, indeed, of the old gentleman.

I have nothing particular to note of the day, but may remark how soon a man left to himself, without the aids and influences of Christian ministry and communion, becomes listless and indifferent in religious observances, and neglects the appointed means for the strengthening and refreshing of his soul. We need the stimulus of the example and offices of others, and especially those of the Church, to keep us up to the standard of vital Christianity.

30th July. I arose at earliest dawn, wishing, if possible, to reach the next camp ere the sun should attain his full power. The path led down a narrow valley, threading some ravines, and penetrating some remarkable defiles, then passing over table lands, until we stood looking down upon the river Shayak and its valley, which lies at right angles to that down which we had come, the distance some six miles. The Shayak's course here I judge to be N.W. A small hamlet with its green crops greeted our sight from the eastern side; all else was bare rock and barren slopes. I had hoped for better things.

We turned to the left, following the river's course, but high up on the rocky mountain-side overhanging it, and, plunging down a deep gorge, came upon Kalsar, our destination, placed as usual by a stream, and looking cool and inviting with its fruit trees, and green crops, and beautiful clear water. We were guided to a nice bit of ground in a small orchard shaded by peach or apricot trees, very large, and one fine walnut tree. I enjoyed the comfort of the foliage after the three days without a tree, and sat down to breakfast enjoying the 'dolce far niente' thoroughly after my exercise. We were three hours and a half on the road without a halt; so I suppose, allowing for the ups and downs which were continual, we must have come about ten miles.

31st July. The morning being cloudy, and my tent under the shade of the walnut tree, I did not notice the first blush of dawn. We got off at a quarter to five. A difficult climb immediately awaited me, the ascent abrupt and the path deep in sand. Nevertheless I got on famously, finding myself, both to-day and yesterday, in excellent working order, and in good wind. I put Mooktoo, still ailing, on the horse. After an hour's travelling over a plateau intersected with deep ravines we descended to the bed of the Shayak, along which the path now led in a direction due west. A level waste of sand had now to be crossed, its width occupying the valley or river-bed, some three-quarters of a mile in width here; its length interminable as the river, perhaps, which here was a rapid turbid stream of forty or fifty yards in width, depth unknown. On the other side was a village in a small spot of cultivation recovered from the surrounding waste. There was a decided improvement in the scenery, the mountains falling back as the valley extended, giving good distances. Had the valley, or river-bed, been full of water, when it would have had the appearance of an extensive lake, the scene would have been magnificent. But the flat waste of sand destroyed it.

We had to quit the sand, and ascend a steep, rugged spur of the mountain, immediately under the foot of which the river rushed, making a bend S.W. Then down again we went, and had to toil over a good three miles of sand and shingle, our halting place always in view, but seeming never attainable. We crossed a beautiful clear stream, a bit more shingle, and then up a slope to the village of Diskit, a straggling place on a stony plateau looking down on the valley, here some mile and a half wide. Opposite is a valley partly revealed, down which, from the northward, flows another stream, tributary to the Shayak. Up that stream our route lies.

The gopal came to pay his respects, bringing some fruit—very small apricots, about the size of a marble and insipid. I learned to my sorrow that the river was impassable at present, and had been so the last three days. The sun was very hot, and but little shade was afforded by the ragged peach trees. The thanadar's son came to offer his salaam, also bringing fruit—apricots, peaches, and nectarines, all very small and unripe, also some cherries of the colour of greengage. He assured me that the river was impracticable, but might possibly be passable in three or four days. He made difficulties at first about horses; but on Abdoolah speaking somewhat sharply and authoritatively, quoting the thanadar's assurances, the young man gradually softened his objections, and after a time promised that everything should be ready for me, but pointed out that the state of the river was unfavourable, as all communication with the villages on the other side was cut off. He proposed that I should take shelter in a house which, however, when inspected by Buddoo, was reported too dirty and offensive for my occupation: so I turned into a small paddock instead, finding tolerable shelter under a large peach-tree, the trunk of which, I should say, was three feet in diameter. I could not remain in my tent, the heat was so great; so I sat under the tree, where it was more endurable.

It had been agreed that I should inspect the river to-morrow morning with the thanadar's son who promised to have four or five horses ready this evening: but nothing further than reports of their being on the way eventuated, and from this and other significant indications I am of opinion that, under all the superficial demonstrations of anxiety to assist me on my way, runs a strong reflux of concealed opposition. But, if so, I think I can either turn it aside, or surmount it. This delay is vexatious, as I have not a day to spare. I must try and recover the day lost by a double march or two, which will be easy enough as I purpose mounting all my attendants.

It was a beautiful sunset; such as I have not seen for a long time, having been for the most part so closely shut in by mountains as to have had no view whatever of the declining sun; and, moreover, were there distances, there has been usually too little vapour for effect. To-night good distances and a cloudy sky lent their aid to the mountainous landscape. The huge rugged mountains, softened in the subdued evening light, suffused with mellow glowing tints, were certainly arrayed to the best advantage—their massive proportions and gaunt nakedness toned down into pleasing harmonies of form and colour. Long I sat gazing, admiring, and musing—long after all beauty of external landscape had vanished, but enjoying mental visions of charms surpassing even the reality, now faded into the past—when Buddoo broke in upon my reveries with the lantern, and in obedience to the mandate I was soon ensconced in my canvas nutshell, in which confined space I was soon made very sensible of the true littleness of myself and my sphere.

1st August. A cloudy morning—which was welcomed as conveying an increased chance of an early abatement of the floods: because, the sun's powers being intercepted and diminished, the snows on the distant lofty mountains, on the solvency of which the state of the river depends, would be subject to a much reduced action of that consuming orb.

Some wretched tats were sent by the than's son, for which I abused the gopal who brought them; and perceiving it to be necessary to assume a more commanding tone, when the above-mentioned official sent his salaam by a sepoy, I returned him a sharp rebuke which operated favourably, as the sepoy soon returned with explanations and assurances of every effort being made to comply with my desires; that active trustworthy men had been sent to ascertain the state of the river, and orders for horses had been despatched in all directions. Notwithstanding, I thought it advisable to adopt precautionary measures to ensure a true report of the river's condition, so sent off the shikarries on the tattoos to examine it thoroughly up and down; who after some hours absence returned, and stated confidently that the water was going down fast, and that the river would be easily forded to-morrow. They had crossed many mullahs into which it was divided, and had gone through much hard work. They were proud of their performances, exhibiting their wet clothes, and helping each other to exaggerate their aquatic feats. Much pleased with the information, I gave orders for the move on the morrow at 10 A.M., considering that the water would be at its lowest about 11.

The thanadar junior came to pay his respects, and received the news of the river being passable without placing much reliance on it, cautioning us to avoid risking the lives of any of the people. I had a long talk with him. He appeared reconciled to the necessity of forwarding my plans, and promised every assistance. He had with him a brown spaniel, a good looking dog, which was given him, he said, by Colonel Markham, whose promising career was so suddenly cut short, when to human apprehension he appeared to be just at the attainment of a soldier's highest ambition, having been called for from India, it is supposed, to succeed to the command of our army before Sabastopol. He travelled through this country from Kulu through Leh some seven years ago—it must have been just before that summons to the Crimea—and then made this present. I looked with much interest upon this relic of a man whose fate was so remarkable.

Numerous coolies are in attendance, and all things arranged for the morrow's enterprise.

2nd August. Notwithstanding my repeated directions fully explained that we should not start early, the whole camp was astir earlier than usual, everything packed, tats saddled and bridled, coolies ready, and all waiting in expectation of the word, 'March.' This was at 6 A.M. I sat reading, and took no notice for some time, but did at last call Abdoolah, and remind him of the hour fixed for departure, and the reasons, as before given. Then the coolies were dismissed for a time. Now ensued a loud and angry quarrel between Phuttoo and Mooktoo, in the heat of which the former ass threatened the other with bringing his influence with the Maharajah to bear, and having him put in prison; upon which Mooktoo chaffed him with great effect. Phuttoo's conceit is outrageous.

I started between eight and nine, and found the space to traverse to the river much greater than I had imagined—quite three miles, perhaps four—and for the most part over shingle. The river was here divided into many streams, varying from fifty to a hundred yards in width, the current being strong. I had formed no idea of the volume of water from the glimpse of the river I had gained higher up. All the coolies stripped. Four or five men with poles preceded us, sounding; then I followed, and then came the shikarries mounted, with two men to each tattoo, and, far behind, my servants also mounted, and the coolies. An amusing scene took place with my little dog who had swam one or two minor streams, and followed me into a larger, where the current was very strong. A native tried to get hold of him, but the little fellow growled and bit at him viciously, swimming away bravely. The man then put his stick over him to draw him towards him: this he resisted, and was completely submerged. After several unsuccessful attempts the man succeeded in subduing and capturing the poor half-suffocated Sara who made a gallant fight; but the man, the stick, and the water combined were too much for him. The two former opponents bore marks of his vigorous resistance. He then quietly submitted to be conveyed by Subhan in front of him, following my every move with wistful eyes, and trembling violently with excitement.

My little nag had never encountered such a flood, and was quite bewildered by the glare and the rapid passage of the rushing waters; and I had much ado to guide him, ever giving way to the current. Abdool, the guide—not so on this occasion—preceded me, exhibiting in his nude state a sad specimen of legs, spindle-shanks, which were ill calculated for this arduous work: and the poor fellow was obliged to stop in mid-stream, supporting himself with difficulty by his stick. My horse, thus checked, turned aside and got into deep water, but I recovered and held him together: then, passing Abdool, he stuck to the shikarries who kept with their supporters all together. It was hard work, and certainly not without danger, as a stumble would have sent man and horse down the flood.

We thus fought our way on, crossing some score of these streams; in one of which, the widest—I should think two hundred yards across—I got into difficulties. By taking a lower course than the guide had done, I bungled into a sand-bed—quicksand—but my little nag exerted himself vigorously. The shikarries and others were vociferating loudly, 'kubber dar;' as if that was any good when we were in the thick of it. We struggled to firmer ground, and then got to a high bank of shingle with bushes on it. I had hoped that the main stream was crossed, but to my vexation found the great difficulty still to be overcome. A mighty flood swept by, which if we could get over, the passage was virtually accomplished. But was it fordable?

We now saw a party, horse and foot, on the other side making their way towards us. They, too, were brought up by the formidable volume of turbid water rushing between us. We were within hail of each other, but any words indistinguishable, and they were not to be induced by any sign to tempt their fate by showing us the way over. Things now came to a dead-lock. The river guide funking—and no wonder—moved here and there, up and down, making as though he were desperately in earnest, but ever recoiling from the main rush of the torrent. The servants and coolies now arrived all safe, after some few narrow escapes, as Abdoolah informed me—the Cashmiries, poor creatures! of whom there were five, having to be held up in the water, even when without loads: they lost their heads and legs immediately. What despicable poltroons they are! I am confident that my three Punjabies would 'leather' the three shikarries and five coolies combined; though of them Abdoolah is the only one of true 'grit.' He is a first-rate fellow, rough and ready, honest and plucky.

I followed the guide, going up the river, then descending on a bank which divided the main current, the water flowing over it in diminished strength. I was in great hopes we were about to triumph, as we now neared the opposite party; but on reaching the tail of the bank we found the two currents there united which, sweeping roaring through a deep channel of a hundred yards wide, again effectually opposed us. I could have pushed my horse through swimming; and perhaps the tats with the shikarries might have got safe through, though very doubtful: but the coolies and baggage, never. We, therefore, retraced our weary, watery way, and again took downwards below the aforesaid bank, and got into the main stream; but our bewildered guide again retreated.

He and others much amused me by their idea of sounding the depth—just taking stones, and pitching them in, with the notion of judging the depth by the splash and sound; and this in a roaring flood. I now looked upon the passage to day as hopeless, for we had now tried up and down a mile in length; but the goose of a guide still rushed wildly about, entering the water where he could have no real intention of going on: so I hailed Abdoolah from the depth in which I was floundering to beat a retreat, and with Subhan, my only adherent, turned backward—a most disagreeable alternative. I could not halt on that bank in the middle of the waters, though apparently safe, as I know the dangers and uncertainties of floods in mountain regions. And to fight our way back, over ground it had cost such exertions to win, was most disheartening.

Another party of horse and foot had joined mine on the bank, the young relative of Ahmet Shah and attendants, who I forgot to mention came to pay his respects to me, being at Diskit detained by the flood from proceeding on to the Lobrah district of which he is kardar. He is a most prepossessing young man in physiognomy and manner, and is going to his district principally on my account, to aid my arrangements. It was now half-past twelve; and the flood's might, augmented as usual at this time of day by the melted snow, cut off our retreat, so I was the more anxious for my party and effects to hasten their movements, and saw with vexation that there they stuck, like Asiatics, irresolute on the bank. But, seeing me resolutely fighting my way back, they at last got under weigh, and, I am glad to say, all got back safe and sound, men and baggage. The latter had narrow escapes; four coolies, becoming bothered and frightened, lost their way in the middle of the current of one of the biggest channels, and had to be rescued.

I settled down again in my former ground, giving directions for further examination of the river to-morrow; but am resolved not to attempt the passage again, till some one has actually crossed. The delay is very vexatious, but I must endeavour to make up for it by expedition. If I get my extension of leave, it will not matter in the least; but should that be unattainable, I shall have to ride, night and day, through Roopschoo and Kulu from Leh to save my distance. But I must get to these Karakorum mountains, whatever may betide.

We saw numerous trees and pieces of timber remnants of the bridge once spanning the river somewhere above this, which was carried away some months since by the floods. The thanadar junior is here, I believe, to reconstruct it; but that will be a most difficult job from the distance the timber will have to be brought. There is stone enough and to spare; but they are not architects good enough to make use of it. Yet their houses are fairly put together of stone and sun-brick, but the stone rough certainly. They could never form a durable arch, even if they contrived tetes-de-pont, and piers. And now to wait as patiently as may be the subsidence of the waters.

3rd August. Cloudy and showery. I was informed that men had been sent to get information of the state of the river, and in the evening they returned, stating there was little or no change since yesterday. There was rain in the evening, and a heavy storm apparently bursting over the mountains east of us.

4th August. Again a cloudy day. I sent off Phuttoo and Subhan with the Lobrah man, Tar-gness, to get news of the river, and employed the morning in writing. About 2 P.M. Subhan returned with the welcome news of the waters having subsided, and Phuttoo and Tar-gness having gone across to the other side to the village of Lanjoong, he hastening back to give me the information: he said also, that he had marked down some wild fowl in the watery meadows. I despatched my letters carefully sewn up in a bit of sheepskin, being assured that they would be safely delivered at Sirinuggur, under cover to the Baboo; then took gun and shot, and went with Subhan after the ducks which we soon found, and I knocked down one, and wounded another, but, unfortunately, we could not get either. We tried all about, and saw others, but could not get near them, so, after an hour and a half's fruitless endeavours, returned in heavy rain.

5th August. Sunday. A cloudy morning. I took a ramble before breakfast, and enjoyed it much, finding more beauty than I thought the place possessed, but could not select a site that satisfied me for a sketch. The scene is too extended for any view that would include the principal features. There is a picturesque lama monastery high above the village on the mountain; but the village itself is such a scattered, stony, tumble-down place as to defy a definite representation. The valley, looking either way, when lighted, is beautiful—the mountains of fine and varied forms. The effects this morning were very striking, as the fitful gleams of sunshine, struggling through the heavy clouds, threw their shifting light here and there. Looking west, a considerable expanse of rich cultivated plain occupies the valley; east, all is sand and shingle.

I scrambled up the rock over the village, and thence contemplated the scene below me, and did not omit to turn my grateful heart to the adorable Creator of the beauties around me. I wandered leisurely among the rough winding field-tracks; and so came back crossing the brawling rivulet which dashes in several rocky channels through the village. There was no news from over the river; but the gopal came to obtain his dismissal, being ready to start. With many injunctions and oft-repeated warnings from my various followers, by which the poor man, from his perplexed visage, must have been sorely bothered, he withdrew about 11 A.M.

Tar-gness made his appearance, reporting the road to be 'chungy,' that is, comfortable. Phuttoo remained, and I fancy, from observations I so understood, is exercising an assumed authority to a great extent, as I thought he would. I hope to get well across early to-morrow morning, and then proceed on some six miles to a village called Chamseen. It appears that the gopal of this village is the actual kardar of Lobrah, and Ahmet Shah's relative the government moonshi.

After dinner I was talking with the shikarries about the roads and which way we should return, and we discussed the possibility of a road, marked in my map as leading from Kopalu to the Yarkand road, being practicable. A native of Kopalu told us he believed there was a path, but that it was a very difficult one, quite impracticable for horses; but that it was only five or six days from the Karakorum to Kopalu. This would suit me capitally, if we could but get sure information, and make fitting arrangements. Then I should save fifteen days or so of a dismal and uninteresting road. Abdool, guide, sitting with the others, amused us all much by the vehemence with which he denounced the project of this route, declaring it to be terrible, both from its natural obstacles and supernatural; relating how two Bhooties were mysteriously killed by evil spirits who overwhelmed them with sand and stones. He further stated that 'shaitan' himself inhabited those regions, and assailed travellers, tooth and nail: and, while spinning this marvellous yarn, he illustrated it by action and gestures in a truly ludicrous manner. He has a very comical 'phiz' at all times; and when he takes off a large slouching felt hat he wears, leaving his queer comical-shaped cranium (closely shaved) bare, and in excitement indulges in involuntary grimace, he is a certain antidote to melancholy. He is a valuable adherent, always busy at something; even immediately after a long day's march he bustles about, and seems never to think of rest or refreshment. How different from the lazy Cashmiries!

Orders were issued for an early start, as I wish to make up for lost time, and, having crossed the river, to push on another stage.

CHAPTER XI.

TO THE KARAKORUM.

6th August. Away in good time, and high spirits at the prospect of resuming my travels. I found the river very much altered as to its channels, and reduced in volume; but still it was a work of time and labour to cross over. The main channel was considerably enlarged, and I should think some eight hundred yards in width, with here and there a current of tremendous force; the average depth was not above the knees, but in the rushes up to the middle. I got across without misadventure, leaving servants and baggage to follow, and made for a village called Thaga, over a sandy road: in one place the sand, by the action of wind or water, was heaped up in successive ridges, like the sea in a stiff breeze.

I found Phuttoo and the moonshi at this village: the former assured me, with much volubility, that everything was ready at Panamik. The servants and baggage having come up, we moved on to Chamseen, which is, I should think, eight miles from Lanjoong, the path rough and stony. We passed through one village and an agreeable stretch of cultivation, the valley generally as barren as ever, and bivouacked in an orchard, my tent being pitched under a fine spreading peach tree, the shade of which was very enjoyable.

7th August. We quitted this pleasant bivouac before 5 A.M., and travelled over a country in this narrow valley similar to that crossed yesterday, a barren stony hollow, with a hamlet occasionally on either side, where man's ingenuity and industry, invading this domain of rock, has won a hard fought footing. My shikarries and servants are now all on tattoos, and will be thus assisted all the way to the yâk country. We saw two or three hares in the thorn thickets now met with. This rugged valley runs, I think, almost N.W. Some lofty snow-capped mountains close in the upward view.

We arrived at Panamik at half-past eight, the distance not more than ten miles. It is a small village as to residences, but with a large extent of rich cultivation, and a good number of fine fruit trees, and also large willows. I took up my quarters under some peach trees, the fruit abundant; not as we see it in our gardens in England, a solitary specimen here and there on a wall, but depending in bunches numbering some dozens together—small certainly, and nothing to be compared in flavour. They are yet generally unripe. The kardar and moonshi attended to report that all was prepared: I was, therefore, the more vexed and disappointed, when in the middle of the day Abdoolah told me that, owing to a mistake in the maund—the kardar having willfully, as I believe, mistaken the amount which was ordered to be in 'cucha' maunds—there would not be half enough flour provided for rations, and that, as it had to be ground, another day's delay was unavoidable. There was no help for it, so I submitted to stern necessity as tranquilly as possible.

We had great work shoeing the thanadar's horse which I must take with me in default of any other fit for my use. There was no professional 'nahlband' here, nor the usual implements of that operative; but luckily 'a handy-man,' as they call a bungler at several trades in a regiment, turned up—one accustomed to accompany kafilas to and from Yarkand, and look after the horses. I was much taken with the man's expression and manner, and became more interested in him, when Subhan informed me that he was well acquainted with the localities the yâk frequented, and, moreover, was willing to join my expedition—a most valuable recruit, I think. He reminds me strongly of some acquaintance or other, I cannot think who: his voice and way of speaking are peculiar, slow and deliberate: he is the son of a Cashmiri by a Bhoot mother, and I should fancy some twenty-five years old.

The kardar produced two sets of shoes, made in the neighbourhood, of such inferior workmanship and bad metal that, taking one in my hands, I broke it in two to the dismay of the kardar, who beat a retreat, and after a time came back with a set of Yarkand shoes, as light as racing plates, but of the best quality of iron, and a lot of nails to match. Then the work began. A pair of pincers, a hammer, and, after much research, a mortising chisel, were produced, and satisfied with these rude tools my new man set to work with confidence, and, I may add, skill. The old shoes were soon ripped off—there being no file to take off the clench of the nails, I apprehended some damage to the hoof, but all turned out well; then, the hoof being placed on a piece of timber, the other leg hoisted up by the active, useful Abdool, the chisel was applied, and the hoof, bereft of its superabundance, roughly rounded to the form desired, the inner surface and the bridge, frog, and heel, slightly pared with one of my pocket knives, and the shoe affixed in a workman-like manner, the nails right well driven and firmly clenched. Abdool's ingenuity in steadying the hind leg was admirable. He took the long tail of the nag, and wound two turns round the pastern, so getting a good purchase: he then held the leg out at full stretch, and another help placed his shoulders against the other ham to control any attempt at violence, and so the astonished animal was newly provided all round.

I ordered dinner at five punctually to enable me to stroll out and look for a hare in the neighbouring thickets afterwards. At dinner Abdoolah informed me that the rascal of a kardar was intending all sorts of frauds and tricks in respect of the price of the rations and hire of horses, having told him that he had established a tariff differing much from that of Leh, and most exorbitant. As the principal town gives the standard, I told Abdoolah that I would take measures to bring the kardar to his senses, and directed the horses for selection and the officials to be in attendance to-morrow at my breakfast hour. I thought over my plans, and prepared my speeches, enriching my vocabulary from my Hindostani Hand-book. I went out with Subhan, and killed one hare, and wounded another, the only two we saw. On my return Mooktoo and Subhan attended, and informed me that the moonshi had confided to them, that the kardar had collected a wretched batch of incapable horses for me, and that there were some good serviceable animals to be had, if I insisted upon it. He could not speak out himself, he said, but urged them to advise me to assume a high hand, as these people will do nothing unless driven.

8th August. Taking my gun, Subhan, and Sara, I went to look at some hot springs of which Abdoolah had told me, he having visited them yesterday. They were about a mile off: our way lay through the thicket where I shot the hare yesterday. We found the springs gurgling up from under a limestone rock on the side of the mountain, and flowing copiously down into the valley, lining its channel at first with a white incrustation, then further on with a bright ochrous sediment. The difference of atmosphere was very perceptible on approach, a hot steam being generated around. The heat of the water, where bubbling out, was very great; one could not suffer one's hand in it a second. The water was limpid and tasteless; the earth for a considerable space around was coated with a white efflorescence, slightly saline; the grass seemed to thrive in the immediate vicinity. I fancy there was a good deal of soda in the subsidence of the evaporation, but am too ignorant to offer more than a conjecture thereon. The natives ascribe valuable medicinal properties to this water, and, for the purpose of utilising it, have put up a very rough little bathing shed close to the well.

I shot a hare returning, my dog Sara behaving with the most surprising intelligence, considering that she has never been taught, nor has she ever seen game before. Her spaniel blood here shows itself, though sadly contaminated by mongrel admixture. On return I refreshed my mind for the assault of the kardar.

Some time after breakfast I saw the horses being got together, my attendants present, so betook myself to the place, and out of some fifteen animals could only pass three, the others being miserable creatures, wretchedly thin, and with terribly galled backs. The kardar and retinue kept on the opposite side. Having commented on the miserable condition of these animals offered for my use, I let out at the unhappy kardar, alluding to my possessing the Maharajah's purwanah, and the express orders of Basti Ram enjoining on all officials the duty of supplying my wants, and specially, in this instance, good horses, which, I said, I knew were to be had. Then, assuming wrathful indignation, I observed that I had hitherto waited patiently, and submitted with the utmost moderation to the kardar's trickery and evasions, but that I must now adopt other measures, and I declared that if a sufficient number of serviceable horses were not speedily forthcoming, I would seize the kardar, and strap a load on his back, and compel him to come with me. This braggadocio style was the thing. Consternation fell upon kardar, his followers, and all the villagers standing looking on. I remained scowling at them in truly mock heroic style to allow of no hope of my relenting: then, seeing that orders were given, and messengers hurried off in all directions, I retired from the scene; and in the course of an hour or so a capital lot of serviceable-looking nags were paraded, on inspecting which I told the kardar that there was proof positive of the correctness of my information. He, in a deprecating tone, assured me that these were the property of merchants, and depasturing here. I must have them anyhow; and the custom of the country, and the purwanahs I bear, entitle me to them. And I cannot see any difference between a zemindar's and a sandagur's horse, only that the latter is the richer of the two, and can better remedy any inconvenience that he may be subjected to. But I have positive information that these horses have been detained by the government, until some transactions of a suspicious character, smuggling or fraudulent, on the part of the owners (brothers) have been cleared up, of which there seems no present prospect; so, meantime, they may as well serve my turn. I shall have in all nineteen or twenty horses and some twenty-four men in my expedition, for all of which, biped and quadruped, I must carry food, making this a rather expensive as well as arduous expedition.

Tar-gness has now, in addition to his matchlock, added a large, rough, black-and-tan dog to his sporting equipment, which he avers to be no end of a shikarry, and especially good at shâpu and nâpu. I am glad to have him, if only as a watch at nights. I am now told that we must advance four days' journey beyond the Karakorum range for the yâk. I care not if to the gates of Yarkand, if I do but get my extension of leave. I should rather like the fun of a 'chappar' there; but my gunners are such horrid cowards.

The additional rations and some tattoos were promised this evening; and Abdoolah reporting everything delivered, and the officials waiting for my receipt and their congèe, I accordingly summoned them to the presence, and the moonshi reading out all the articles supplied I put them down verbatim, and gave him the receipt, settlement to be made on my return; so I avoided all disputes as to price, and now relieved the kardar from the sense of my displeasure, and we parted apparently mutually gratified.

9th August. I roused my camp, and, after seeing preparations going on for packing and loading, set off as usual ahead. The route was similar to the former, but with more cultivation and grass meadows, and also large patches of thorn thickets, about which we saw many hares, two or three together. The last four miles to Chanloong were very barren and sandy. We crossed a large stream which Abdool said flowed from Sassar, a mountain we have to cross. We arrived at Chanloong at ten, the distance some twelve miles. There was only one hut that I could see, and an enclosure containing a number of willow trees, and some patches of grain. I was very glad to shelter myself from the sun and glare, the latter being excessive. My followers and luggage arrived all safe at 2 P.M.

A tremendous dust-storm assailed us in the afternoon, rushing up the valley with prodigious violence, and filling the air with clouds of sand and dust, obscuring everything, and particularly disagreeable. It lulled about 5 P.M.

Just as I had finished dinner, Buddoo informed me that Tar-gness was going to display his skill with his matchlock, firing at a mark; so I joined the group of spectators. He set to work in a very methodical manner, carefully loading the gun, and, having adjusted the match, he put another man in a befitting attitude to do duty as rest; then, placing the barrel on his shoulder, aimed and fired. The ball struck very low: the mark was a piece of paper on a stone, about eighty yards off. Poor Tar-gness was much chaffed by the shikarries and bystanders, and all his implements examined and criticised with much ridicule. He bore it all with the greatest good-humour, and proceeded to try his luck a second time. His rest was too lively, and could be got into position with difficulty. This time the ball struck only a foot below the mark. Tar-gness was encouraged to try again. He now put in more powder, loading more deliberately than ever, testing the amount of charge by the finger measurement on the ramrod. And now, his looks denoting determination and confidence, he posted his rest, aimed carefully, and fired—when down came the mark. "Sha-bash!" was the exclamation; and the triumphant marksman looked round with conscious skill upon his quizzing tormentors of whom Abdool had been prominent, taking a stick and imitating Tar-gness' motions to the great amusement of the lookers-on, his queer little wizened face being irresistibly comic. The sporting appointments were all home-made and very ingenious; the bullet-mould of a black soft stone in two pieces, fastened by wooden pegs; the bullet was an elongated sphere, crossed in its length and breadth by thin raised bands, the spaces they left containing an ornamental dot. This was Tar-gness' talisman—very curious.

I passed a disturbed night, noises in every direction around me; men and horses passing to and fro all night; a dog barking in a desperate manner; and a shrill cock, mistaking the moonlight and the unusual movements for dawn, keeping up a horrid chanticleering.

10th August. I was glad of the first symptoms of dawn to rise and rouse the camp. We had a tough job before us as I knew; but I had not quite reckoned the full extent of it. The path now turned abruptly from Chanloong to the right, out of the valley, over the eastern range which, seen from our camp, did not look formidable, but was in fact the stiffest climb I have had. It occupied us three hours, of which I walked two, and then, seeing the summit still high above us, I mounted, which was a great relief to me and to Abdool who was pulling on my horse. The difference in the dispositions of the three shikarries was here noticeable in their treatment of their ponies. Subhan got off, and led his nearly half-way; the other two never once got off, but when compelled to adjust their saddle-gear, or something of that kind. An hour after we had started, the baggage animals were still to be seen down below stationary in the enclosure—provoking sight.

The crest of the mountain was very grand; but the view from it, however magnificent in its scenery, was by no means inviting to travellers. We looked down a very steep descent of rugged and sandy slopes, into a valley of utter sterility up which we had to make our way. Nor did near approach improve it; for the heaps and masses of stones, through which we had to scramble and pick our way, were strewed with the skeletons of the unfortunate horses that had succumbed to the terrible difficulties of the road. Numbers of them lay bleaching on either hand; sometimes singly, and at others in dismal groups of four or five, making this unattractive valley horrid with their ugliness.

We stopped on the bare stones to breakfast, there being nothing better in prospect, a stream dashing by to the river flowing down the valley; then, on through the same wilderness of stones. I cannot think how they came there in the positions and proportions they exhibit. It appears as though the sides of the mountains had been forced open, and torrents of rock and stone vomited violently out, and hurled into the valley; or that the mountain peaks had been riven and shattered by some tremendous shocks of earthquake, and toppling down had spread their fragments all around.

We crossed the river by a bridge, and arrived at twelve o'clock at a shepherd's encampment, our halting place, close to a huge mass of ice and snow, filling the end of the valley, miles in length. Some rough loose stone enclosures constituted the abodes of men and cattle; of the former some half-dozen presented themselves and salaam'd. The whole place was redolent of the strong smell of goats. There appeared nothing whatever in the vicinity to eat. All was wild desolation.

I took shelter under a huge stone, the shikarries putting up some wrappers on sticks to form a screen; and but for the essence of billy-goat, so pungent as to take one's breath away, I should have done well enough. Hours passed, and there were no signs of my traps. I became extremely anxious as the road was so bad, and at five o'clock went off to reconnoitre alone, and took post on an elevation from which, through my glass, I descried three horses on a green patch the other side the river, some three or four miles off, but far above the bridge. This I could not understand. After a time I saw three men, my servants, mount these horses, and deliberately ride up along the river the wrong side, on which the path was but a sheep track, and terminated in the river at a point where it would be hazardous to attempt to ford. A coolie appeared in sight on the right side, so I was comforted in the belief that it was only my three servants that had gone astray. I watched them anxiously. They rode down to the river, and there stopped a long time; then into it, but kept in to their own bank. I became quite nervous for them—quite painfully alarmed lest the poor fellows should try to remedy their mistake by risking the passage. They were far beyond sound or sign from me; so I made my way back to camp, and sent off two Bhooties to render assistance.

I found the shepherds milking their goats, and suddenly bethought me of a syllabub which, as I was hungry and should not in all probability get my dinner for hours, would be a pleasant refreshment; so with a modicum of brandy from the flask and a spoonful of sugar I concocted a pleasant cheering beverage, vulgarly called 'doctor'—from its medicinal properties, no doubt. I felt much comforted thereby; and when the coolies arrived and told us that the servants had turned back to cross the bridge, and that the animals and baggage had met with no mishap, but were coming on, I felt I could wait most contentedly their arrival. We lighted fires both as beacons and for warmth, and also to be ready for cooking. It was now bitterly cold, and black dark. The coolies came straggling in; then Abdoolah and Buddoo who reported that Ali Bucks had got a fall and a ducking, but no harm done. At last all the baggage came in, at 8.30, and I had a stew warmed up and dined.

I ordered every horse two seers of corn, and went after dinner to see if it had been given. The grain had been issued, but most of the rascally drivers had gone off to the Bhoot huts, and left their disconsolate horses famishing. I kicked up a great row, and Abdoolah and others rushed about frantically, lugging, hauling, and abusing, until I saw each 'quad' munching his feed. Poor things! they have hard times of it. These Bhooties have a most absurd idea which Abdool revealed, he firmly believing in it, that in this country the horses should never be allowed grass until sunset, or they swell up and die. He would have starved my horse on this principle, but that I overruled his stupid attempt; and the poor baggage cattle would have got nothing till morning, after their great fatigues and long fast—-another idea—had I not interfered.

11th August. At the first inkling of dawn I halloo'd loudly for Buddoo: they were all fast asleep, and, after I was ready to start, Abdoolah and others were still ensconced in their blankets. It was a cold raw morning, which made me anxious to be moving. The horses were all astray, except mine, no one having had the sense to send for them. Mooktoo came to me with a whine, saying that his horse had not eaten half his corn: I took the opportunity of rebuking him for his selfish want of consideration to the poor beast yesterday, attributing its being amiss thereto.

I left the shikarries to await their horses, and went on with Abdool. It was bitter cold, and I walked long ere the circulation was in full play, and longed for the sun's now genial beams. The path was a great improvement on yesterday's, and there was a good deal of grass scattered about. The route lay due east. Ascending a stiff rocky hill, an opening in the mountain peaks appeared, which I found to be the pass of Sassar. I had decided last night to halt at the bottom of the pass, by the advice of Abdool, and there to pass Sunday, enabling the poor cattle to rest and pick up a bellyfull of grass which Abdool stated to be plentiful there; but if it turned out that there was no grass, we should cross the pass on Sunday morning to the next halt, where grass was abundant, and wood also. We are carrying wood with us at present.

The valley, as we approached the pass, was blocked up by masses of stones, in the midst of which were occasional pools of water. Clambering over these rough heaps, we came in sight of the grand obstruction to our progress, in an enormous glacier which completely choked up the valley. Masses of snow lay in all directions, and several pools of clear water; around which, and elsewhere, I was glad to see a sufficiency of grass for the horses. I selected a spot for the camp, and then the shikarries came up, and I found that Phuttoo and Mooktoo had changed their horses, having knocked theirs up yesterday. I gave them a bit of my mind, and forbade such tricks in future. The wind was very cold, blowing off the masses of snow, but the sun excessively hot—a most unpleasant contrast. This being a short march of about eight miles, all the baggage came up in good time. Abdool had tied up the shikarries' tats, and remonstrated at my orders to loose them: the silly fellow would have kept all the animals fasting during the day. No wonder so many perish under such cruel privations. Subhan is unwell, complaining of headache—the effects of the sun and wind, no doubt. I had the foot of my shuldary closed in with turf-clods to exclude the biting blast, and prepared plenty of clothes to weather out the night.

12th August. Sunday. I had a very uneasy night of it, suffering from indigestion, although I dined at five—hare stew too rich, perhaps—but the principal disturbing cause was the difficulty of respiration, owing to the extreme rarification of the air at this great height, many thousands of feet. I waited in painful disquiet till the sun rose; then turned out, the thermometer in my tent 33°. From the past night's experience I was doubtful of my health, but after a wash and a cup of tea found myself all right. Abdoolah told me they had all suffered from shortness of breath as I had done; so, quite reassured, I went forth to stroll.

We are in a basin formed by rugged mountains whose many gorges are filled with immense masses of snow, in ridge and furrow, having the appearance of mighty rivers suddenly congealed in all the irregularity of their downward rush. In this basin are many stony hillocks; at their bases clear pools. I wished to see how the poor horses fared, and was much pleased to see them apparently enjoying their repose and pasturage, many lying down, their stomachs proving by their rotundity that they had made good use of their time. I sat down and watched them, and was forcibly struck by the wisdom and mercy of the Sabbath ordinance. Poor wearied beasts! your aching limbs and galled smarting backs would now be causing you renewed tortures, but for that merciful decree of the Divine Will. I enjoyed a grateful, peaceful sensation at my heart in this recognition of the Almighty Creator's loving-kindness.

I came back to camp and enquired after Subhan, who emerged from the shuldary, and reported himself somewhat better, but that Phuttoo and Mooktoo were ill; the latter's whining voice was heard in corroboration, complaining of the cold. These men are in every respect as comfortable as my domestics, and have the advantage of being inured to the rigours of a cold climate; whereas the others are denizens of the sultry plains of the Punjab, and yet they do not complain; though shivering, they are content and cheery, and, I believe, quite despise these unmanly hunters.

I continued my stroll up the valley, and ascended a high hillock near the glacier which presents a truly formidable aspect, its congealed masses being broken into a multitude of conical peaks which look as though they bid defiance to any attempt to scale them. Viewed from this eminence, the icy scene around was grand in the extreme. I overlooked the upper gorges of the highest mountains, all of which appeared to converge towards a centre, their immense contents of snow and ice radiating, as it were, and uniting, the distance blending them and mysteriously concealing the vast and irregular spaces that really separated them. The sun was warm and genial, the air sharp and fresh, under which influences I felt simple existence delightful, and rejoiced devoutly in being the creature of the Beneficent Creator of these mighty works.

In the afternoon I walked to the foot of the glacier to examine the path, and went over a considerable tract of snow, but could not discover the track up the glacier, which must be very steep and difficult. On my return the unhappy shikarries, who had remained all day rolled up in their blankets, crawled to my tent and expressed their shame at being 'hors-de-combat' without any apparent reason. They all complained of severe headache, which I attribute to rheumatic pains contracted from exposure to the bitter cold blasts here blowing. The stupid fellows have left their tent-poles too high; so that the foot of their shuldary allows a space of two feet open for the draft to rush through, and as they sleep on the ground the effect must be striking. I had advised them on this point, but Asiatic-like they would adopt no precaution. I again pointed out to them this objectionable gap, and cheered them up—the miserable beings!—telling them they would be all right to-morrow, as we expected to meet game. I got them out of the dumps, and gave them some sugar for their tea, and they retired, and immediately docked their poles. It was intensely cold, so I retreated early to the shelter of my canvas.

13th August. I got comfortably through the night under piles of clothes, and roused up at dawn, the thermometer in my tent at freezing point. The shikarries had allowed their tats, after being driven in, to run off again, so I started with Abdool. We got well across the snow to the foot of the glacier, where we found no regular path, but had to scramble up a mass of stones and débris on one side of the ice, almost perpendicular. I feared for the baggage animals. The road was execrable; nothing but rugged masses of loose sharp-pointed stones. Of course, riding was out of the question. One side of the pass—the northern—was free from snow, but piled on high with these masses of stone: the south side was filled with snow to the consistency of ice a foot or so from the surface. I should calculate its extent to have been some four or five miles, with an occasional break where was a basin and a pool of green water. The route was most uneven, presenting a succession of ups and downs all but impracticable from the stones. This gorge was strewed with the skeletons of horses, of which we must have passed a hundred or more. When I thought that we must have got over the worst, I found the whole pass blocked up with a distinct glacier over which we had to climb. But it was less difficult than it looked, the surface being rough, and crumbling under the tread. There was about a mile of this; and then a gradual descent to masses of stones similar to those already passed, through which we scrambled and stumbled until well down the pass, where the path appeared again, and I mounted.

As we rode down towards the camp, Tar-gness' dog, which was a little ahead of us with Kamal who carried my breakfast, pursued a large flock of shâpu, scattering them here and there: a large body of them, however, stopped and recommenced feeding high up above us. This looked promising for sport. I alighted at half-past nine, after five hours' hard work. We found some stone screens, and, piled up by one, a number of bags of 'charras,' there deposited by some merchant whose horses had died. I am told that an immense quantity of valuable merchandise is thus lying about on the Karakorum mountains, awaiting the owners' leisure for removal. They say it is never robbed, which says much for the honesty of the natives who pass to and fro; though I suppose the fact is that none but merchants *do* travel this road, and they naturally respect each other's rights, and compassionate their misfortunes.

The scenery was very grand. Immediately in front rose two enormous mountains looking black like coal, composed of a slate-like stone; and beyond them was a broken range of light sand-coloured mountains, seen through the gorge dividing the former, where I believe our path runs. Right and left of us lies a valley of the usual sterile appearance, huge snow-capped mountains shutting it in. It lies, I think, north and south.

A kafila was announced; and in time there arrived a merchant from Buduckshan. He had about twenty-five laden horses—small, well-formed, compact animals. He pitched his tent, a gay, green, flimsy thing; but, after some conversation with the shikarries, he struck it, and pursued his way. And a horrible rough one he will find it, poor man! He has never travelled this road before. I fear he must lose some of those nice horses, although they are in marvellous good condition. He halted ten days to refresh them at a place called Sugheit, where is abundance of grass, and for which I am now making.

My servants and horses arrived all safe, after much difficulty and one or two falls. I went with Subhan to look for game, and after a length of time we found, in a deep nullah. I stalked carefully up the stony hill, and was but just in time, as the herd of nâpu were on the alert, and fled as I arrived. But I struck true, and saw one lag behind as they darted down the steep. Blood shewed on the side, and it just crossed the ravine, and dropped. I fired into the lot going up the opposite side, and dropped another. We made our way to the prey, two female nâpu, on which Subhan performed the 'hallal' duly; then, placing a conspicuous mark by the carcases, we returned to camp, where our success was a subject of much rejoicing, and sent for the meat.

Two merchants journeying to Yarkand had followed me closely, and joined my camp. They came to see me while at dinner, and on my jokingly proposing to accompany them into Yarkand they assured me I might do it with perfect safety; they would answer for it with their lives. I talked with them for some time, and felt quite elated at the idea of visiting that famed city, hitherto hermetically closed to Europeans. I was quite resolved to attempt the adventure, and what with the day's sport, this exciting object, and a glass of sherry, I turned in quite jolly.

When the two animals were brought in, the coolies petitioned for a halt to mend their shoes, and Tar-gness, who had been out on the other side after shikar, coming back with the news that he had seen some fine large-horned nâpu, I consented to a day's halt, and ordered an early start to hunt.

14th August. A bitter cold morning: and there was a stream to cross, the stones of which were coated with ice, so that Subhan, the plucky Subhan, who volunteered to carry me across, fell just on reaching the other side. We had most difficult climbing up stony steeps: found a herd of nâpu, male and female, but tried in vain to approach them, as they first got our wind, and then sighted us; so we descended again to breakfast near a rivulet. From this spot we descried the herd crossing a ridge on the mountain, and the males, some ten, remained behind and lay down. I gazed at them through the glass, and admired their massive horns. After a time we determined to try and circumvent them, and pursued our way along the stony slope of the mountain, low down. But these 'cute creatures spied us, and, I believe, detected our plot, which was to station ourselves in a ravine crossing their probable line of retreat, when roused by Tar-gness who was to approach them by a long detour down wind. I noticed that the suspicious animals had already faced about in the direction of the new danger. I had hardly any hopes of success, and told Subhan that I feared Tar-gness would never go back far enough to drive them in our direction: but the attempt must be made, and a terrible struggle we had up a ravine, the surface of which was one mass of loose sharp stones, causing one to slip back every step. After many a pause to take breath we reached the requisite height, and I posted the shikarries—Subhan and the guns with me commanding the passes, Phuttoo and Mooktoo guarding the two ends. A bitter keen wind nearly blew Subhan and me off our perch, to which we had climbed with difficulty. Here we waited perhaps two hours, and then, neither hearing nor seeing anything, descended; which was not effected without danger. Indeed, I was nearly coming to grief getting up, as Subhan ahead of me detached a large stone which, by a convulsive effort, I avoided: had it struck me, it must have hurled me down below, when nothing less than a broken limb would have resulted.

We made our way down the stony ravine, Subhan and Mooktoo having their sandals cut off their feet, and completing the day barefooted. We went back by the river bank, the sand of which better suited the shoeless pair, and on the way fell in with some ten pair of nâpu horns, some very fine ones, the animals supposed to have perished in the snows.

It was a bitter cold night, snow and sleet driven by a furious blast sweeping over the encampment. The poor coolies, how I pitied them! It was lucky they had a good feast of flesh to keep them in heart.

15th August. To Moorgaby: a march of some twelve miles, rendered very uncomfortable by having to cross the river which came up to my knees on my horse, and was very rapid, nearly carrying the horse off his legs. The shikarries' tattoos, with supporters, got through with difficulty. The water was as cold as ice, and my extremities being saturated I dismounted, and tried in vain to recover a pleasant warmth; so sat down and wrung the water from my socks, and then got on better; but had soon to remount as the path lay between the two huge black mountains, up a narrow, savage gorge down which flowed a torrent. This we had to cross continually. And as, each time, my wetting was renewed by the splashing of my high-stepping nag, and it was freezing, I endured agonies of cold, which quite blinded me to the magnificence of the savage grandeur of the scenery. After two hours of this misery we turned abruptly from the ravine, and ascended by a gulley to the hill-side, and, surmounting a stiffish ascent, found a fine open valley before us.

I now thoroughly restored the circulation, and strode on vigorously. A caravan came in sight; on arriving at which, composed of about twenty horses, we pulled up, and I chatted some time with the proprietor, and tried to deal for a horse. But the price did not suit. Some fifty more laden horses came up; and I tried to bargain for some Thibet boots for my followers. The first merchant was reasonable, but had no stock for sale; the others were exorbitant, and the business concluded by the former, after much altercation with his partners (I presume), presenting me with two pair, saying he had received more kindness from the 'saheb-logue' than he could ever repay. He is an Affghan. The merchants accompanying my party are from Cabul, and also profess the utmost regard and respect for the English. This liberal fellow gave us most encouraging accounts of the abundance of game at Sugheit, and at another place nearer, where he himself had killed a fine antelope which intruded amongst and frightened his horses. There were numbers of kyang there. This place is three or four stages off. My new acquaintance is going to Lahore, where he promises to pay his respects to me, should he have left Ladâk before my return.

We continued our march, much exhilarated by the reports of shikar; and after some three or four miles of level ground, the valley narrowing to a mere ravine, we halted in a sort of swamp affording a good bite of grass. We found five or six pair of nâpu horns, but could perceive no recent traces of those animals. The baggage arrived in good time, except the sheep and goats which had to be carried across stream, a work of much time and trouble. When they did arrive at night, one of the poor goats appeared with a horn broken, and evidently suffering much. The evening set in very cold. A storm driven by a furious blast roared down the valley; but shortly expending itself, the swift-passing clouds made way for the welcome sun whose departing beams were most cheering.

After dinner, which I eat shivering with cold, and at which, by-the-bye, figured a dish of rhubarb I had gathered on the hill-side, of which there is abundance, I went to warm myself at the small fires of my followers, where they were preparing their frugal fare; that of the Bhooties consisting of simple hot water and bread. A large copper vessel was on the fire round which they sat, and one ladled out this mild liquor into the cups of the squatting group. These cups are remarkable, being carved from a very handsome brown striped satin-wood. They come from our hill-states. Each Bhoot carries one which constitutes his entire stock of *crockery*. From this party I turned to my kitchen fire, where cakes were in course of preparation. I got a plate of tea, and returned to the Bhoot party, and, to their infinite delight, produced the tea which, however, they intercepted as I was pouring it into the vessel, reserving half for a future meal. They greeted me with many 'johoos,' and eyes glistening with pleasure. Poor creatures! a little kindness is excessively appreciated by them.

Now took place a very curious and important operation—the brewing the real tea—not the 'make-believe,' as the Marchioness styled the choice liquors she concocted for Dick Swiveller. The tea being immersed, a ladle of ghee is put in, and four or five table-spoons of salt added: then much stirring and mixing takes place, a curious implement being used to froth the beverage, like what in the navy in my younger days—perhaps, the very name now forgotten—was called a 'swizzle-stick' which, by rapid revolution between the hands, aerated the grog in the tumbler, giving it a pleasant sparkling appearance and freshness of flavour. Many a time I applied it in my first voyage from England to Hobart Town, viâ Canada, instructed by the veteran purser, Tucker; and a by no means contemptible beverage it made in tropical latitudes at eight bells. Well, the tea well mixed, and frothed, and repeatedly tasted, was ladled out to the anxious party, and much relished; of whom some, opening their flour-sacks alongside of them, concluded their meal by mixing up as much flour as would soak up the tea, and form a paste which was kneaded with the fingers, and then devoured with much relish. This is the ordinary mode of tea-drinking among this people; but when a tea-fight is given, the compos is, of course, entirely prepared in the one vessel, and served out, of the consistency of strong gruel.

16th August. To Bursey: a long fatiguing march of about fifteen miles. Our route now lay north, and led up the sandy bed of a much-divided river. We ascended and descended two formidable heights, bulging out from the mountains, which was very laborious work, the path being deep in grit. About twelve o'clock, from the wide sandy channel we were moving up some animals were discovered, which on examination turned out to be shâpu. They looked as large as bara sing. I dismounted, and, leaving the horses with the trusty Abdool, went in pursuit with every prospect of success. We followed a nullah, screening us and leading to the rear of the position; from this we cautiously emerged, but our advanced scout, Subhan, in vain strained his eyes for a sight of our game. We moved from place to place, and at last were compelled to accept the unwelcome conviction that the quadrupeds had instinctively outwitted the reasoning bipeds, and defeated their well-contrived plot. And, indeed, we soon saw them far in the distance; so we made straight for our horses, and resumed our weary way up the sandy plain—excessively wearisome—every hundred yards crossing the stream, or one of its innumerable offsets. My endurance was greatly taxed by holding in front the fidgetty Sara whose feet, poor little fellow! were very sore from the stones. We passed one or two places which we thought would prove the halt, but the inexorable Abdool, his thin wiry limbs apparently unsusceptible of fatigue, pointing ahead, still strode on, helping himself over the streams with a staff, and grinning and muttering something unintelligible when addressed, like a menagerie baboon.

At length, we did halt on a bare expanse of shingle under a rock, without a vestige of vegetation—a bad look-out for the cattle. It was now about 3.30 P.M. The equestrian party arrived about five; but the coolies, carrying the kheltas and provisions, were far in the rear, nor did they come in till eight or nine. Luckily I had some remnants of cold meat from my breakfast, on which, with some fresh chupatties and tea, I dined as well as though I had been at mess. I attended the Bhoot tea-party again, and watched their operations, warming myself by their fire. I also had another confab with the merchants about Yarkand, and the feasibility of an invasion on my part: they are not so encouraging as they were. I saw each horse provided with two seers of grain (wheat), and turned in. An exceedingly sharp frost.

17th August. To Pulu: a long march of, I should think, little under eighteen miles. There was a great improvement in the road, the first part of which led up the wide sandy channel as yesterday: the running waters were covered with ice, and the air was bitterly cold. The many streams necessitated riding, the consequence being extreme suffering from cold in hands and feet. After four or five miles, a tract less intersected by streams allowed me to dismount, when I led off at a sharp trot, but had hardly sped sixty paces, when I was summarily checked by suffocation, my lungs heaving up and down violently, craving for inflation, but deriving no relief from the thin atmosphere. I fell leaning upon a large stone luckily at hand, and then underwent something very like death. I asked myself, 'Is this death seizing me?' The paroxysm did not—nor could it—last more than a few seconds, when with many long-continued gasps I gradually felt my lungs in play again, and will take good care not to put them out of gear again in a hurry.

We threaded some wild narrow ravines, only allowing the torrent which cleft them passage; then we emerged into sunshine, a valley opening out, and hills and peaks stooping down, until we found ourselves ascending a smooth gradual elevation, from the top of which, rolling away from our feet, was an immense, wavy, undulating table-land, stretching away on all sides, bounded in the distance by much-broken ranges of snow-clad mountains, but presenting no remarkable features. This elevated plain being some 17,000 feet above the sea, its excrescences did not, I imagine, protrude more than 1000 or 2000 feet out of its surface. The utmost sterility imaginable held desolate sway around. But the vast expanse spread out, after our long intercepted vision, and the beautiful tints and varied forms of the distant mountains, composed a magnificent landscape. Abdool, recognising some familiar features, broke out into exclamations, hailing the objects interesting him, and turning round to us with a glowing face—if such an expression can be applied to such a mummy-like phiz—to notice the impression made upon us. There is some enthusiasm in that scarecrow, I do believe.

The track through this desert was lined by the bleached bones of horses, strongly recalling the old route from Suez to Cairo, and, here and there, large fragments of a skeleton form—portions of the vertebræ, for instance—were propped up by stones to serve as landmarks to the traveller. On mounting the crest of a rise, I noticed an object in the path below, which looked like a huge animal, by the side of the remains of a horse. It proved to be an enormous hyena: from its size and appearance, I should think a rare species. After a short scrutiny it leisurely cantered away, giving many a backward glance at the unwelcome disturbers of its morning meal. From many tracks of these animals on the path, I suppose them to be numerous here, following the caravans, and revelling on the carcases of horses, victims to the privations of the journey. This unclean beast was a fitting object to complete the dismal 'ensemble' of this dreary waste.

Looming in the distance fronting us now appeared an approaching caravan, undergoing those strange transitions of appearance, those transformations under the mysterious effects of mirage, so common in the atmosphere of the desert—now swelling out laterally, then diminishing and towering aloft to most unnatural proportions, all the time swayed and agitated by glimmering waves of chiaraoscura, defying the eye in its attempt to define the forms immersed in this ever-oscillating, quivering, atmospheric flood. Startled by this alarming vision, a dozen or so of antelopes came trooping down, giving our party a wide berth. And having now been some four hours on foot, and there being appearance of water at hand, we determined to halt and make an attempt on the antelope, pending the arrival of the far-behind Kamal with the breakfast.

The leaders of the caravan came up, with some thirty horses, and we exchanged courteous greetings, and received confirmatory intelligence of the merits of Sugheit, both as a place of refreshment and shikar. One of the sandagurs carried in front of him a large bundle of clothing containing a child—a boy, I imagine—looking, poor little chap! pale and sick with cold. It was an uninteresting, mealy-faced child, with a very marked obliquity of vision, but I felt much compassion for him; he wore such a look of patient suffering. They vanished in space: and we, leaving Abdool in charge of the horses—what a desolate, forlorn creature he looked thus forsaken!—set off on our excursion. And far we wandered, but only on our return saw animals far in the distance—perhaps of the herd before seen, or may be others—when we turned our steps towards our living mark just visible, an undefined, quivering heap.

The remainder of the caravan hove in sight, a seemingly long string of horses, also exaggerated and palsied by the flickering medium through which we looked on them. I sent off Subhan to bring Abdool and Co. to a point we would make for, intersecting the road, and so saving us a long round: we then continued our route towards the mountains, and on arriving at their lower spurs connecting them with this table-land we descended to an extensive valley, watered by a rapid and a wide, but shallow, river. Some patches of grass were visible, on which were some animals grazing here and there. The ground was too level and void of covert to admit of much hope of stalking them; but I made the attempt with Subhan, and in spite of every precaution of tactics experience lent us—crawling a long distance on all fours, much to our personal inconvenience—the wary creatures (antelope) kept out of reach of harm, contenting themselves with keeping us at arm's length, as it were. Thus baffled, we rejoined our party, and pursued our journey, I resolving after these repeated discomfitures not to attempt again to approach these knowing inhabitants of the desert, they being as wild as though they had been hunted every day the last six months.

A gradual ascent crossing two shallow rivers brought us to Pulu, where on a bare plain, under a spur projecting into it, and under its angle abutting on the bed of a stream, are three rude huts; all around which are closely strewed the bones of horses, of which I counted fifty from one spot. A whole caravan must have perished here in the snow, I should think. The baggage (equestrian) arrived about five, but there was no hope of the coolies for hours. Abdoolah, however, had provided against such a contingency, having with him a reserved portion of the game killed the other day, and the canteen for cooking; so I fared excellently well, the chops being exceedingly good and tender. I ordered each horse two seers of grain, and one in the morning, this being the second day without a bit of grass. The cold was excessive; the huts a great comfort to my retinue.

We cross the mighty Karakorum range to-morrow—a great event. The ascent is said to be easy, and the road good. Indeed, I believe the great difficulties in our journey to have been surmounted at Bursey. But the want of grass and fuel still attends us. The night was horridly cold, the difficulty of breathing great. I heaped all the clothes on I possessed; but the keen frosty wind would not be denied, and found entrance through the chinks of my armour.

CHAPTER XII.

SUGHEIT.

18th August. The passage of the Karakorum mountains effected—and no great feat either, as the heavier work had been already accomplished 'en route.' On turning out of my tent this morning, everything congealable was frozen. I was informed that a horse was down very ill, and went to see him; and there the poor creature lay in agony, a nice creature in good condition, which I had noticed as one of my best. There he lay struggling, the steam of the death-sweat exhaling on the cold frosty air: his nostrils were full of blood. Alas! I could do nothing for him. And even while I turned to move away, death seized him, his teeth set, an universal shudder convulsed him, his legs were stretched out stark and stiff, and with a hollow groan he expired. Poor creature! it was a distressing sight. I attribute his death to inflammation from the severe cold. This is the second casualty, as I had to consent to the maimed goat being put out of its misery at Bursey: its moans were shocking. The coolies made a good meal of the poor thing. And so I added my contribution to the piles of bones at this melancholy spot.

Some six miles of tolerable travelling, mostly along the watercourse, brought us to the foot of the Karakorum, up which a portion of the winding path was seen, nothing formidable about it. I breakfasted, and then rode up the mountain, pausing every twenty paces or so to breathe the nags. Here we passed our mercantile companions who had given us the go-by, when at breakfast. A zyarat—a pile of stones with some rags on sticks—was on the top of the pass. I thought it was Buddhist, and rebuked Abdool for doing reverence to it, but was informed that it was a Mahomedan pir. We descended into a level valley, watered by a stream which Abdool states to be the source of the Yarkand river. Bones and carcases of horses lay in all directions, the loads of many left beside their bearer's remains. Huge bloated ravens flapped and croaked around. Footprints of the hyena, too, were seen, which foul ugly beast had skulked from the glare of day to some lone den in the rocks around.

I rode slowly on ahead of my party, pondering on subjects suggested by the savage wildness of the scene, when I was quite startled by the rushing sound of two monstrous ravens which, quarrelling for a morsel of carrion, swooped down close by my head. I thought how, in darker ages, this would have been regarded as an augury for good or evil. We descended gradually, following the watercourse, the valley widening to some two or three miles extent; at a bend in which, taking us to the eastward, our course having been hitherto north, we saw some of the wild horse (kyang)—two or three in the valley, others on the hill-side, and some up a creek down which came a tributary stream. Exciting as this sight was, nothing could be done. To attempt to stalk such wild, sagacious creatures, with every natural condition in their favour, was hopeless; so gazing in despair I rode on, and saw two large antelopes equally unassailable. The valley narrowed to a gorge; then opened out on to an extensive plain of shingle, miles broad and more in length, intersected in all directions by streams which, if united, must form a large river. We crossed over this plain to a grassy bank, lying between it and the sandy hills which represent, as it were, the projected roots of the mountains, stretching out far and irregularly from the main body. The country is now evidently opening out, showing wide expanses between the mountains, and giving hopes of better lands to be soon reached.

Another caravan passed on its upward course, but some way from us. We saw some startled antelope hastening from them, and went after them; but after having toiled long, performing a circuitous course to reach them, we viewed them where, from the direction of the wind and absence of all covert could not approach. I sent Phuttoo to try to drive them to us, but he failed entirely. We wandered about this shingly plain, viewing other antelope equally unapproachable; then returned to camp ground. None of my people had arrived. Nor did they till 5 P.M.; when I learned that another horse had knocked up, and was apparently in a hopeless state, but the blood being extracted from its nostrils, and its burden removed, it recovered and was being led on.

After night had closed in, I was sitting anxiously awaiting the arrival of the coolies still behind, when I heard sounds of human voices in distress, faint and distant. There were answering calls from camp. This continued a long time. I then enquired if any one had been despatched to direct the wanderers to our haven, and was told one had; but think not till I spoke. A long time elapsed; and then the voices drew nearer, and at nine o'clock all had come in safe, to my great relief. They had naturally followed on the main track, from which we had turned off to camp, and so they had strayed some miles beyond us.

I had given orders for an entertainment to be prepared for all hands to-morrow, including our mercantile friends, to commemorate the passage of the Karakorum, as also to freshen up my exhausted coolies, who have had four consecutive hard days' work. The whole party look worn and haggard. Much pleasure was evinced at the prospect of the morrow's rest and refreshment. I got out additional clothes to sleep in, and, having carefully scraped up the dirt and stones against my tent-foot to exclude the piercing wind, hope to make out the night comfortably.

19th August. Sunday. I enjoyed a tolerable night's repose, thanks to the precautions taken to render my shuldary proof against the icy blasts coming down from the snowy summits around. I strolled out, and selected as favourable a site as this wild offered, where to sit and ruminate. My reflections were not altogether satisfactory, not unmixed with growing apprehensions of disaster, from loss of cattle extending to loss of men. I have reduced the coolies' loads to a mere trifle; still they get on with difficulty. It is not the burden, but the difficulty of respiration, that oppresses them. Another goat was obliged to be killed on the road yesterday. The want of natural nourishment is terrible: and the fact of this region not producing sufficient herbage to support a goat may well define its inhospitable sterility. The few wild animals existing must pick up a precarious and meagre sustenance in and about the watercourses, where alone a vegetation, coarse and scanty, may be found. The horse that knocked up yesterday was led in at night, and having fed we hope to save him.

From these gloomy forebodings I turned me to the more cheerful subject of to-day's festivity, and descended to carry out with Abdoolah the designs already chalked out. I desired that all the mussulmans should eat together, merchants, shikarries, domestics, and Bhooties—the Hindoos separately—and the Buddhist Bhooties. About 12 P.M., Abdoolah reported that the banquet was spread, and going out I found the party busily employed on an ample provision of well-cooked pillau, helped into its resting-place by tea and coffee. All seemed much pleased and thankful.

In the evening a large caravan of some eighty horses came in. The principal man was a Cashmiri of Kishtewar, and being slightly acquainted with one of his countrymen, the shikarries, he was most accessible to all our queries, and most voluble in his replies. He had not come by the Sugheit road; had seen numbers of antelope to-day. He entered into a long history of the murder of the brother Schlagentweit, which agrees in the main with that already known, but with the important difference that the bulk of the victim's property, including his papers, was with him when Walli Khan so brutally murdered him, and is still in that ruffian's possession. A few things were previously 'looted' on the road, which were following in the rear of the ill-fated traveller. I enquired as to the probability of obtaining the effects, at least the papers of the unfortunate naturalist, and was told that certainly, if I wrote authoritatively to the khaltai newab, or hakim, who rules Yarkand, he would cause their restoration; though it must be a work of time, as all sorts of evasions and falsehoods would be put in practice to mislead me, and induce the belief that the effects were beyond recovery.

Here is a matter for serious consideration. A great advantage to the public may be obtained by my instrumentality, but can I, a servant of the government, take upon myself the responsibility, wholly unauthorised, of using my influence as belonging to the government, in a direction altogether beyond my office and functions?

20th August. To Waad Jilgo: a pleasant march of some ten or eleven miles, in my case agreeably diversified by good sport with antelope. Our route lay down the extensive plain of shingle, the streams of which were thickly coated with ice which jingled merrily under our trampling feet. A smart pace was necessary to keep up the circulation, so I strode on ahead of Abdool. The shikarries were detained, waiting till their tats had finished their seer of corn. The poor animal that knocked up on Saturday disappointed our hopes and expectations, after all his improving symptoms dying in the course of the night. He was one of the strongest of the lot, and in fair condition.

Many antelope were seen on either hand; but the ground presented no facilities for stalking, so I did not check my course for them. After about five miles' tramp, the shikarries came up. We now left the shingly watercourse, ascending on to some uplands yielding, here and there, a light sprinkling of grass, the blades few and far between, but just tinting the spot where they grew. A fine buck antelope suddenly stepped into view, as he surmounted a rise; gazed at us a second or two, and leisurely took himself off. This was tantalising. I dismounted, and with Subhan sought to circumvent him; but he had put many a hundred yards between us. We again descended to a bed of shingle of wide-stretching dimensions, on which moving objects were indistinctly seen in the uncertain hazy light, at first thought to be kyang, then decided to be antelope. Two peculiar features were now observable in our direct route, lying close together, apparently rocks which would be islets when the floods were out. For these we steered, determining there to breakfast. As we alighted, a buck antelope sped along far on the other side, coming down a shelving bank on to the shingle, as though he were about to cross it. He was far away; but Phuttoo handed me the Whitworth. I said, "Well, we have lots of bullets and lead; how far off is he?" They said, "three hundred yards;" so, putting the sight to three hundred, I rested the rifle against a rock, and aimed high and forward. The ball was seen ricochetting far beyond the buck, which had started, and then stood, head drooping. "Mara, mara," exclaimed the shikarries in great excitement. And so it appeared. The animal did not move: so, making arrangements, I advanced on him, and, as I neared him, he lay down—evidence enough of his being mortally wounded. Gaining his rear, I finished him; and a fine, handsome animal he proved, in prime condition, a different species from the black buck, the antelope of the plains; being of a rufous colour, with a thick felt of fur, the winter coat, and fine tapering horns with sharp points bending forwards, with regularly placed transverse bars from the base to six inches from the tip in front, smoothing off to the rear: there was a curious puffy lump at the nostrils.

Continuing our way, I observed something shewing above the level of the gravelly plain, so checked my horse, and called the attention of the shikarries, and asked if it were not the horns of an antelope. They said, it was a stick. But, while thus conjecturing in an under tone, the single object doubled, and proclaimed its character beyond any further doubt. I dismounted, and prepared for action. The buck, benefiting by our audible doubts, aware of danger, sprang up, and moved away, but not rapidly; so, using Subhan's shoulder as a rest, I levelled Whitworth, and with similar effect to the former shot, the missile being seen skipping far away, and the animal stopping with drooping head. He soon lay down, and on our approach rose and made off at a laboured trot; when an Enfield bullet, striking him in the rear, and traversing his body, stretched him lifeless.

We had ridden on some eight hundred yards, when another buck suddenly rose, and stood bewildered, beholding us. Phuttoo fumbled so long with the Whitworth ere handing it to me, that the buck had turned, and was going off at a brisk pace, when I aimed and fired. "Mara, mara," was again the exclamation. We thought he was another victim. But it was only to this extent; his left horn was struck off close to his head, to the intense discomfiture of the poor beast, which threw itself into all sorts of contortions as it dashed away. We left the carcases in Kamal's custody to be cleaned and brought to camp; where we shortly pulled up in a bight of an indent, down which trickled a thread of clear water which produced a patch of unhealthy-looking turf, and some scattered blades of grass in the vicinity.

Subhan and I started after an antelope we had seen near by. He had vanished. We saw others—but does, too wary to get near. We wandered up and down; found tracks of kyang, and made for a gorge, where they might harbour. There we spied a buck; and, as he appeared to have spied us, retreated, and, creeping up the dry watercourse, surprised him feeding on the bank, and rolled him over. Now we turned towards camp; on reaching which I was informed that another horse had knocked up, and been left on the road. It was a poor, lanky, diseased animal, but had stood out well hitherto, although I had, from the first, predicted its giving in. I sent two men to try and lead it in; but they could not succeed, so I fear, though there is both grass and water close to it, the poor creature is doomed. Just before dinner I climbed a hill overhanging the bivouac, on which I found the head and horns of a yâk, a truly massive head. This had probably been killed by a shikarry, there being no other bones near. From this eminence I noticed antelope in to-morrow's line of march, and anticipate sport. There is now great frizzling and kabobbing of flesh.

21st August. I did not turn out very early, but, when I did, found that the horses had not yet been driven in, the Bhooties continuing their cooking. I took the Whitworth from Phuttoo, and, followed by Abdool and nag, started off. We saw antelope on every side in numbers, but could not get within five hundred yards, so wild were they. There were fine grassy uplands for this barren country, *i.e.*, sandy downs bearing a greenish hue, caused by a blade of grass every square yard or so. But it was extremely agreeable to see even this scanty herbage—a wonderful relief to the aching eye. We could not get near the antelope; so, after footing it some five miles, I took the path, as usual, in a wide river-bed, and mounted. I rode on some five or six miles, and then, finding water, halted for breakfast, when Phuttoo and Subhan came up on foot, having tired of waiting for their tats. After an hour's rest, leaving them till the nags arrived, I pursued my journey, and about 3 P.M., after a most wearisome five hours of foot's pace under a burning sun and intense glare, pulled up in a dismal hollow under the mountain leading to Sugheit. This spot, being soon in shade, was bitterly cold, and it soon froze sharp. These rapid alternations of heat and cold are very trying.

It was long before any of my people arrived. I then learned that four horses were left behind, having strayed away—Moosa, Ali Bucks, and Mooktoo remaining behind to bring them on. These came in during the night, but several coolies did not arrive. I gave orders not to move till after breakfast, having on enquiry been assured both by Moosa and Abdool that it was but three hours to Sugheit, and I wished to get all the people together.

22nd August. A bitterly cold morning, and the coolies still absent. I was, notwithstanding, in good spirits from the near prospect of reaching our shooting quarters, the far-famed oasis of Sugheit, rich in grass and timber, and abounding in game, only three hours off; and I cheered up my shivering followers with visions of unlimited quantities of meat. The coolies came in at seven, looking only a little pinched. We set off at 8.30, and had a steady, even pull for some three miles up a hill, from the top of which we understood we were to gaze upon the verdant charms of Sugheit; when, to our utter dismay we looked down upon a long valley of complete nakedness, shut in by mountains equally devoid of clothing. Moosa and Abdool endeavoured to explain that 'the happy land' was not distant, pointing down the valley. But I now thought it prudent to reduce my expectations, although I had received such glowing descriptions, from so many, of the surpassing merits of the fertile Sugheit.

We went some six dreary miles down this vale of disappointment, in which, however, we saw some traces of yâk; and then we turned easterly over another mile or so of barrenness, with an occasional patch of grass by the stream. Then, coming to very rough, broken, rocky ground, the stream became our road; and a very awkward one it was, full of boulders, and the incline now very great. Grass began to form a regular border on the bank, gradually widening until we descended into a narrow valley, or rather gorge, and the grass filled the bottom. The stream was fringed with willow-like bushes, which also grew here and there in large patches. And this was the much-vaunted Sugheit. But it is not to be wondered at, that the natives of this desolate region should imagine this strip of fertility a perfect paradise, and magnify its beauties and merits accordingly.

We passed a Yarkand merchant with a few horses, who stated that he had seen a dozen or so of yâk in a spot known to Moosa. We had noticed tracks of those animals, as also of shâpu, on first entering the valley. We passed on through some fine rich herbage—a sort of lucerne abundant—and finally dismounted at a spot where were two Yarkandies, apparently known to Moosa and Abdool. Here we were to halt. These men did not give a cheery account of our prospects, as they had seen no game.

Thoroughly down-hearted at having come thus far to so little purpose, I took my choga and namba, and lay me down moodily under a bush, and went to sleep. When I awoke, Subhan and Moosa came and begged me not give way to despondency. These Yarkandies, they said, had at first been alarmed at the awful apparition of a saheb; but, having recovered, had declared there were plenty of yâk in the neighbourhood; and one of them, though now doing a mercantile turn, was a professional shikarry, thoroughly acquainted with this country and the haunts of the yâk, and as one of his mares had recently foaled, and he must be detained some days, he would accompany the saheb, and shew him plenty of yâk for a consideration. Ample 'backsheesh' was promised, and things looked brighter. But the wretched aspect of the land, as compared with my anticipations, still kept me down-hearted.

I took Subhan with me in the downward direction in which we were to move to-morrow; but there was no improvement visible in the country. This valley debouched upon another which crossed it at right angles, its enclosing mountains as bald as ever. I announced my resolve to prosecute my travels on to Yarkand, if we found no game, and questioned the Yarkandi as to the reception I was likely to meet with, and whether he would accompany me. He replied that, as Yarkand was ruled by the khaltai padshah people, he could not answer for his accompanying me, his present business would not permit it: he would shew me shikar, that was all.

A 'bunderbus' was made to move camp into the transverse valley to-morrow, to a place on the river affording grass and wood in plenty; and in the afternoon the hunting party, equipped for two days' excursion, were to start for the yâk grounds—the place where the merchant and the Yarkandies said they had seen yâk three days back.

23rd August. I passed a pleasant night of undisturbed repose, the air here being soft and mild compared with that we have recently been subject to. After breakfast we moved off, and, passing down a declivity of some three miles, crossed a fine clear stream into a sort of wild meadow bottom, producing a good crop of grass and abundant thick-growing bushes. It looked a nice place to camp. On the way we found a yâk's head, and at this place other remains of the same animal, a large bull, apparently victim to some shikarry. On arrival of equipage, we selected clothing, bedding, and victuals; but on mustering the party I found, to my astonishment, that the Yarkandi was not coming, shuffling off his engagement under pretext of headache. I do not know to what to attribute this breach of engagement.

Our party rode off, following the regular road; then turned into a narrow defile up which ran a rocky track, occasionally used by travellers. Old tracks of yâk were visible. Having made some three miles, we dismounted and sent back our horses; fixed on our bivouac; and, leaving Phuttoo and coolies to arrange it, climbed a hill-side to reconnoitre. We looked over a table-land, and into a valley threaded by a stream, but found only old tracks; those very numerous. We returned, doubtful of our chances; but thought that, if our informants had not deceived us, we must find game or fresh tracks on the morrow. I supped, and turned into my bed, snugly occupying a space between some bushes, the air fresh and cool, the night bright, recalling many an 'al fresco' couch in Australia. I enjoyed it amazingly, awaking occasionally, and fully appreciating my comfortable position—bright starlight, a young declining moon, a fresh breeze rustling amid my protecting screen of bushes, and plenty of warm bed-clothes; all but the leaves still as silence; no voices of the night here, save an occasional dissonant grunt from the direction of the sleeping attendants.

24th August. We were up at daybreak, and soon off; and made for a grassy bottom by the stream, where Moosa made sure of a find. But there were no fresh tracks: old innumerable. We followed up river, and crossed over, Mooktoo carrying me; still only signs of distant date. And so on; until I called a halt for breakfast and a consultation, all now growing despondent. Poor Mooktoo was barefooted, Tar-gness having carelessly lost one of his shoes which he was carrying across the river. And it was no joke traversing this rough stony ground shoeless. I resolved to penetrate some distance further, to a point giving a long view up the valley. There I halted the party, and sent on Subhan and Moosa to search for sign, and Tar-gness in another direction; deciding, if they found fresh sign, to send for camp things. The two former returned on the opposite side of the river, and beckoned me. I rode Mooktoo across, noticing pleasure beaming on their faces. They had discovered one fresh track of a well-grown male, and thought they had found tracks of the lot seen by the merchant; so I sent back Kamal for the traps, and after a bit started off on the trail. This we ran some six miles; and as it did not lead to others, and a long distance visible presented nothing, we pulled up in despair, and I announced my opinion to be that it was useless to try further in that direction, the yâk, which had the previous year crowded this locality, having certainly found other feeding grounds. To this all assented; and it was decided to move back, meet the coolies, then halt for the night, and move on to standing camp in the morning; and thence make a fresh start in the opposite direction, which will lead to the grounds where Nassir Khan and his followers told us they saw yâk in hundreds. Moosa had deferred leading us there, because, when tending horses two years back in this valley, the yâk pastured here in herds, and fed mingling daily with his horses. This the tracks abounding verified.

Back we went. And, no way discouraged by this failure, I trudged on ahead, and selected a snug turfy retreat, amid thick overhanging bushes, for our bivouac; and then discussed our prospects and projects with my retainers. Yarkand, and the possibility of recovering poor Schlagentweit's effects—his papers useless to the barbarians amongst whom he fell a victim—a favourite every day topic of mine, was renewed; and Subhan told me, to my surprise, that Moosa, my Panamik recruit, had been employed together with his father by government agents to obtain intelligence, and procure any effects possible of the murdered saheb; that he had discovered the saheb's servant in Yarkand, and got from him a boot and a book, which he had delivered to a Mr. Leake in Kulu, who had rewarded him, and given him the black tattoo now with us, and a certificate which was at Ladâk. He further stated, that this servant had in his possession the saheb's head, which he had sought for and found where he was slain, some months after the event, he having been imprisoned, and only having escaped death by turning mussulman. Much astonished at this unexpected revelation, only now divulged, I sent for Moosa who distinctly affirmed the above to be strictly true: he added minute particulars fully bearing out his story. My interest in this sad affair was much augmented by this fresh and important intelligence, and I questioned Moosa on the possibility of my obtaining an interview with the ruler of Yarkand. Moosa now confessed that he dare not venture, as had been decided, to procure fresh supplies for my party, as the Affghan merchants now gone ahead would have given information of a saheb having come to hunt at Sugheit, and the destination of such supplies would be at once suspected. Here was an additional argument for me to risk the adventure; so, after much cross-questioning, I find that five days' journey from Sugheit—the road rough, but grass at each halt—is an outpost, or thanna, where are stationed five or six Chinese soldiers, whose duty is to detain travellers, merchants, and others, sending information to the authorities in Yarkand of any unusual arrival; and according to the orders returned is the party permitted to proceed, or detained, or repulsed. Moosa thinks that, if I give notice of my arrival, and explain to the officials at this thanna my desire for a friendly interview with the ruler of Yarkand, that functionary will accord it, and will assist my enquiries after this servant and any effects of the saheb to be had, and will also order supplies for my party to any extent. The Yarkand people had nothing to do with the assassination of poor Schlagentweit, so will the more readily co-operate, perhaps. I fully determined to try and carry out this scheme.

I must allow the poor, galled, jaded horses some few days' rest and refreshment, in the meanwhile hunting; then, selecting followers and the best cattle, will move on Khylian, this outpost, giving entrance to the Yarkand territories. It is a ticklish adventure, as we are at war with China; but I trust to the ignorance of these singular people, either not to know or to recognise this fact. Moosa and my whole council seem much pleased with this resolution; and the more so, as I tell them that, in all probability, if I succeed in recovering the papers of the deceased, government will reward any native assistants liberally; if not, I will myself. I talked this project over at length, and retired, my mind full of it and its execution.

25th August. We had a long stiff pull up hill, of some five miles, ere we descended to our former bivouac; then on, down the rough glen, till we debouched on the valley where was our standing camp. Crossing some level sand through which the path runs, Subhan gave a low peculiar whistle, and pointed to fresh tracks of yâk, some four or five, and two of them bulls. Much struck by the oddity of the animals we had taken such trouble about having thus in my absence gone straight to my camp, and cheered by the omen, I strode merrily on, and followed the tracks right into our bivouac, expressing astonishment thereat, and laughing over the consternation they must have created in the dead of night. But Abdoolah at once dispelled our illusive thoughts by the information that a Yarkandi had come in yesterday with four bullocks, tame yâks, whose tracks had so excited us.

The newcomer was an old man with two servants, a gun, and a dog, and was proceeding to the syarat of which Nassir Khan had spoken, whence the stone of the Delhi musjed had been quarried; his object being to possess himself of a supply of specimens of this holy stone which, conveyed to Yarkand, was bought at a ridiculously high price by devout mussulmans. It was also the old gentleman's intention to hunt yâk which were there plentiful: but, finding a saheb in his path also after those animals, he had most courteously expressed his intention to await my return, accompany me, and aid me to his utmost in procuring sport, which I should enjoy to my satisfaction. This quite compensated for the mistake of the tracks, and, summoning the stranger to an audience, he came and confirmed his good intents on my behalf. I stepped to his fire close by, where was a large rough dog, useful in the chase of the yâk, which he attacks, and so distracting his attention from the hunters gives them the chance of getting a good shot. He had a long matchlock with rifled barrel, and a forked rest attached. This, he said, was of Russian manufacture, and cost only twenty-four rupees—£2. 8*s.* We could not do it cheaper in Birmingham. He said it shot right well. I sent him a leg of venison, an acceptable supply of meat; and in the course of the day the good man appeared with a return present of a pair of ornamented saddle-bags and a dish of flour. The bags being a necessary part of his equipment, I declined them with thanks. He said, were he but at home, he would have offered me something really worth having. He is the lumbadar of his place, only some four days' journey, whence he says he can supply my party with any supplies required. This is well.

I retired to my tent, and was writing up journal, when Subhan appeared, and to my enquiry as to his wants, he said, "The saheb's servant, of whom we were talking last night, is here." Thinking that I must have misunderstood him, I repeated his words interrogatively, "Here, in camp?" "Yes; and awaiting an interview." I was amazed at this extraordinary coincidence with my wishes and designs, as were all my followers who had been made aware of my intention to proceed in search of this very man. A feeling of awe seemed to hold them all in silent expectation, from which they were released by exclaiming at my wonderful 'kizmet.' I now took my chair outside, a circle of anxious attendants sitting round; when the cause of all this excitement appeared on the scene—a stout burly man, with a round red face and grizzled beard, wearing a red cloth skull-cap, fringed with black curly wool. He was agitated at the meeting, and enquired if I was a countryman of his late master's. He spoke no Hindostani, only Persian and Toorki; so the interpretation necessary was tedious—Moosa first interpreting into Cashmiri, then one of the Cashmiries into indifferent Hindostani, which Abdoolah helped me to understand. The gist of the narrative was as follows.

This man, a native of Bokhara, was travelling from Delhi to Yarkand with merchandise, being a regular trader, when in Kulu he fell in with M. Schlagentweit who entered into some agreement with him, by which they became apparently connected in some speculation in furs—ermine I imagine—as M. Schlagentweit gave Murad an acknowledgment for three hundred skins, value six hundred tillahs, which was dated July 3rd, 1857, and written at that place: a concluding paragraph states that the amount was to be paid on arrival at Kokand, or, in case of the writer's death, by the government treasury at Kangra. This bond is somewhat obscure, as it makes some reference in favour of the reverend missionaries of Lahoul, which I could not make out. This is probably owing to the writer using a foreign language. The party arrived at this place, Sugheit, M. Schlagentweit having many attendants and several horses with him; and from this place he despatched his khansamah to Leh with his journal and letters, and, while asleep at night, his property was plundered, and his servants ran away, and deserted. M. Schlagentweit, it would appear, had determined to personate the character of a merchant, and had with him much valuable cloth, and some forty horses. Over this business transaction a complete mystery hangs. The probability seems that M. Schlagentweit, fully aware of the difficulty of travelling through a country reputed so barbarous and hostile to Europeans as Yarkand, adopted the disguise of a merchant: but the bond in question shows some transaction ostensibly undertaken on account of Government.

The robbery was effected with such dexterity, it would appear, that it was only discovered in the morning, and then reported by Murad to M. Schlagentweit who ordered him to search out which way the robbers' tracks led. They pointed to Kargalik, a district of Yarkand. The robbery was committed in the ravine where I encamped on Thursday night. M. Schlagentweit, Murad, and a Yarkand servant, by name Mahomed Dahomey, and a Bhooti, proceeded onwards on the Yarkand road. Arriving in Kargalik, they found the whole country in anarchy, one Walli Khan, with a considerable force of some fanatical tribes, being arrayed in hostility against the Yarkand authorities who, in that city and elsewhere, had shut themselves up. This news troubled M. Schlagentweit, and he hesitated how to act. But

Mahomed Dahomey informed him that Walli Khan was a native of Kokand, which country was under the British government, and therefore there could be nothing to apprehend from him; on the contrary, he ought to apply to him for assistance. M. Schlagentweit was persuaded to write to Walli Khan, reporting the robbery of his property, and its having been tracked into Kargalik—the thieves had taken off eleven of the best horses with their loads. This letter was entrusted to Murad who preceded M. Schlagentweit, and despatched to Walli Khan; who causing search to be made, the goods were found exposed for sale, and the whole restored to M. Schlagentweit to whom Walli Khan sent most courteous messages and invitations to visit him. He was then in Andejan. Mahomed Dahomey tried to persuade M. Schlagentweit to go to Walli Khan, but he expressed his desire to go straight on to Kokand, saying, "My road lies here: why should I go out of my way to see Walli Khan, into the midst of fighting?" But by some fatality he did yield to this man's persuasions, and arrived at Walli Khan's quarter's; where, his arrival being reported, that villain ordered his boxes and packages to be opened and examined. The keys were taken from the khansamah, a Cashmiri, and everything looked at; and a report being made to Walli Khan, he ordered that the saheb should pay duty upon them. Mahomed Dahomey went into the presence of Walli Khan—no one else of M. Schlagentweit's attendants—and spoke two or three words to him. M. Schlagentweit expostulated at the demand made upon him, saying, "he was on his road to Kokand, and this exaction was unjust," or expressions of like character. At this time the horses setting-to fighting, M. Schlagentweit directed Murad to go and quiet them. He did so, and on his coming back M. Schlagentweit was lying murdered by his property. Murad, the Cashmere khansamah, and the Bhooti, were imprisoned. The Cashmiri was released after some few days' confinement, and went in guise of a faquir to Cabul. The Bhootie was killed: and Murad, after some three months' lying in irons, embraced Mahomedanism, being a Jew, and was then released. For six months Walli Khan held possession of the country, but the cities and the forts held out against him; when, a strong Chinese force being despatched to the aid of their beleaguered countrymen, Walli Khan's force broke up and dispersed. He himself is now in prison under authority of the ruler of Kokand. Murad's brother was resident in Yarkand, and now befriended him. He now made search for the remains of his late employer, and found the head, which had been severed from the body, near the place where the murder was perpetrated. Though much decayed, he identified it by a remarkably prominent foretooth; the other portions it was impossible to recognise, as some hundreds of men had been slain in battle on that ground. He made search for property, and bought a horse, an instrument, and a book, that had been the saheb's, and was now on his way, accompanied by his brother to Kangra, where he hoped to find the brothers of his deceased master, and deliver these relics to them. The head of the unfortunate gentleman is wrapped up in wool, and sewn up in a bag, with a view to avoid unpleasant scrutiny, looking like a pillow.

The narrative is here given in a much more connected form than that in which I received it, having asked many explanatory questions. When Murad described the horrid deed, or rather his finding his master murdered, he burst into tears, sobbing violently. Phuttoo and Subhan, in deep sympathy, wept aloud, and all the listeners were much affected. From the difficulty of understanding the expressions, the narrative fell with less force upon me.

There is much in Murad's statement which one would wish clearer. Why has he so long delayed communicating with the friends of the deceased? Merchants have gone to and fro, and enquiries have been made by government, but now three years have elapsed he turns up with a bond worth 3,600 rupees, and otherwise in good circumstances. His brother's aid may account for this, certainly. I hate to suspect any one. Bella Shah and the thanadar, Basti Ram, stated the Bokhara servant to have been an accomplice to the theft and murder. However, I have taken the man's statement for truth, and lest he should meet with molestation at Ladâk, or elsewhere, on his journey down, have offered him my protection, giving him clearly to understand that he is perfectly free to pursue his journey and objects, if he chooses. He expresses himself most anxious to stay with me; saying, he feels sure that Basti Ram would seize the relics, and send them to the British government on his own account. Not improbable. Murad, therefore, leaves the party of merchants with whom he has hitherto travelled—and they number some two or three hundred horses, I am told—and joins my party to-morrow.

After dinner I went out to a fire lit for me, it being excessively cold, a bitter wind still blowing, the concluding blast of a storm which has covered the adjoining mountains with snow. My principal retainers gathered round, and talked over the story of Murad, and canvassed its merits. Many doubts were expressed as to his veracity and complete innocence. I now sent for the Yarkandi, thinking it advisable to lose no time in sending for additional supplies, as some twelve days must elapse ere their arrival. The old man came, and took up a berth among the others, and negociations went on rapidly. He entered into our views with alacrity, and promised to procure the flour and corn we required, some rice, and a quantity of fruit, apples, grapes, apricots, and melons, as a present for me. He said, this stock should be laden on horses which I might purchase, if I pleased. He was to receive six rupees in advance, for which I went to my tent, and on my rejoining the group he had withdrawn to give directions to one of his servants to start on this business in the morning. Everything now seemed to work smoothly, and promise success.

26th August. Sunday. I slept well, and waited to gain a glimpse of sunshine under the tent ere turning out. There had been a sharp frost during the night, and it was a beautiful, clear, fresh morning. I sat in my chair idly sunning myself, when a sense of the sanctity of the day, and an imperative impulse to express it, took hold of me; and I made my way through the thick bushes to the river, where its divided waters poured noisily over many boulders, and, selecting a stone for a seat, gave myself up to devotion.

Coming back to camp, I was met by Abdoolah who told me that the old man, who had promised to do so much, now declared that he dared not venture to send for any supplies for me, lest the Yarkand authorities, hearing of it, might wreak their vengeance upon him. He had come to this conclusion on consulting his servants. This was most unexpected. Food for man and beast must be had; so, enquiring of Moosa the distance to this man's residence, I resolved to fulfil my hunting plans, then to return, bringing the patriarch with me 'nolens volens,' and, so accompanied, proceed to his village, and there obtain supplies by force, if needs must: the constraint put upon the old man would secure him from harm. I then bethought me of ascertaining what stock should remain, and found by my account that there should be twenty days' rations for men, but very little for horses. Thus there would be enough for ten days shikar, and ten days to Panamik, and then corn might be procured from some kafila. I now directed an order to be written to the gopal of Panamik to send out a horse-load of flour and corn to the foot of Sassar, on this side; which note was despatched to the merchants just starting for delivery, and I hope we shall have enough without adopting my scheme of violence and rapine.

Murad joined my party with his brother and three horses, and, to my dismay, has brought with him neither atta nor corn. I have directed him to obtain stock from some of the passing travellers who are yet expected in numbers—crowds of hajis now proceeding to Mecca, their pious pilgrimage having been checked these last three years by the mutinies, perhaps. This he promises to do. He brought a German book, a volume of scientific geography, having no owner's name in it, but being purchased, he said, in the bazaar of Andejan, doubtless poor Schlagentweit's property. He brought the pillow containing the head, and was proceeding to open it, but I desired him to desist.

The bunderbus is complete for a move to-morrow, the old Yarkandi expressing the utmost willingness to shew me the hunting grounds. I take provisions for four days, and look for sport ere my return; until when, I must leave this my diary.

CHAPTER XIII.

THE YÂK.

27th August. Under the guidance of the old Yarkandi's servant who bore the long rifle, with only my bedding and three days' provision, we started on our hunting excursion up the valley. We had but about five miles to go, then bivouacked amid the brushwood opposite a deep gorge running far back into the mountains, where we were to try our luck after the yâk. I had expected to commence operations this afternoon, but the Yarkand hunter objected, on the just ground of the wind blowing up the ravines in the day time, and down them early in the morning, therefore advising a very early start. I dined at five, and at sunset went to the fire, where, summoning the Yarkandi and Moosa to interpret, we questioned him as to the nature of the ground we were to go over to-morrow, the habits of the kutass, as he calls the yâk, and the prospects of sport. He said, the place was not far, and the yâk plentiful, and that we were sure of finding them, as he had never yet failed to do in this spot; he had been hunting here some three months back, and with two other men had killed nine, three of them close by us. This intelligence set us quite cock-a-hoop.

28th August. We were all afoot ere dawn, and off up the mountain. Having gained some distance, we came upon tracks which in the dull light we pronounced recent, and continued our toilsome ascent, cheered by the discovery. A bitter sharp wind came off the snows, cutting one's face like a knife, and here, as in all this region, respiration was most difficult. The Yarkandi, to my surprise, suffered more than any of us from this inconvenience, stopping every ten or a dozen paces for relief. We reached the grassy slopes under the snows, where yâk were wont to be invariably found; but, one after the other, they were anxiously reconnoitred, and found blank. As the light had increased, I carefully examined the tracks, and felt sure they were many days old. The Cashmiries were quite at fault here; they are truly indifferent hunters. We now ascended a steep sharp ridge which gained us admission to a lot of ravines, in which the Yarkandi made sure of a find; but these we traversed with like ill success, and then, having stopped an hour for refreshment, went on to a third favourite haunt, equally empty, and the signs of the same date. While resting on a ridge, we saw a kyang crossing a hill-side behind us: he looked like a large donkey, with a disproportionately large head. The wind being adverse, we could not attempt to do anything with him. The traps and attendants had been ordered up the main valley to the entrance of another gorge, for which we now directed our steps; and, after a tiresome descent, and a long tramp over a shelving flat of some six miles, we reached our camp, much beat, and our anticipations greatly reduced: yet the Yarkandi persisted in the most confident assurances of success, and said we must inevitably find to-morrow. I turned in, in a snug bower which Buddoo had constructed for me in the bushes.

29th August. We were off again, ere the first blush of dawn, and, entering a wide ravine, held our course up it. Numerous tracks of yâk were seen, but none fresh. After two hours' gradual ascent came the pinch, a steep slope up the mountain, on which, to our joy, we met with fresh tracks, unmistakably fresh, and our spirits rose accordingly. Our path lay up a wide ravine, penetrating into the mountain-side, and giving entrance to a wide basin-like indent, on the level bottom of which were extensive patches of grass, on which were plainly visible recent signs of yâk. We crossed a steep rocky ridge, abutting into the basin, and shutting one re-entering angle from view, but, to our infinite chagrin, all was void as before—signs fresh and plentiful. Here we halted for breakfast.

It was now proposed to ascend one side enclosing this basin, and, resting on the summit, examine the adjoining ravines, and wait the probable appearance of yâk, from out some retreat or other, to feed on the grass below us. We climbed accordingly, and found a yâk path leading over the ridge, and fresh signs of their passage. Here we lay down some couple of hours. Looking about, I saw a ravine towards which I felt sure the yâk had gone, from the converging tendency of their footprints, and communicated my ideas to Phuttoo who made an examination, and confirmed my suspicions; and we decided that we would explore that spot after a while. Shortly after came Subhan, all excitement and pleasure; he had from a high point, commanding the said ravine, therein distinctly made out the objects of our search. Now all was bustle and preparation. Subhan described the animals to be so situated that there appeared no reasonable doubt of complete success; and I only thought of how many I should knock over, and told Subhan he must scrutinise the herd, and discover the position of a huge bull whose enormous footprints had been the object of our admiration. We held much sanguine talk of this kind, as we descended towards the prey in expectation. But, alas! it turned out that the game was far away up the ravine, some three miles; that the wind blew strongly straight on them; and there was but the one direct path up to them—no side-slip by which to turn their flanks. But yet, there they were; and, scanning them through my glass, I counted, big and little, sixty-three. There being apparently nothing else for it, we advanced, hoping from the favourable direction in which the clouds moved there might be also a favourable current of wind further up the ravine: so we made the attempt to stalk these wary animals whose power of scent, their principal security, it is said is wonderfully acute and far-reaching. And so we found it. We approached right well, as far as concealment from sight went; but the brutes winded us, and gradually drew away. This leisurely retreat deceived the shikarries who pressed me to pursue, in spite of my repeated assurances that it would be utterly futile. Having hunted the bison in the west of India, I was up to this seeming apathy to our approach.

Subhan, as always, eagerly leading, kept on the advance, until we suddenly viewed the whole herd, closely packed together, moving slowly forward, out of shot. The shikarries would have it that they were not alarmed; so we made an onward move again to gain a rise, whence they hoped my battery might open with effect, though at a long range, on so dense a mass. We gained the stony height, but found the herd again scattered, some still retiring in the distance, others lying down, some feeding at some six hundred yards off, but with a smooth slope separating us, which offered no chance of getting at them. Here we lay behind stones, watching, admiring, and longing. From hence I saw the huge old bull of the enormous foot-prints, carrying a very heavy pair of horns, slowly and, as I thought, feebly descending behind a rise: others, fine fellows, lay down on the rise. We waited long, hoping against hope; till at last evening, growing apace, and the frosty air admonished us that we must make up our minds what to do. I had no covering but the suit I wore, and nothing to eat, so that passing the night here on guard was out of the question. Subhan proposed a dash at the enemy for a chance shot—so like him! I proposed to withdraw quietly, and seek the foe next day; so the decision was left to Moosa who directed the retreat. Back we went; and now a terrible long trudge awaited us, and it was long after dark ere the straggling party following Subhan and self had come in, some quite sick, Mooktoo and the Yarkandi 'hors-de-combat,' and all thoroughly fatigued. I, therefore, proposed to remain in camp to-morrow, and send back for more provisions, on arrival of which in the afternoon we would shift quarters, moving up the mountain near to the place the yâk were left in.

30th August. Moosa returned about 4 P.M.; and as soon as the fasting hunters had cooked some bread, we started for our new quarters which we reached at dusk. We were yet a long way from the yâk ravine, but at any rate two hours nearer. There were no bushes here for shelter, so I selected a hollow trench-like place for my couch, Subhan digging up the ground to soften it; and, on arrival of the traps, I was not long ere I sought the protection of my blankets, first fortifying the inner man with a little well-diluted eau-de-vie, there being no fire, no tea. I rose up once or twice, and looked around on the imposing mountain scenery which the moon lit up with her softly bright clear beams; and again dived into the woolly comforts of my blankets. But ere the night was half spent, a change came over it. I awoke feeling that something unusual was taking place, and lo! the surface of the earth was sheeted with snow, and I was fast disappearing under its fleecy mantle. I luckily had a long felt namba which extended beyond my pillow, covering my head, and I drew the blankets over and round my shoulders, and quite closed myself in. The snow drifting pressed upon me, and kept me warm. But I got too hot from the confinement of my breath, and was forced to stir myself, and open a hole for ventilation; when unluckily moving the namba over my pillow, down came an avalanche of cold snow about my shoulders. Clearing this away as well as I could, I made a hole on one side at which to place my mouth, and once more resigned myself to await events—not, perhaps, thoroughly comfortable, yet enjoying the novelty of the situation. I gave many an anxious thought to my poor attendants whose voices reached me occasionally. Perceiving dawn approaching, through my peep-hole,

August 31st, I at once disencumbered myself of namba and snow, and proceeded to survey the surrounding scene. Everything was buried. My followers looked miserable enough, poor fellows! but there was no real suffering. All was soon recovered, and in marching trim, and we set off for our hunting ground. It was very bad travelling, the natural difficulties being much increased by the melting snow. The wind blew downwards, and we augured favourably of our day's chances. But hardly had we gained the long ravine, where we hoped to find the game, than the wind shifting blew directly upwards. We halted some time hoping for a favourable change, as the clouds, as on the previous day, were sailing towards us rapidly. But we waited in vain: so, there being nothing in sight, we went on upwards, and reached a point whence a general view being obtained revealed bare grounds only. Here we breakfasted in a storm of sleet; and then we spread ourselves out to search for tracks, which appeared to take downwards some two or three miles, then across the high ridge westward; in which direction Moosa and the Yarkandi said there was no knowing were to find the animals. We continued looking for tracks, hoping that some of the yâk might have separated, and gone to the place we searched the other day. For this we pointed, and I had given orders to climb the high ridge intervening, when the wind suddenly shifted, coming down upon us violently with a fall of sleet, and from a quarter that would have given the yâk, if any, our wind. I then said it was useless going on, and the shikarries, dreading the fatigue, cheerfully assented; but there being a yâk's head and horns on the other side, poor Tar-gness, much against his will, was directed to make his way over, and bring the same to camp, we ourselves turning at once in that direction. We reached our bivouac, having passed, in an angle of the torrent's bed, under a precipitous cliff, a number of nâpu horns, none of which animals we have seen.

I ordered the traps to be packed and taken below, intending to go into standing camp to-morrow. Snow had long since disappeared, save on the mountain summits, and the descent was tolerably easy. Soon after our arrival came Targness in great excitement, having seen no less than thirteen yâk, of sizes, in the basin we had intended visiting, when that untoward change of wind made us give up our intention, and return. A consultation decided that Abdoolah should go in for provisions tomorrow, and bring out the shikarries' ponies, and we ourselves resolved to start at 3 A.M. for the yâk.

By the way, I have omitted to mention that Kamal was sent on Thursday with orders that, if on reaching camp he found they had not been able to procure supplies from passing travellers, he was to make the best of his way, with a Bhooti, to Chanloong, and there having got three mds darra, and two mds atta, to bring the same on tattoos with all despatch to meet us; so that with this, and that previously written for, we ought to manage well.

We chatted long at the fire, hoping that our luck was at last turning. I told the shikarries that to-morrow was the first of September, and explained to them our game laws in respect thereof; and I myself really, amid all my disappointments, had a sort of superstitious feeling that this sporting date would be signalised by the slaughter of yâk. Impressing upon the shikarries the necessity of as early a start as possible, not later than 3 A.M., I turned in, and, awaking once or twice, examined my watch by the bright moonlight; the first time it was 12—then, 2—then, 2.30, when I roused myself,

1st September, And was up, and dressed before 3. The moon was beautifully bright, and full, or almost so; our path, therefore, opened plainly before us. It was, however, very cold, and freezing sharp; and the way was long, and the ascent laborious. On reaching the base of the steep slope, leading direct to the basin, we stopped some time; then, slowly struggling upwards, pausing every fifty paces, we gained the upland, the light now becoming dawn well opened. Nothing met our view on attaining the general level of the basin. But there were many dips and hollows: cautiously advancing, we examined them, and they were all empty. Tar-gness was sent up the ridge, and had gained such an elevation as I thought would discover every nook; and, saying so to Subhan, I proposed to move on to the spot where the head and horns, before mentioned, lay. As we moved on, Tar-gness broke into violent gesticulations, and came springing down; and, when we could get an intelligible reply from him, informed us that he had discovered two yâk moving up a hollow near us. Now all was excitement and preparation; guns were uncased, and the shikarries only to the front. The wind was right, and everything seemed such as to ensure success; when, as we stole forward, we saw a yâk on the hill-side over the hollow; another, and another, came in view, moving upwards, cropping a blade of grass here and there, and looking about them. I fully believe they were systematically reconnoitring, having acquired some suspicions. They turned, and three of them lay down on the hill-side. Here was a predicament. We could not stir without certain discovery; so we squatted as patiently as we might. It was bitterly cold, the ground covered with hoar frost. We waited and watched, and watched and waited, when all but one impracticable animal moved down into the hollow. This one, in the most elevated position, commanding a view of the whole plateau, remained watchful, and, I believe, uneasy, every now and then giving an impatient flourish of its bushy tail. All we had yet seen were females. What was to be done? I proposed to station myself in the line of their probable retreat, and send men round to give them the wind. Subhan disapproved, and the other two seemed to have no idea of their own on the subject, trusting all to luck, to 'kizmet,' not even venturing an opinion.

Well, we waited some hours in this icy locality, not being able to stir for cloaks or breakfast. Looking up from a doze, into which all had fallen under the sun's genial influence, I saw yâk moving upwards—one, two, three—then off bounded our persevering sentry, cantering off, whisking her tail, and leading the way over the ridge. Then out came others in succession, to the number of twenty-five, old and young, a fine bull in rear, and took their way up the ridge, disappearing over its crest. This was the ridge running into, and dividing, this plateau; so, as there was a nice grassy flat on the other side, we were charmed with the move, and our improved prospects. Away we went, making the best of our way over the stones, and crossed the spur of the hill, instead of the crest—fatal error of our leader, Subhan—and, gaining the reverse, to our surprise saw nothing. The herd had vanished. We moved along the hill-side, and found the tracks leading into the bight of the bay, as it were; and there, sure enough, was our chase. But the wind was now blowing direct to them, and our wary, active, suspicious foe already indicating alarm, and mischievously elevating her tail. There were only about twelve in view; the others must, therefore, be concealed by the ground, and be somewhere nearer, below us; so we pushed on and down, no concealment possible from the first lot, now much agitated.

Now we opened the others, among them a fine bull. We were some four hundred yards off, and above the animals, but their alarm was so evident that Subhan advised me to fire at the bull; but the brute kept his stern to me. However, waiting, my rifle resting on a stone, he turned, disturbed by the agitated flurry going on around him. I fired, and evidently hit. He thundered down the slope, passing from view, and then coming out of a nullah, his left fore-leg apparently broken, and, by his puffing and roaring, his lungs injured. "He's hit, he's hit, all right," were the exclamations. The herd, with tails aloft, scampered about, and finally halted nigh together, bull and all, some five or six hundred yards off, and I discharged my whole battery at the group, certainly striking one, if not more. Then, away they all careered, the big bull hanging behind, and labouring heavily. They gained the opposite hill-side, and seemed undecided how to act, which way to turn, and broke into two parties, one pausing, the other making backwards along the hill-side to gain the place they had originally come from.

The guns being reloaded, Subhan proposed a chase—he to cut off the lot on the hill-side, we to advance on the other. Away we went best pace, but that very bad. Our lot soon followed the other, the wounded bull limping, and labouring heavily in rear. I sung out to Mooktoo to run and intercept him; but there was no 'go' in Mooktoo. After running a dozen yards, he was as done up as the bull.

Subhan was now seen on our right, gaining a position cutting the path of the retreating foe. He struggles on—the first batch pass him, some two hundred yards off. On, then, comes the second—they go by—and we shout to him to await the bull, lumbering behind. He drops to a position. On comes the huge brute, and bang! bang! go both barrels, only accelerating his flight though he flourishes his tail frantically. Phuttoo and I now make for a point to cut him off, which he divining leaves the herd, and slowly goes straight up the hill, now and again stopping and looking back on his pursuers, his roaring lungs audible a mile off at least. Subhan slowly follows—Oh! how he crawls! I shout to him to follow on, *close*. Mooktoo seems shirking the work, stopping at the foot of the hill. I yell at him, calling him no shikarry, a soor, &c., and, in a frantic state, urge them on. The bull, ever gaining ground upwards, at last disappears over the ridge. Subhan, having gained but half-way, there stops, and halloos Phuttoo down below, and a short conversation takes place. Mooktoo, of course, stops and joins in. I vociferate, and abuse them all. Subhan is asking Phuttoo to send a man with food after him. Now they crawled on, seeming to make no progress, and constantly pausing; and, full half an hour after the bull, Subhan went over the ridge on his tracks—Mooktoo in another half-hour. Phuttoo and I sat down. He said, they must secure the brute, there could be no doubt of it. Having known them fail so often in pursuit of mortally wounded animals, I had my doubts. Phuttoo was sanguine.

Now came up Tar-gness and the coolie with breakfast; the former, remarking on the roaring breath of the bull, which he had heard a mile off, said he was hit in the lungs, and must die. We despatched him also in pursuit, and, when half-way up, he turned to tell us there was a quantity of blood. We waited here till 4 P.M.;

and then, believing the hunters would return by another route, whether successful or not, we moved down to camp. The Yarkandi had joined in the pursuit, so we were satisfied on the score of their coming back the best road. We gained the bivouac, and Abdool, soon after, hove in sight. He said, they had as yet received no supplies whatever from passers by, and I now learned that there were but some six seers of corn. I made up my mind to go to the old Yarkandi's village, and there obtain supplies; dined, and remained anxiously looking for the hunters. About six o'clock the Yarkandi came in alone. The bull, he said, had escaped, and the shikarries had stopped behind; he, being cold, had come in; they were, no doubt, following. All our hopes were now at an end. The others came in about seven, looking very woe-begone, Subhan declaring that the bull had been only struck somewhere below the knee, and slightly injured. He had followed him, I can't say how far, and he stopped every now and then to eat grass, and moved away, when gained upon. Whether true or false, it mattered little now. The chase was over, my chance of a yâk ended. I felt, of course, much disappointed, and, sitting with my melancholy group round the fire, discussed my plans of going into the Yarkand territory for supplies. Moosa and the Yarkandi were called into council, and the latter was delighted at the idea of shewing us the way, if ordered, describing his land as one flowing with milk and honey, corn and wine; so we considered the matter settled, and I determined those to go, and the number of horses, as also the formation of our depôt.

2nd September. Sunday. I allowed the sun to shed his first ruddy beams abroad, ere emerging from my retreat, my coverings white and hard with frost. Taking a stroll to look at my nag, I passed some swampy ground, out of which silently sprung a snipe, a true snipe, and, settling again, permitted a close inspection. His colour and markings were duller than those of the English bird—like the Indian—and his bill somewhat shorter. There were snippets also here, so I could compare them. I also saw a couple of teal; these, with some hares and chakores, are all the small game seen; except, by-the-bye, the gigantic chakore which are in numbers on the mountains. One day I saw, I should think, from one spot a dozen coveys, each numbering nine or ten birds, fly over; they appear as large as a full grown hen.

3rd September. We returned to standing camp, and found all well. I had the amount of flour and corn correctly ascertained, and found that we had of the former ten days' supply, with economy, and five and half mds. of the latter; quite enough for our wants, until we should meet with the stock ordered out. I had no idea that we were so well off in point of rations; and now came the necessity of again taking into consideration the propriety of my contemplated expedition into an enemy's country. The actual necessity no longer existed, and although I would have given much to have carried out this plan, and obtained a glimpse of the Yarkand territory, the question of right or wrong, after mature deliberation, was given against it. There was the uncertainty of the extension of leave, and the trip to and fro would extend over twelve days. I should have no valid reason to urge for not returning now. I had food for my party, and my horses were sufficiently in condition to commence the return route, excepting two, which from bad galls would not be well for a month or six weeks. I had, therefore, no justification for the gratification of my curiosity, and accordingly gave orders for the return march to-morrow morning, deciding to take the route up the valley we had just come down, thinking that there must be some good reason for so many caravans as we had observed taking it, and our experience of the other left anything but pleasing recollections.

All was now preparation. A caravan being reported at hand, I sent Abdoolah and the shikarries to endeavour to coax the merchants out of some atta and corn. They returned laughing, the newcomers having fled on their appearance, leaving their property to its fate. They were soon recalled, and their alarm dispelled. They are hajis all, and journeying to Mecca. In the evening they sent a deputation to pay their respects, bringing with them a dish of rice, and, with Moosa's assistance, I conversed with them. They are quite in ignorance of the nature of the countries through which they have to pass, and the length of the journey; but they know that the greater part is under the rule of the 'saheb-logue,' and, therefore, feel sure of good treatment, and prefer this route, in consequence, to any other. The justice and liberality of the 'saheb-logue,' they say, is proverbial in the most distant provinces of Asia: they, as have others, expressed a desire to see their countries in possession of the English. They requested my sanction to their travelling in my company, and, of course, I acquiesced. With regard to the supplies requested, they replied, that they had only brought their own stock, but that we should be together, and should I run out, then they would supply me. This was satisfactory.

In the evening I summoned the Yarkandi to receive 'backsheesh.' He had toiled hard, and done his best, to obtain sport: he was delighted with two Co.'s rupees, and made a profound salaam, with more grace in it than I could have imagined him capable of. The Yarkandies I have seen are very like Europeans, quite as fair, the climate considered, and exhibiting great variety of feature and style. This man had the most decided snub nose I ever saw, completing a good-humoured face.

All is prepared for the return to-morrow. What a distance I have come, and through what a horrid country, only to meet with disappointment! And the prospect of retracing my steps amid such dreary scenes is not cheering. I have added to my geographical or topographical knowledge at any rate, and shall be the first European, I believe, who has penetrated thus far, and returned to tell it—should it please God to spare me.

CHAPTER XIV.

THE RETURN.

4th September. There was a great to-do with the horses, which were anything but disposed to resign the life of ease and good cheer which they had recently been enjoying: they careered about in every direction, Murad's being the most intractable. I left the Bhooties in hot pursuit, and, starting ahead, breakfasted at our first bivouac, and halted for the night at our second. While waiting the arrival of the baggage, Subhan came and reported a 'jamwar' present. I supposed it was an animal, of course; but it was a bird of the curlew kind, glossy black. I took the Whitworth, and, retiring to about eighty yards, squatted down, fired, and the bird subsided on its tracks, shot exactly through the middle. Subhan rushed up, and performed 'hallal,' and accepted the bird joyfully, as they had had no flesh for many days. The things came up in good time, horses fresh and strong.

5th September. We continued our journey up the valley, the route due east, for some ten miles, with occasional patches of grass and bushes of considerable extent; then turned up a defile to the right (southerly), which leads out of this valley, and gives us a passage through the mountains to Waad Jilgo, where we meet and pursue our former route. Neither Moosa nor Abdool have been this road, so all is conjecture as to distance and quality. I believe it will prove a march longer.

After ascending a couple of miles or so, we halted in a glen affording grass, wood, and water, essentials for a camp not always forthcoming in this desolate region. The baggage arrived in due time. I admired two ghoonts of Murad's, and accepted his offer to ride one to-morrow. Abdoolah telling us that a sandagur had told him the distance to Waad Jilgo this way was but three marches, I determined to try and reach there to-morrow. It will be a great thing, if we are able to get from this place to another yielding grass, without a halt in a complete desert as on the other road.

6th September. We have severe frosts every night now, and the mountains are coated with snow from summit to base, from recent falls. This looks like the beginning of winter here, and, if so, summer must be short indeed, of but a few days' duration; and it is well I did not fulfil my project of entering the Yarkand country, for twelve days may make a serious difference in these mountain regions. The scenery is magnificent in its canopy of snow which removes the unpleasant impression created by the universal sterility, the pure mantle of snow leaving ample scope to the imagination. All around was exceedingly beautiful in the early doubtful lights.

I set off, attended as usual by the shikarries and one coolie with breakfast, Abdool leading Murad's ghoont. A stiff climb at once awaited us; then down into a narrow rocky ravine, up which we scrambled, and became aware we were off the horse-track, having been misled by a yâk path. Much delay took place ere we hit off the track. Then we had a gradual ascent of some six miles over a barren stony tract, a nullah on our left hand. The morning, hitherto sparkling and fresh, now became overcast, and a violent storm of sleet assailed us. I know nothing more miserable in travelling, than riding at a foot's pace, your horse stumbling at every other step or so, and a chilling blast cutting you to pieces, with its horrid accompaniment of stinging sleet and hail. The wind, which had been behind, now veered round and blew direct in our faces, as we descended into a desert plain of boundless extent. My borrowed nag's pace was so far from agreeable that I dismounted, and trudged doggedly on, head down. Gaining a little warmth, I got on better as the storm abated; but that coming on again with increased bitterness, I at last pulled up, and sat down with my back to it. After a time, I again trudged on. How this 'maidan' seemed interminable! But at length we came to a deep gorge with a stream running down it. It was now about one o'clock; and, but for the idea I entertained that we must be getting near Waad Jilgo, I had stopped here. Being far ahead of the riding trio, I was forced to follow my own ideas, and pressed onwards. Another interminable plain presenting itself, on, on I trudged, without any seeming alteration in its extent, until half-past three, when the shikarries overtook me with the ghoont, thinking I must be tired. I did mount, and rode on some six miles. There was now a ridge of low hills in front of us, and a range of higher ones immediately on our left. I hoped we might find water at any rate on the other side, intending to stop at the first place where was water. We had come a long distance, and there was hardly a chance of the coolies coming up. Abdool, being questioned, could give no information about the localities, nor could we understand his gibberish.

We reached the hills in front, and looked into a low flat, where was every appearance of a watercourse, for which we made, but found it dry. A violent snowstorm now setting in, and, having no knowledge of what was before us—all our people and things miles behind—I thought it best to halt here. Bad as this choice was, there was something in favour of it; a quantity of roots for fuel were at hand; so here we dismounted, tied our horses together, and, collecting roots—we had some sticks with us—with some little trouble we got up a smoky dull fire, round which we sat shivering, our prospects for the night decidedly comfortless.

The snow came thicker and thicker; there would be drink for man, if not for beast. Murad and a haji arrived, and joined our group, and at dusk the trusty Buddoo, with a horse carrying my bed, tent, &c., so I was all right. I had also a cake and bacon remaining from my breakfast. My tent erected, I turned into bed, the better to shield myself from the severe cold. I could not eat.

Buddoo said that the other servants and baggage were far behind; so the probability was, what with the night and snow, that they would not be able to find the path or, therefore, camp. I had no fear for them; they had everything but water with them. But I felt deep anxiety for the poor coolies, with nothing but their loads;

what would become of them? I felt truly miserable. I told Buddoo, that he and my other two servants, when they might arrive, should shelter themselves in my tent, there being just room for them to huddle themselves up on the floor, and the closer the better. Poor Buddoo was extremely thankful; remarking that the snow descended thicker than ever, and the cold was intense, he closed the entrance, and left me to my gloomy reflections. Sleep was beyond my reach: fretting and restless, I lay listening to outward sounds. Subhan brought the guns, and had no comfort to offer, on my questioning him, but that those of the party here would not die, as they had fire; for the others, the coolies, there was much danger. As he talked, a loud whistle came down the wind, some of the party approaching; and, ere long, I heard with delight the strong cheery tones of Abdoolah who, soon arriving, was bustling here and there, giving directions, and apparently making light of the difficulties that beset us.

All with the horses had arrived safe; but of the coolies there were no tidings. There was strong reason to hope, however, that they would find shelter with the haji kafila, also on the road. The servants' shuldary was with them, so I sent an invitation to the shikarries to put up in mine; they, however, preferred a screen they had contrived, and a good fire. My mind to a great extent relieved, I tried to sleep, but the intense cold, in spite of all the clothes I could heap on, rendered my rest troubled and broken.

7th September. I heard the people quite merry and laughing in the morning. At the appearance of sunshine I turned out, and went to the fire, where I found all in good humour, though recalling bitter experiences of the past night. Snow, of course, lay thick all around. No tidings of the coolies. Abdoolah busied himself melting snow in the kettle to give me some tea (a tedious process, resulting in a smoky slop, for which, however, I was thankful), accompanied by the cake of yesterday. The poor horses stood coupled together, with heads drooping, and teeth grinding. I had ordered them each two seers of corn at night, and gave them one now. Some of them, by-the-bye, had augmented the influences disturbing my night's rest, by coming close to my tent, and grinding their hungry jaws, and uttering uncouth sounds, expressive of distress and suffering, as though to reproach me as the author of them. I did all I could for the poor things.

It was supposed that we were distant from Waad Jilgo some two coss; so a move on was resolved, as water must be had, and the coolies might follow on. The sepoy was despatched to see after them. Hoping to kill an antelope or two, we hunters went on ahead, I as usual on foot. The exhilarating influences of the fresh sharp air, the sparkling snow, and surrounding, many-tinted, diverse-featured mountains and hills, soon dispelled all my gloom, and I trudged cheerily along, enjoying many a pleasant fancy and reflection. But we had short reckoned our distance. It was at least ten miles to the first water and grass; not the spot we had previously stopped at—a couple of miles short of that; but as the grass was abundant, there was every inducement to rest here, which we did. When the breakfast coolie arrived at twelve o'clock, I found that Abdoolah had put me up nothing, and I was now extremely hungry, having had very short allowance of late. The shikarries, however, soon cooked me a couple of cakes, and, Abdoolah and baggage arriving soon after, I started off with Subhan to try for antelope. We went a long way round, and saw numbers, but could not get near one, and came back, disappointed and weary.

As we approached camp we saw sheep and goats nearing, a good sign; and I was told that the coolies were all right, except being hungry and thirsty, and were coming on. They did not arrive, however, till dusk, and then two were stated to have given in, and were remaining far behind, helpless. With some trouble and personal superintendence, I got off two Bhooties with a supply of water for them. The coolies had, as was supposed, stopped at the haji camp, and so were as well off as if they had reached ours, but that they assert that they could get no food from the hajis, which, however, I do not believe.

8th September. The night was bitterly cold. I could not sleep; experienced much oppression of chest, and could not contrive to keep my feet warm, all I could do—three pair of worsted socks on, drawers and trowsers, double blanket, felt namba, and flannel jacket and mackintosh over that, on the foot of the bed. In the night I got flannel trowsers, and wrapped my feet in them, but produced no warmth. The frost was very sharp, the stream turned to ice. The sun, however, was bright and cheery, and under its genial influence all were in good spirits. After breakfast we hunters started in advance. We soon saw a herd of antelope. But they also saw us, when we reached a low hill, behind which they slowly retired. I went after them with Subhan, and opened them about three hundred yards off. They soon increased that to four hundred, when some five or six being grouped together, I took a shot at them with Whitworth, and the bolt only just cleared their backs by an inch or so. Off they scudded, and I fired the Enfield, both balls seemingly falling right amidst them, but stopping none.

We crossed the plain where, on coming, we were so fortunate, bucks jumping up under our very noses. Now we just caught a glimpse of some in the distance, which were off at once. A piercing blast, blowing off the snowy Karakorum, met us in the teeth, cutting us through and through. I never felt anything like it. It seemed to enter my eyes, and wither my brain. My nose and lips were in a terrible state. Moving on, head down, I was aroused by Subhan's signal, and saw in front, in a watercourse we were about to descend, five antelope apparently asleep. I dismounted, and strove to get at them; but, the ground offering no covert, no nullah, they soon saw us, and away they sped into space. I now walked on, and descended into the wide interminable shingle plain, stretching from the base of the Karakorum. On turning an angle, I saw something move. It was a miserable horse left here to linger out its last moments in agonies. Two days, I suppose, it must have lingered, deserted by the unfeeling owner, a Bokhara man, who had passed us at Sugheit. He must have suffered heavy loss, as we have already passed eight or nine of his dead horses. The throats of the others had been mercifully cut. I put this poor animal to rest with a bullet in his brain.

Hence, on to our former bleak and dreary camp ground, the wind if possible more keen as we neared its primary source. I was glad to dismount, and wrap my head in a blanket, turning my back to this inhospitable blast. Soon up came Buddoo, the trusty, ever-cheerful, quiet Buddoo, and not very long after, the invaluable, energetic Abdoolah; and all the coolies came in by dusk. I have resolved, in consequence of our very limited quantity of rations, to make a short march to-morrow, though Sunday, to a place in the middle of the Karakorum gorge, where I hope to find a little sprinkling of grass, as we saw many antelope there, on coming through. This will give us an easy march over the pass to a spot beyond the wretched charnel-house, where we camped last time, and lost our first horse—offering the important advantage of a bite or two of grass, and, I think, fuel. I ordered a sheep to be killed, intending to regale my servants and shikarries with flesh, the better to enable them to stand the cold—an addition to their simple farinaceous diet most acceptable. Resorting to every possible precaution to promote warmth, I put on three flannel shirts, one amazingly thick, drawers, flannel trowsers, flannel coat, nightcap tied on by a voluminous merino neckcloth also encircling my throat, and on my feet, my principal place of suffering, three pair of woollen socks, then over all a woollen gun-cover, in which my feet are inserted, then the long ends folded round and secured. Thus clad, with double blanket, felt ditto, mackintosh, and warm choga enveloping me, I may surely hope for enough of caloric for comfort and repose; though that terrible wind is howling its menaces, and the frost set in hard. I wish I was safe in the Lobrah valley. Well, well, a few days—say seven—and we shall (please God) be at Chanloong; formerly, how despicable a place! now, how ardently longed for!

9th September. Sunday. A very indifferent night; my feet numbed and chill, in spite of all my manifold coverings; my lungs much oppressed, and continually calling me to consciousness by a sense of impending suffocation. On the sun's rays being distinctly recognised by the growing transparency of my tent, I emerged from my many wrappers. The outer atmosphere was intensely severe; ice everywhere it was possible; and a wind that found its way to one's marrow. My tent had been well secured at foot to exclude this assailant, as also, by-the-bye, the poor goats, which, unhappy sufferers, made several efforts to repeat their invasion of Friday night, when two of them established themselves under my bed, driven to this bold intrusion by the severe cold, and little Sara, as though in appreciation of their sufferings, and compassionating them, offered no opposition. Nor should I have taken measures to exclude them, poor things! but that they kept me awake by their constant restlessness and unusual noises.

I attempted to be, and to look, cheerful—on the Mark Tapley principle. My attendants looked very black and pinched. No wonder; there is some difference between this temperature and that of their fervid plains. At breakfast Abdoolah told me, that the party generally would prefer halting here to-day, as they needed rest. The coolies wanted to mend their boots, and promised to go through to the halt I had designed to-morrow. He observed, too, that the flour was all but out, and as the Yarkand kafila would come up to-day, we could indent upon them for their promised contribution. I had no objection at all to remaining; on the contrary, it would enable me to maintain my Sunday practice, proposed to be interrupted only on necessity.

I passed the day within, reading and writing; received report of the death of a horse, knocked up yesterday, one with a dreadful sore back, which I had remarked, and predicted its certain death. The Bhooties in attendance on the horses cannot be induced to look after them, or attempt to remedy the effects of the saddle-galls, by mending or altering, or applications of any sort. The loss will be theirs and their employers', as I have explained to them, with repeated injunctions to look after the animals; but all in vain. The Yarkandies came up in the afternoon. Abdoolah went to beg, and only succeeded in obtaining twenty-six seers of atta. I was angry with him for having either deceived me as to the quantity of flour in hand, on my making particular enquiries on Monday, or for having exceeded the proportion of issues he had then told me was necessary daily, having led me to expect that we had ten days' supply, when here on the sixth we were consuming the last day's rations. He made some unintelligible explanations of having omitted in his estimate some of the Bhooties who had hitherto subsisted on their own provision; but all this should have been correctly ascertained. I suspect that Abdoolah, in his anxiety to prevent my prosecuting my intended inroad into the Yarkand territory, rather exaggerated our resources, or under-reckoned our wants knowingly—a very grave fault in our circumstances. But we have the provisions, written and sent for, to hope and expect. Kamal is a thoroughly trustworthy messenger, and will be probably fallen in with at Bursey or Moorgaby.

The thermometer this morning at 7 A.M. was six degrees below freezing in my tent.

10th September. While yet dark, poor shivering Buddoo came in to take out bullock-trunk and chair for the coolies, now ready to start. Oh! how cold the rush of external air! The tent again closed, I enjoyed a sort of sense of comfort by comparison, and waited till the first appearance of dawn; then speedily got ready, and, muffled up, moved off. All the streams, though rapid, were frozen over thickly. I tramped on as fast as the rough shingle and a pair of new ammunition-boots, of great strength and corresponding hardness and stiffness, allowed me. A gentle ascent of some eight miles, I think, had to be surmounted ere we reached the actual pass of the Karakorum, and this up a valley or river-way. Having gained partial warmth after two hours' walk, and my boots chafing, I mounted, and took Sara before me. But, though the sun was now illuming this valley, the frost did not yield, and my moustache and beard were firmly united in a mass of icicles from my congealing breath, so that it was inconvenient (to use no stronger term) to open my mouth, as it needed the parting or extraction of some hairs to effect. With every contrivance to wrap them up, and with two pair of woollen gloves—one, certainly, all rents—my hands became so painful I could no longer keep poor little Sara under my cloak before me, so set him down; and, soon after, we made a turn to the left, opening the pass, from the snowy peaks of which came rushing an icy blast that quite curdled my blood. My eyes ached, my brain seemed congealed, and a pain in my back and side, and every now and then a gasping for breath, completed my misery. I was soon obliged to dismount, in spite of sore feet, to endeavour to restore the circulation by walking as rapidly as possible. But the difficulty of breathing was terrible. On I struggled, until a bend to the right into a narrow ravine presented itself, whose lofty banks gave some promise of shelter from this killing blast. For this I hastened; and, finding a little nook in a bank, down I threw myself, lifting my face to the sun, and so sought, and soon found, partial relief.

The shikarries came up, and we were all, I should think, half an hour before attempting a remark. Then, having thawed a little, we could find an objurgation or two against the country and climate. My breakfast bundle unfolded displayed milk frozen in bottle to a lump—tea, ditto. This was enveloped in a thick blanket, and carried on a man's shoulder. It was soon liquidized in the sun. I remained an hour or so basking: then, the worst over, away and up over the pass, and down, down into the valley beyond, where the temperature under the sun's increased power was tolerable. We passed the former halting-place, Pulu, and, after resting an hour, continued our course to Dupsang, where we chose our camp on an extensive plain, with a scanty patch or two of grass. The effects came up late, coolies later; but all got in. I determined to start the coolies very early, and leave, myself and mounted party, at 8.30, after breakfast, to give the horses more time to get a bite of grass.

11th September. On turning out I found a very severe frost, as I had expected from my experience within. Abdoolah proposed to give me an omelet for breakfast, but produced chops instead, explaining that the eggs were frozen into stones, and he had hard work to separate the meat.

We had to cross the elevated table-land, before described, now just covered with a thin layer of snow. A bitter wind blew in our teeth, putting all enjoyment of the scenery, or any pleasing train of meditation, out of the question. All was silent endurance, grinning discomfort. Yet I did give a glance, and sentiment or so of admiration, to some magnificent forms of mountains in their pure and brilliant garb of snow. But I was glad to be rid of their frozen features, and descend into a narrow ravine, where, screened from the wind, and cheered by the sun, my temperature and temper regained their customary tone. Here we met a party conveying goods of Bella Shah's—dyed leather—to Yarkand; and one of them was the unfortunate owner of the horses with me, a merchant who had been long in prison at Leh, and recently released. On gaining freedom, he, of course, looked for his horses, and was very glad to hear that they had been engaged for me. He now collected his clothes, and turned back with my party, much questioning and answering going on between him and the shikarries; he had read my first note to the kardar at Panamik for supplies, and had pointed out to that individual the necessity of implicit compliance; had met Kamal on the hill over Chanloong, now six days back. This was satisfactory. We need now have no apprehensions, but of a day's scarcity—perhaps, a half ration. We continued on, far beyond our original halt, and finally pulled up on the shingle, near a small thread of a stream which was lost in the shingle. When we previously ascended, this water-bed was intersected in every direction by rapid streams: now water was difficult to find. The traps arrived late, and I did not enter my tent till dark. There was a perceptible difference in the atmosphere, though still frosty.

12th September. I intended to start the whole party early, in order to bring the horses to the grass at Moorgaby, as soon as possible, but found them all astray, having wandered away in search of grass during the night. I could not wait in the cold, so started, my horse at hand following as usual. I strode away best pace, and passed coolies and Murad's party, and was deep in thought, when a rattling of earth aroused my attention, and looking up, there were some thirty nâpu close by me, on the hill-side on my right hand, not above fifty yards off, all of a heap. They were leisurely moving upwards, a capital shot. No shikarry, no gun near, that wretched Mooktoo having lagged far behind. Abdool coming on, driving my horse before him, I made frantic gestures to him to stop; but, head down, eyes on the ground, not heeding, in stupid absorption, on he came, nor could I gain his attention, till I picked up a stone and threw it at his head. Then he ducked, and halted, and began to talk. Mooktoo, awake to the circumstances, now came running up, rifle in case; fumbled at that, then to cap—his fingers so numbed, I suppose, he bungled sadly. The animals were now far up the mountain. I got the rifle, and pulling trigger, no effects—the cap bad. At last I got off both barrels, but the objects were too far off for this weapon—a polygroove.

We arrived at a point where the path, quitting the river-bed, ascended the rugged mountain-side to a great height, and re-descended. There being now no water, I thought we might go straight on, but Abdool would not hear of the horse going. He said, "man might go, but no horse could;" so Mooktoo and I, followed by Lussoo, breakfast-bearer, entered the defile which delighted us at first by its easy, accessible ingress. We soon, however, learned to respect Abdool's opinion, at which and his experience we had been scoffing. We found ourselves entangled in a confusion of rocks which at last quite blocked up the passage. There was nothing for it, then, but to retrace our steps, or climb the steep on either side. I set to work at one point, Mooktoo at another. Making slow progress, and slipping back often—for I had no staff to support me, and my boots were ill fitted for climbing—I gained the ledge with much exertion, and, after clambering along some hundred yards, found I must re-descend into the bed of the torrent, all further progress being cut off by a yawning precipice. Nerving myself for the attempt, I succeeded in getting down, showers of loose stones accompanying me. I could not pause for observation, but fixing my eyes on certain points apparently firm I dashed at them, and off again before my weight had detached them, leaving them to fall with awful resounding crashes into the depths below. I got down all right, not a little pleased and relieved thereat, and found the way now practicable. Looking up, there were Mooktoo and Lussoo craning over the chasm. I hailed them to try another place, and then went on, and heard stones and rocks thundering down the steep. Reaching the point where Abdool and horse should cross, they were not yet in sight, but soon appeared, and in due time joined me. Half an hour had elapsed since I left the other two in difficulties, and, becoming alarmed, I despatched Abdool to look after them; who after ten minutes or so reappeared, abusing them and Cashmiries in general as good for nothing. They were close at hand, and came up, Subhan and Phuttoo also. They had to extricate Lussoo who, terror-stricken, had stuck half-way down the steep.

Here I breakfasted, and then went on to Moorgaby. No Kamal: but an encampment—some of the people, and horses, and goods of the Bokhara man. Horses lay dead around; and a man was engaged in skinning and cutting up one for meat. My people did not make their appearance till six or seven hours after me.

13th September. A cold frosty morning. I stepped out smartly for a couple of hours, and then mounted, and found the Bokhara man encamped, who to enquiries said that he had lost six horses, and the others were so feeble that he must leave his goods behind, and take them on to Lobrah to recover their condition. I found the torrent, from wading and crossing which so many times, when coming, I had suffered such agonies of cold, now a narrow gentle stream, much to my satisfaction. On nearing Sassar a man with a loaded ass appeared, who turned out to be one of the party come with my supplies: the others were at Sassar. Kamal remained at Panamik, footsore. We found the river at Sassar, so formidable when last crossed, now easily forded in any place. Men, donkeys, and loads there: others encamped with yâks designed for hire by merchants whose horses might knock up.

Subhan rummaged out a sheepskin bag containing some dozen letters and heaps of papers for me. I greedily seized and ran through the former. Good news from home—all well, thank God! Excellent accounts of the corps at Amritsir; no casualties from the date of my leaving to the 20th July. The Baboo, writing the 20th ult., makes no allusion to the receipt of my packet from Leh, or from Diskit. This is perplexing and serious. If my letters, application for extension of leave, &c., have miscarried, I shall be in a considerable fix. He says, however, that he had previously despatched these letters by a coolie who, after twelve days' absence, returned, saying that he was taken ill on the road. Perhaps, in his letter first sent he mentioned the receipt of those packets, and forgot to note the same in his second. I hope so; but must suffer suspense and anxiety till my arrival at Leh.

14th September. Up betimes for the arduous passage of the Sassar, which I quite dreaded, so frightfully rough and fatiguing is it, without a redeeming feature. The coolies had preceded us, so we had no idea of meeting with shikar up the valley; but as I strode ahead, Subhan signalled me, and I at once saw a large flock of nâpu feeding in tranquillity on the steep hill-side on my right hand. They might have been three hundred yards off. I took the Whitworth from Phuttoo, and, followed by Subhan with the Enfield, moved gently up the hill, straight for the animals, there being no other course. Luckily the wind was down. I got to a big stone about a hundred and fifty yards from the flock, scattered feeding a few yards apart, and was obliged to wait some seconds for breath and composure. The animals were quite unconscious of our neighbourhood. At last, taking the opportunity of two coming together, one of which seemed to me the largest there, and to have horns, I aimed. It was most difficult to aim surely and with nicety, owing to the grey light of morning, the grey colour of the animals, and that of the ground, rendering the object very indistinct. Whispering this to Subhan, I let drive, and down rolled one of the animals; when, to my infinite astonishment, off dashed little Sara at speed, whose presence I was not aware of. He had, however, followed silently my every movement. He flew straight at the wounded animal, and seized it as it struggled. I called him to come back: but in vain. So, taking the double rifle, I looked for another shot, and fired at two passing nâpu, I believe without effect, but the ball seeming to go through one.

And now ensued an exciting and ludicrous scene. The wounded nâpu, an animal as large as a fallow doe, partially recovered the blow, and, shaking off the worrying Sara violently, came with irregular bounds rapidly down the hill, pursued frantically by the gallant little dog close at its haunches. I raised the rifle. Subhan adjured me not to fire, lest I should injure the dog. But fearing that the animal, apparently yet vigorous, might escape, I aimed well forward, and over it rolled. Sara was at its head immediately, and seized it by the ear, when a desperate struggle took place. The animal bounded into the air; but the tenacious little rascal kept his hold firm. Down they came, the dog undermost, never relaxing but to get a better grip. And thus the contest continued, until I got hold of the hind legs of the violently-struggling creature, and Subhan the head. Then Sara, coming to my aid, fixed his teeth in the haunch, and there held on, never yielding till life was extinct. His excitement then subsided, and he lay down panting, and looking as if really ashamed of his exploits.

Cheered by this incident, we pursued our way which was yet terribly trying. However, the passage was in time accomplished, and after reposing and refreshing for a couple of hours or so, during which time Buddoo and tent passed us, and the other servants came up, we went on and bivouacked on the hill above the Bhoot goatherds' encampment, a spot producing a fair supply of grass. At Abdoolah's suggestion I had engaged three of the yâks to relieve my tottering horses and carry the baggage, the horses coming on unloaded, by which plan I hope to save their lives.

We intend to go through to Chanloong to-morrow—a stiff journey, with the tremendous mountain to get over, which, however, is not so bad from this side. We are all elated at the near prospects of a better land and a better climate than we have recently sojourned in. I hear a deal of good-natured banter going on around, and feel very 'koosh' myself, and have been congratulating everybody upon our having bid an eternal farewell to the Karakorum and Sassar horrors.

The Bokhara man sent for some corn. He lost three horses yesterday. Two or three of mine look as though they would not survive, poor wretches! in spite of being freed from their burdens.

15th September. Still bitterly cold, my camp being close to enormous glaciers, in addition to the snow on the mountains. I led off at a round pace down to the shepherds' huts, and saw donkeys there loaded, which turned out to be an additional supply convoyed by the faithful Kamal who had been detained by a sore foot. I renewed the well-remembered horrors of this vale of stones and bones, to the latter of which there were now many additions. The air breathed on the mountain-side was quite pestiferous from the many rotting carcases.

It was a terrible long drag up. Having reached the top, I ordered a general dismount, or Phuttoo and Mooktoo would have assuredly bestridden their poor jaded beasts all the way down. We stopped a few minutes at a fine clear spring to refresh; and then on to the willow groves of Chanloong. The descent occupied about an hour and a half, best pace. How delightful and refreshing appeared the struggling willows of this scrubby piece of cultivation! Selecting the most umbrageous, I threw myself under it, and experienced such delicious sensations as the privations I had recently undergone could alone have procured me. Bees and insects in numbers were buzzing and humming about, and the freshness of vivid vegetation was strongly perceptible in the atmosphere. Excepting the valley of Sugheit, the air of which was fine and agreeable, that I have been breathing and exposed to may well be likened to a perpetual east wind, the rawest and most intense experienced in March in England. I revelled in the pleasant change, lying down in the shade, giving the reins to memory and imagination, until gentle slumber stole over me.

My attendants, baggage, and cattle, except one horse, came in. The absent animal was obliged to be deserted on the mountain summit. I ordered a man with corn to be sent up to make a last effort to save him. How delighted all the poor fellows were to get down!

I eat my dinner again 'al fresco,' and sat out as long as the light enabled me to read, occasionally casting a glance over the scenery, always grand though savage, and in the evening-subdued light endued with softer beauties: then turned in anticipating a good night's rest.

16th September. I did enjoy an untroubled night of calm repose, such as I have not experienced since I left Sugheit; no violent palpitations and struggles for respiration, no biting wind penetrating my every covering, and—oh! satisfaction indescribable—warm feet.

I rose early, the air cool and fresh, and just sauntered about among the straggling bushes, feeling truly sensible, I trust, of the mercies and blessings vouchsafed me. So far I had returned safe and sound. I now look forward with pleasure to my return to my duties and usual avocations. I passed a pleasant, cheerful day; and retired in suitable mood again to enjoy a night of delicious, healthy sleep.

CHAPTER XV.

LEH AND LADÂK.

17th September. Everybody astir early. Even the coolies were anxious for a start. Not their wont by any means: it has always been a hard matter to rouse them up. But they, poor mortals! have their affections, and are now looking forward to return to their homes and families.

Having seen many hares and partridges when coming this stage, I had my gun and shot ready, wishing to give little Sara some diversion. Arriving at fields and cultivation after six or seven miles of horrid barren country, I dismounted, and flushed a snipe in some swampy ground, whilst a hare was visible running off in the distance. I thought Master Snipey a certain bag after the hare, so did not fire at him, though an easy shot. The hare made off through a fence, and a teal rising I knocked it over. Now I tried for the 'long-bill.' But whether the report of the gun had awakened dormant hereditary suspicions—for he could never have been shot at—I know not; but he proved himself the most 'cute and wide-awake creature imaginable, and, after many dodges, finally took flight. So I tried after the hare. No find. Then I took down a stream, and shot a long-billed bird which, when sitting, I thought must be a woodcock: but it was only some kind of plover, the head and bill exactly like the woodcock's. I saw the 'long-bill.' There was but this one, and again I sought his life. In vain: he was off long ere I got near him. Then I tried a swamp; found nothing, and stopped to breakfast. All the people and traps came up and passed. I felt resolved to have that snipe. And, as he had gone off in the direction of the spot first found in, I had no doubt of seeing him there, so went back. There he was, quite conspicuous, feeding about, but still wide-awake, and ever fluttering on out of shot; and at last, when my attentions became too pressing, he took a long flight, but came back a long round, and settled in some sedges. I was relentless, and resolved to compass his death by treachery; so, taking advantage of a fence covering my approach, I stole upon him. Reconnoitring carefully, I saw him evidently on the 'qui vive,' and had to advance still some way to make sure. I peeped again: he was not visible. Suspecting a 'ruse,' I went on a little further, and looking over the hedge saw my fine fellow, his head on one side, evidently listening. Without any compunction, I blew out his brains then and there. Soon after, I shot a hare, and then, turning towards the horses, a good long beat lying between, I fired at four others ineffectually; a just punishment for the persecution and murder of the solitary snipe.

I found my tent pitched at Panamik in the old spot; and in the afternoon transacted a deal of business. The moonshi, Ahmet Shah's relative, met me on the road.

He and Abdoolah had come to some understanding on prices and charges, and we got on very well. The horse left on the hill died yesterday, making five in all out of the seventeen taken from Panamik, which gives a fair idea of the nature of the journey. The hire of each horse for the forty days, after due deductions, is eight rupees, one anna. I was very glad to have the matter settled, and attacked my stew with additional zest. Some turnips and pumpkins obtained yesterday were a great treat after a month's forced abstinence from all vegetables. No fruit to be got here. I push on to-morrow beyond the corresponding stage when coming, and, as the river is now low, shall probably avoid Diskit altogether.

18th September. A more than usually tiresome march, the glare from the surrounding bare sandy ground excessively trying to the eyes. The moonshi overtook and accompanied me, and on arrival at Lanjoong procured me some melons and apples which, though indifferent of their kind, were most acceptable. Here I discharged Tar-gness who appeared delighted with his rate of wages, doing obeisance in a most servile manner. The kardar arrived from Diskit, and I tipped him five rupees, much to his satisfaction.

19th September. A long and most wearisome march, repeating all the disagreeables of yesterday in a magnified degree, the road lying through an interminable tract of shingle and deep sand by the river side. I shot a hare at the village where we stopped to breakfast, and disturbed a young brood of chakore there. The hen bird exposing herself to certain destruction to draw off attention from her nestlings, I forbore to injure her, respecting her maternal solicitude and magnanimous self-devotion. We finally brought up at a small village on the right bank, having passed by Diskit and Kalsar, and thus gaining a position almost opposite the ravine leading down from Karbong. The sheep arrived from Diskit looking well, all but the solitary survivor of the Wurdwan lot which, whether from pining in strange company in an uncongenial climate, or other cause unknown, is in very poor case.

20th September. After two or three miles of very deep sand, we crossed the river where divided into several channels. Its waters are diminished in depth and force, otherwise it is not fordable when comprised in its main channel. We had now a rough path up a rugged ravine, with some very steep pitches to ascend, and did not reach Karbong until eleven, and had to wait for breakfast till twelve. The owner of the horses of my expedition, who is accompanying me to Leh, there to receive his money, came up and reported that five of the coolies had bolted at our camp, and every male had disappeared from the village, so that Abdoolah had adopted the only course left, and gone back to another village with the sepoy to impress other coolies. This mishap compelled me to give up all thoughts of going further to-day, which will necessitate a double march to-morrow, including that horrid mountain.

21st September. A very severe frost, and the cold intense on this elevated plateau, surrounded by snow-covered mountains. I rose at the first glimpse of dawn, and tramped fast and long before acquiring any glow. After a heavy drag up hill for four hours I halted to breakfast about a mile and a half from the foot of the ascent; which I then accomplished, not without sundry slips and tumbles, the ice beneath the snow being hard and slippery. The descent was steep and rugged, down a horrid stony path running through corn fields now under the reapers' hands, to the immediate precincts of Leh, passing under the rock and its crowning palace; and thence turning across the fields we entered the enclosure where was our camp, and were warmly welcomed by Suleiman and domestics. The former was much relieved at our appearance, having suffered, he said, much suspense from want of authentic information regarding us, and flying rumours of misfortune.

Major Tryon had taken his unfortunate servant with him in a doolie. He had lost some of his fingers which had dropped off, but was thought to be getting better.

No letters or papers for me, nor any news of those transmitted hence having reached the Baboo. I am thus in a fix, not knowing whether I have leave or no, nor even if my application for leave was ever received. I must hasten on to Cashmere, expecting to meet the Baboo's explanations 'en route.'

The thanadar was very civil in messages, sending apples and a sheep, bed and bedding too. Abdoolah arrived and reported things on the way, yet far behind. Buddoo and bedding arrived, so I was well provided for. I sat chatting by the fire some time, and then turned into my large tent, quite a mansion, and read for an hour or so. One small snooze—and then I was roused and kept awake for hours by an inharmonious combination of sounds—people wandering about, coolies arriving holloaing at each other, servants and followers all jabbering away together, horses neighing, a jackass braying, yâks grunting, and Sara and Fan rushing out of the tent and adding their shrill yelps to the general outcry. I summoned patience, and dwelling on my safety and comfort forbore to interrupt my retainers in the outpouring of their mutual gossip on reunion; but lay and endured it all, hoping for a lull in the storm, which at length arriving, I submitted joyfully to the sweet bonds of sleep.

22nd September. A delightful fresh morning. I just sauntered about around my tent, and ordered two sheep, rice, flour, and tea for the entertainment of my establishment, to commemorate the safe return of the expedition. Suleiman reports that he had distributed all the Scriptures and tracts, but a few which he had kept in reserve in case we should visit Kopalu. He had met with some attentive listeners, one a Sikh from Lucknow, now resident in this country, who said his mind was full and troubled after reading the Gospel, and wished he could consult with a 'padre.' He is going to Kopalu, and Suleiman was going to entrust him with some books for the Rajah of that place, a very intelligent man, and one with whom Suleiman, in his former travels in this country with Colonel Martin, had held communication and discourse, of whom too he was hopeful. But we learn that the Rajah is now in Sirinuggur attending the durbar, so we hope to meet him in person.

There is also an old man, a bunga, native of Feruckabad, who has been here some years, and has married a native woman, by whom he has three young children: he is earnest in his enquiries, and professes a conviction of the truth of Christianity. He proposes to go under my escort to the mission at Amritsir. But to remove and deport a family of the Maharajah's subjects without full sanction would be going much too far. And, then, how would my friends, the missionaries, approve of my burdening them so heavily? After pondering over the subject, I resolved, if the customs and laws of the land permitted, to run all risks and encounter the trouble and expense, for the sake of the children—nice, lively, dirty, naked, little wretches, always merry and chattering. So I sent Abdoolah and the moonshi to enquire of the thanadar about the matter, who replies that, when a foreigner marries a native of the country, he ought not to quit without due authority from the Maharajah. So I thought the utmost prudence necessary in such a case. I was sorry to reject the poor man's petition, and, pitying his disappointment, said I would endeavour to get a purwanah from the Maharajah for his exit, should I have an interview with his highness.

Poor old Basti Ram is ailing, and obliged to be bled, so I have announced my intention to pay him a visit.

23rd September. Sunday. A quiet morning. About breakfast time Bella Shah, the moonshi, Murad, and other folk and attendants came to see me. Murad, who looked remarkably down and conscious, excused himself from going on with me, stating that his horses were lame, and, when this was contradicted, he then declared that he owed Bella Shah money, which if I paid he would go. Bella Shah had then taken leave. I declined it, and told him he was at liberty to choose his own route, time, &c., and so dismissed him.

24th September. I paid all wages and claims before breakfast, and afterwards off to the town to Bella Shah's, and inspected some rugs, and damask silks, and other goods. The silks were described as from Russia, but had a stamp with the arms of England, lion and unicorn, on them. If they are from England, a far less circuitous route might be found for such merchandise. Questioning Bella Shah as to Murad's being indebted to him, he said it was true; he had borrowed money at Yarkand from his nephew to be repaid here, but that this should be no obstacle to his accompanying me. I had thought much last night over Murad's conduct, and the best course to take in regard to it, and had come to the conclusion that it was my duty to take possession of the head of the deceased gentleman, leaving the other things with Murad.

I now went to Basti Ram's, and was ushered into the old gentleman's presence with due ceremony. He is feeble, but his eye is bright and his voice strong. A large group of slovenly attendants and my own suite were admitted to the presence. We had much chat about my journey, and then brought Murad upon the 'tapis.' Basti Ram became excited and energetic, declaring that he would force him along with me, and send an escort with him: had he not come under my protection, he would have been imprisoned immediately on his arrival, so strong were the suspicions entertained against him: there were merchants of the first respectability now in Leh aware of all the circumstances of M. Schlagentweit's murder, who distinctly taxed Murad with connivance and complicity in the treachery that betrayed him to Walli Khan. The old man was quite roused as he dwelt on this topic. I now made up my mind, and explained my wishes to Basti Ram that he should summons all the credible persons from Yarkand, who were cognisant of any of the facts of this wicked business, examine them, and duly and officially record their depositions in Persian, attaching his sign manual thereto; and that the same parties should also give evidence before me. To this he readily assented, issuing the necessary orders on the spot. He told me that there was a merchant, a man of importance, in the town, who was actually present when M. Schlagentweit was killed. This arranged, I took leave.

There was food for reflection in the information just received, and my resolve thereupon at once taken I sent the jemadar, who followed me from Basti Ram, to bring me the head from Murad, and then returned to camp. After a while the jemadar arrived with Murad, the head, book, and instrument. The head, taken from the box and unwrapped, exhibited a skull complete with facial bones. Earth and dust adhered to it as when it was exhumed. The upper front teeth were remarkably prominent, the two centre ones large. The jemadar, who had been well acquainted with the deceased, had no doubt of the identity. There was a deep cut in the bone just above the nape of the neck. The few roots of hair on the skull were black. I ordered these relics to be placed in my tent, and Murad was made aware that he must accompany me. He only demurred at the difficulties of feeding himself and horses on the road. But this was at once overruled, as Basti Ram had engaged to settle all such matters, or I would have done so. The witnesses are to be paraded before me this evening, when something definite, one way or the other, may be elicited. I have taken measures to have them interrogated separately, and much ado I had to get this understood. Natives will follow their own train of ideas, and pervert one's words in conformity thereto.

Murad and the witnesses having come, after fruitless efforts to conduct an examination in any useful form—it being impossible to obtain definite answers, and equally out of the question keeping a witness to the point, and preventing interruptions from my attendants, all wanting to have a say—I gave up the attempt in despair, and sent the whole party off to the thanadar to be examined on their oaths.

Abdoolah returned from the inquisition with Murad and a paper containing the summary of evidence taken on oath before the thanadar, who sent me word that there was nothing whatever stated, which could in any way incriminate Murad; his suspicions against him were now entirely removed, and he believed his narrative to be substantially true. This result gives me the greatest satisfaction. I congratulated Murad upon it, and pointed out how necessary it was for his own sake that the rumours to his prejudice should have been sifted and refuted. He now holds up his head again, and is quite ready to accompany me, but requires an advance of cash; so I gave him the sum he asked, twenty rupees.

25th September. Bella Shah and his nephew and other people came to see me, and we had a long and interesting conversation on the circumstances connected with M. Schlagentweit's journey and death. Bella Shah's relative says, that the Chinese authorities of Yarkand are not inimical to the British, and would have treated M. Schlagentweit hospitably and with honour. The borders of the country of Andejan are three days' march from the city of Yarkand. This territory contains eleven large cities, is a month's journey in width, and joins its frontiers to the provinces of Russia, which country has recently erected and established a military cantonment on its frontier, after some opposition and fighting. Peace now prevails, and a large amount of trade is carried on. Even British goods find their way by this route through Bokhara, where only any duty is levied, and that light, computed at two and a half per cent. I questioned Bella Shah as to why he, an eminent merchant, did not introduce British manufacturers by the Ladâk route. He replied, that the exactions were too heavy, and the difficulties of the route caused heavy expenses. He did send calicoes and piece goods, but sometimes found the market overstocked by consignments from Russia. It was so at present: such goods were selling in Yarkand for half their original value. It seems unfortunate that the Indian government did not support Moorcroft in his schemes for opening up these vast regions to British commercial enterprise. Russia has now established her influence here, and makes a good thing of it.

I have been purchasing some warm articles of felt clothing for my fat friend the lumbadar of Eish Mackahm; then took a warm farewell of Bella Shah. Yesterday evening, when Murad returned from the thanadar, that functionary sent with him a man denounced by Murad as having in his possession property to the value of 1008 rupees of M. Schlagentweit's. The man admitted to having been entrusted with goods to that amount by M. Schlagentweit who had sent him on arrival at Khylian to a neighbouring village to dispose of them. He followed M. Schlagentweit on to Yarkand, thinking to find him there, and was himself made prisoner. The goods, he said, were safe in the hands of other parties in Yarkand. Mahomed Dahomey had sent a sepahu to him from the Andejan country to give up this property, but he had refused to comply without due authority. The thanadar sent me word that, if the man did not give up the goods at my bidding, he would send him to Lahore to be dealt with. I sent directions to the thanadar to act himself in the matter, and take such steps as he deemed best to procure the property, and transmit it to British authority. He sent to me this morning to write him an order so to act. I have, therefore, given him an official authority, as a British officer, in the absence of other legitimate authority, to search for, and possess himself of, all or any effects or papers of the deceased, and duly apprise the Punjab government when he may succeed. This seemed to me the rational course to take.

26th September. Every one astir ere dawn amid a scene of bustle and confusion. The shikarries and even all my servants, Abdoolah told me, had resolved to indulge themselves with tattoos. Not the remotest objection on my part, as I would only pay for Abdoolah's and the moonshi's. I tipped jemadar, gopal, and the old bunga who was anxious that I should not forget his name, in order to bring his case before the Maharajah. Abdool, the whilom guide, appeared and undertook to lead the way out of the labyrinth of paths, and then took his leave with proper salaams. I believe the poor creature is really grateful for the treatment he has received from me, a rare feeling among Asiatics.

We arrived without any adventure at Mimah, and camped in an enclosure. The evening was delightfully fresh, even rather chill, rendering a clear crackling fire pleasant to sit and think or chat over. My nights now, unbroken by that terrible oppression of lungs experienced further north, pass in tranquil and refreshing repose. If I do awake, it is but to enjoy the realisation of my condition of health and security under God's blessing and providence.

27th September. We altered our course from that in coming, Subhan recommending the road by Sassapool instead of Hemschi, the abatement of the waters of the Indus now having rendered the lower road practicable. No ways loath, mindful of the stony hilly demerits of the other, it was so ruled. The road as far as Sassapool was very fair. Subhan recommended a move on to Noorla, as it was yet early, about 9.30 A.M., and that place not distant. In this, however, he was much mistaken. The path led along the banks of the Indus, up and down precipitous rocks, rough, difficult, and most wearisome, the distance such that we did not reach Noorla till 4 P.M. There was little hope of the baggage coming up till night, and the Cashmere coolies could hardly be expected at all. I determined to make the best of the lots of walnuts to be had for the pelting, and some apples.

At dusk Ali Bucks came up with the disagreeable news of all the Bhoot coolies, who were taken in relay at Sassapool, having bolted; that a few things only were coming on, and that Abdoolah and the sepoy were endeavouring to press other people. I soon had some chupatties made, which with some cold meat formed an excellent dinner: I got some Yarkand tea also which was quite flavourless, but being hot did well enough. Buddoo and the large tent now came up, but no bed or bedding. However, I contrived very well with part of the outer fly of the tent and one or two nambas spread on the ground; and Abdoolah, the sturdy, invincible Abdoolah, having arrived and reported things all on the way, though far distant, describing the difficulties and struggles attending the flight of the former coolies and the forcible enlistment of the new lot, I rolled myself up, little Fan nestled close on one side, and Sara stretched out under the covering on the other, and passed a fair night, though often disturbed by the irregular arrival of the grumbling coolies. The gopal of this place was reported to be drunk from 'bang,' when we arrived, and was not only useless, but saucy and obstructive. I sent him a threatening message, when the fumes were leaving his faculties somewhat clearer, which had the desired effect of providing for our wants.

28th September. Finding that everything had arrived during the night, I determined to reach Lama Yurru to-day. I enjoyed a pleasant walk at a good pace to Kalsee, to which place Kamal had been despatched an hour ere dawn to direct a relay of coolies. It was here that I purchased the crop of corn for my camp. On enquiring of the gopal, he pointed to the produce remaining stuck up in the walnut tree. I amused myself by the consternation with which he received my demand for the restitution of a rupee in consideration of this harvest. My followers, however, helped themselves liberally to walnuts on the strength of it. The jemadar of the bridge fort, who had been uncommonly civil and obliging when coming, advanced from his fortalice to salute me, and, on my entering the doorway, presented a tray of apples, congratulating me on my safe return. A Co. rupee 'backsheesh' called forth abundant thanks, and I passed the wooden bridge over the Indus, and was soon in that tremendous gorge leading up to Lama Yurru, the scenery truly magnificent in its savage grandeur, the road full of precipitous ups and downs, and running as a mere ledge over fearful depths and chasms. My old nag, on which I was mounted, was a little nervous at these slight shelves so projecting, some of which were formed on pieces of timber let into the smooth side of the perpendicular cliff, and, besides having an ominous leaning downwards, were very shaky and full of holes. The old Yarkandi snorted with alarm, craned in front, and dashed forward when urged, trying to jump the suspicious spots. But for this pusillanimous conduct he sought to make amends by dashing at the stairlike path up hill, and springing up at full gallop. I much enjoyed the excitement of this hap-hazard ride. The weather was delightful, and the surrounding scenery full of romantic charms.

We reached the halting-place, and things arrived in due time. I made enquiries after the yâk I had wounded. The villagers interrogated pretended ignorance, which naturally persuaded us that the animal had recovered, and on the gopal arriving he at once told us that it was so. My ponies' shoes requiring replacing, nailing, &c., I had sent off for a smith who resided some six miles off. Night approached, but no man of iron. Lamenting this as a serious mishap, the gopal volunteered to do the job, and set to work, and in such a manner as to keep me on tenter hooks, lest he should lame my nags; his hammer, a little round-headed tool, falling with unsteady aim, driving the nail this way and that. One only having been driven home, and another with difficulty extracted, he relinquished the attempt until morning, daylight now quite failing. Should I ever undertake a similar journey in such barbarous regions, I will go provided with farrier's tools, shoes, and nails, and do my own shoeing.

It was very cold here, snow falling on the mountains; and a bitter cutting wind blowing with sharp frost reminds me of the Karakorum. But I can find means here to repel the cold, which there no precaution could effect.

29th September. Leaving the gopal at work at the horses, I marched off, wishing to outstrip the coolies already started, as there was some chance of seeing shâpu as on the former occasion. But many people were passing to and fro, so that any animals were scared from the neighbourhood of the path. It was a stiff pull up the mountain to the pir, but I did not dislike the work, the lungs here playing freely; then, down again by a long slope into a valley where the trusty Kamal had provided a fire and fresh milk. Having breakfasted, I mounted and had gone but a few paces, when a duck rose from the stream and resettled. The gun was at hand, and the bird soon potted. On nearing Karbo, our halting place, as I was descending to the stream watering the valley, the shikarries signalled me and I was at once aware of a number of teal in the ford just under us. I got the gun, and creeping to a position to enfilade them delivered right and left as they rose, stopping six of their number. As they appeared to settle some way down stream, I followed along the bank, and again came upon them. Three fell to one barrel, the other did not go off. But I had committed slaughter enough.

Waterfowl are not numerous in this country, there being no 'jheels' or feeding grounds for them apparently. But in Chan-than and Roopschoo, where these qualifications are plentiful, they abound. In Cashmere, at this season, they swarm in the lakes and rivers; snipe also are numerous, and that splendid bird, the woodcock, not rare in the jungles; so that, what with pheasants and partridges, the shot-sportsman may find ample amusement. Should I obtain my extension, I must try a day or two by way of experiment to see what there really is to be got.

30th September. Sunday. An exceedingly sharp frost. I took a stroll, morning and evening; the weather all that could be desired, and scenery magnificent, though monotonous in colour. The remains of an extensive fort crown the lofty height immediately over the village. One is led to wonder under what condition of circumstances this small valley could have been of sufficient importance to be worth such a considerable defensive work. Many like ruins are met with in these valleys, mostly perched on inaccessible rocks. The shikarries—not reliable historians—tell me that the population generally inhabited these strongholds, prior to the conquest of Lower Thibet by Golab Sing, being subject to frequent inroads and depredations by roving bands of freebooters. So, in fact, I suppose that the cultivators of every one of these strips of valleys retired from their daily labours to the security of these forts, their only residence.

I enjoyed my day's halt and repose, and took the opportunity of pointing out to the shikarries and others assembled round the fire the wisdom and beneficence of the Sabbath ordinance, well exemplified in the enjoyment displayed by the coolies and horses in this respite from their toils. I tried to describe a Sunday in England, with the general stillness and tranquility prevailing, save the bells ringing out from the many churches, and the troops of worshippers to be seen wending their way in obedience to that cheerful mandate. My audience seemed to approve much of such a rule and practice, but did not, I imagine, think it applicable to themselves.

CHAPTER XVI.

THE BARA SING.

1st October. A fine, sharp, frosty morning. I got off at half-past five, my usual time of starting now, as the sun's fierceness is much abated at this season. The path followed the stream which was broken into many rivulets. A brace of teal were espied, which I potted at one shot. We had then a long hill to get up, and descending the other side came to a village where Kamal had prepared a fire and fresh milk. He goes on ahead for the purpose now every morning. We reached Shazgool at mid-day. Looking about over the valley, I saw some birds, and when viewing them through the glass found them to be chakore. I took the gun, and went after them, but they were on the alert and off ere we got well up to them. However, I knocked two over, right and left; but on Subhan running to pick them up, one found strength enough to fly away, and the other gave us a chase. At the report of the gun down came the dogs from camp, and commenced hunting: they would both do well with practice and teaching.

2nd October. To Kargyl: a long stage this, but midway very pleasant, traversing a cultivated vale, and passing under a long grove of trees whose shade was agreeable, although the air was fresh. Through Pashgyam, and then over the bare uplands where the sun was oppressive and the glare great, till we descended into the smiling valley of Kargyl, with its many willows, fine brawling river, and unsightly whitewashed fort. I noticed here, as several times previously 'en route,' some curious cooking vessels from Iskardo. They are chiselled out of solid stone, of various sizes, from half a gallon to two or three, are no thicker than the ordinary earthenware pots, and, I am told, stand the fire better. Although there must be much labour and skill required in their manufacture, though left quite rough, the price is but six annas or so, according to size. The colour of the stone is grey. Another description of vessel of smaller size is carved from stone at Iskardo, of a greenish-yellow colour, and soft in substance. These are more for ornament than use, I believe. The former are highly esteemed for ordinary purposes, and supply the place both of metal and earthenware utensils in these parts.

3rd October. To Tazgan: a long and very rough march, the path hanging on the mountain side over the torrent descending a narrow valley which leads to the pass of Soonamurgh. Some patches of cultivation with two or three huts here and there on either side—evident signs of increased fertility of soil—are now discernible. Straggling bushes, some stunted fir trees, and many deformed, limb-twisted junipers, dot the sides of the mountains, which are broken into stupendous ranges of magnificent forms, and shew bright tints in the watercourses seaming their declivities, where rank grasses and thick-growing shrubs find suitable soil and moisture. Other coarse herbage also gives a pleasant hue of green, though now yellowing, to the general surface—all being a prelude to the coming beauties of Cashmere.

The halting place is by a sort of warehouse for the deposit of the Maharajah's merchandise in transit, who I find is the principal merchant of his realms, speculating largely in all produce, and exercising a monopoly of tea and pasham, chiefly imported from Las; yet, not to be called a speculation, because he must always make immense profits, as he pays no dues, fixes his own prices, and forces sales on his unwilling but submissive subjects. Thus he always ensures a winning game.

4th October. On turning out, I found that many coolies had deserted. They were engaged to complete this day's march to Dras. I thought there was something amiss last night, as the fellows kept up a jabbering uproar long after I had turned in. Leaving the energetic Abdoolah and the sepoy to extract other 'slavies' from the few houses straggling in the neighbourhood—which must shelter a population of forty or fifty, I imagine, exclusive of women and bairns—I stepped out quickly to the tune of the crackling ice and crisp ground under me. The scenery was similar to that of yesterday, except that more open levels were met with, and the path much improved. The valley widened, admitting a considerable extent of grassy undulations and flats as we neared Dras—a large maidan, boasting a fort of the usual form, in good repair and of unexceptionable whitewash. A large enclosure serves for camping. A jemadar and some twelve sepoys are here. Enquiring about my last letter forwarded, I learned to my vexation that it had only left Dras three days; so I arranged to send in Kamal by tattoo dâk to Sirinuggur, where he will probably arrive a day sooner than the so-called post, and rejoin me the other side Soonamurgh. The traps arrived in good time, coolies having been provided.

5th October. The people all astir unusually early, long before dawn. I turned out by moonlight—a severe frost, and so fine and fresh—and tramped away merrily over the frosty, ringing ground, and crossed many an ice-bound stream; and after some eight miles or so, during which I had left all my followers far behind, I reached a hamlet called Pendras, and sending for the head man (mukadam) requested fresh milk and firewood, shewing a 'jo' as the compensation, which I always find assists my vocal appeals admirably, and invariably succeeds in obtaining the trifles I require. After a bit, Mooktoo and others came up; and then, on again. Ere long a signal from Subhan, close behind me, brought to notice three fowl below us in the river, a duck and two teal. I stole down upon them, and dropped the duck as it neared the opposite bank, and the two teal with the other barrel. Further on I spied half a dozen teal across the river. We rode down to cross at a shallow, when a couple of ducks rose, and, having gone down stream, returned and were passing high over head, when aiming well forward I fired and down whirled the leader, falling into some bushes. On reaching him I found Sara already in full possession. I thought the teal seen were still undisturbed. Syces, Subhan, and moonshi came up and reported them still visible from above; so, cautiously stealing to the place, I found three remaining, and waiting till their dabbling brought them together knocked them all over. Sara, at the discharge, rushed into the stream, and dragged a struggling victim to shore. 'Sha-bash! Sara.'

We had a stiff pull up a hill abutting into the valley, at the base of which two streams, issuing severally from deep narrow gorges, united; and following up the course of that on our right hand, high up above it, we wound along many a bend and turn. The mountains on our left were now well clothed with birch woods stretching downwards. Rich heavy growth of vegetation is now general from rocky summit to base, and the watercourses are distinguishable by the bright emerald tint of their grasses, diminishing in brilliancy outwardly, the colouring gradually assuming a yellowish hue as it recedes from the water. The foliage, generally, has now assumed a yellow hue from the effects of the severe frosts; and some of the more sensitive shrubs already glow in the deepest tints of orange, portions here and there showing like broad red stripes down the mountain; so vivid is the colour, and the whole effect of outline and detail is enchanting. Feasting my eyes on these lovely scenes, I suddenly became aware of an unusual object on one of those emerald slopes. A moment for the eye to dwell, and I was convinced, and shouted, "Balloo, balloo." There was the first bear. He was far away—high up on the other side the river.

Now descending a bit, we came to three stone huts at the foot of an enormous glacier, whence issued a torrent from eastward. Our further route lay up the prolongation of the valley we were ascending, southward. But our day's march was terminated. The bear was on the opposite mountain-side, straight across; and lying down I watched its movements, not thinking it worth while to undergo the fatigue of an attempt on him, from the open character of the ground, and the extreme probability of his soon returning satiated to his lair. Still he grubbed, and now and again ascending a rise to reconnoitre returned to his repast. I dozed: woke up, and there he was still. And so the parties remained till the arrival of Mooktoo who bore the spyglass. Through this I now inspected the distant beast, and found it a very large one. Very soon he moved off; and, after patiently following his eccentric movements, I marked him down, behind a jutting rock high up on the mountain. Summoning Phuttoo and Mooktoo, I made my own bunderbus for the assault; rode Mooktoo across the river, and was obliged to ascend the mountain by a gulley to windward of the bear's retreat, but hoped, by getting above, to weather on him. It was hard work getting up—the grass very slippery, and I had only common shoes on. We reached right over the spot I thought Bruin occupied; closely examined the rock I thought he harboured by; but of him we saw nothing. Nor could we get a glimpse of him elsewhere; so, supposing he had withdrawn unobserved, we prepared for our difficult descent, in which we were engaged, Phuttoo assisting my sliding feet, when he uttered an exclamation, and, following his eye, I saw the dust flying, as the bear, till now in a fast snooze, scuttled off. Phuttoo handed me the Whitworth, and, luckily, the brute turned round on a rise far above us to have a look at the disturbers of his repose. That moment of curiosity was fatal; as, taking advantage of the glimpse of him, I sent a bolt into his neck, and staggered him. Growling savagely, he made his way some little distance, and climbed on to a prominent piece of rock—a fine mark, about a hundred and fifty yards off. Phuttoo, quickly loading, handed me the rifle, and the discharge of its contents brought Bruin from his lofty perch. Mooktoo, who was far above us, made for the spot, and dragging the carcase from a cleft in which it had lodged, it came spinning and rolling, over and over, on to a snowdrift in a ravine. I hastened to inspect it—a fine large female, in full fur, and fat as butter. I resolved to pack off all the traps, and wait till the skin and fat were brought in, in the morning.

6th October. All the baggage off, and Mooktoo with two coolies gone for the spoils, I sat by the fire two hours at least ere the skinning party returned; then off immediately, and crossed several snowdrifts—the valley narrow with a gradual, almost imperceptible ascent. We had arrived at an extensive mass of snow over which ran the path, when Subhan, as I was crossing it, pointed out some wild fowl on a frozen pool below. They were far off, and rose wild. As they squattered over the ice, I fired both barrels and dropped one bird, a duck; then crossed the snow, and scrutinising the stream saw wild fowl in a bend under some overhanging snow; crawled up and dropped five of them—a duck, a widgeon, and three teal.

We continued our route, crossing over to the other side on an enormous mass of snow filling the ravine—no longer a valley—and bridging the torrent. A sharp climb up, then a gradual ascent, and we were on the top of the pass, though not on the top of the mountain. A view of transcendent magnificence and beauty opened upon us. Every conceivable form and colour of loveliness in landscape seemed here united. The mountains, opening out into valleys and dells clad in the richest verdure, with foliage of infinite variety—only, perhaps, rather too general a tint of yellow—stretched in ranges on either hand far away back, giving beautiful distances with their infinite shades of blue. Close at hand, their savage rugged crests, riven and split into all imaginable forms of pinnacle and peak, here and there a snow-covered mass more level separating them, frowned overhead. Lovely peeps downward to the torrent glistening below were offered through the vistas of the foliage. Indeed, all was seen from out a frame, and from under a canopy, of bright foliage. While from below was wafted up a delicious fresh fragrance of rich and abundant vegetation, giving an idea of teeming fertility, but all of nature's wildest. I felt that had I done nothing more in this long excursion than just bring myself to this spot to feast upon these charms of nature, I had been amply repaid.

I had dismounted, and now descended, the way running down in short sharp zigzags, the declivity on this side being of great length and extremely steep. Pausing, now and again, on some prominence to gaze out upon the glorious picture around, thus I went down my way rejoicing into a fine grassy vale: then mounted and rode some ten miles along it, with an occasional stretch of intervening pine woods to cross—the mountains on either side glorious; those on the left more thickly timbered. Luxuriating in such scenery—so widely different from that recently quitted—I reached our halting place, a sweet spot, a level turf close by a river, over which is thrown a rude but picturesque bridge. A straggling hamlet being hard by, a few acres of cultivation, irregular and unfenced, are spread around, the grain now in sheaves. The valley has opened out into an expanse of downs; but lofty mountains, mostly covered to their summits with vegetation or timber, overlook and shut it in. One remarkable mountain, richly clad below, but his hoary summit bare rock broken into countless pinnacles, stands as a gaunt sentinel over the hamlet.

I was charmed with so delightful a spot for a bivouac, and determined to halt to-morrow (Sunday), though I should have to send for provisions, that is, flour. Subhan went off on his tat to visit a shepherd on a neighbouring mountain, and obtain reliable information of shikar. He returned after my dinner, the moonshi Suleiman with him, who had taken a fancy to accompany him on foot. The shepherd declared he had heard the bellowing of a stag for the last four or five nights, and had seen several hinds with one enormous stag in their midst a few days since; and that there was a pool with a well-trodden track to it, where these animals passed constantly. Coming back Suleiman, having started before Subhan, encountered a bear midway. It was now dusk, and, being unarmed, he had fled amain. Subhan, just seeing him from an eminence going at top speed, and disappearing in the distance, could not imagine what possessed him. Poor Suleiman had evidently exerted himself. He was streaming with perspiration—his long locks in great disorder. He is too short and stout for continued speed without disagreeable consequences. I had a little fun with him, which he enjoyed too. The shepherd had promised to come to camp early in the morning, and bring further intelligence of the voices of the night.

7th October. Sunday. The morning very cold, a sharp frost as usual. The sun was well up, and the depths of the valley even smiling under his genial beams ere I set out for a stroll towards the place indicated as the shepherd's encampment. All around me replete with picturesque charms—a perfect landscape—and the atmosphere clear and deliciously invigorating, my mind could not divest itself of the thoughts and speculations conjured up by the previous day's reports of the game hereabouts, which the aspect of the surrounding scene was well calculated to encourage. It seemed the very 'beau ideal' of a sporting locality. I strolled on to the top of a hill overlooking a deep valley covered with rich vegetation, and the woods standing thick around it. This must be the haunt of the deer, I thought. An old deserted wooden hut stood on the left hand, but I saw no trace of the shepherd's camp.

Retracing my steps I paused to admire one or two charming sites for a sketch, bringing in my camp, the village, river, and bridge, with a long perspective up the valley descended yesterday, and on the left the huge hoary-headed mountain, conspicuous above its fellows, and remarkable in its serrated ridge. What a picture it would have made! But I have quite given up sketching, feeling how entirely incapable I am of portraying such sublime magnificence—how inadequate would be my most successful efforts to represent such scenes!

The shepherd had arrived. Indeed, I had met him, but took him for the mukadam. He had not noticed the bellowing of the stag during the night, but thought there was no doubt of his being still somewhere thereabout. I arranged to move up to his place in the evening after dinner, simply taking my bedding and food for the day following, and to give chase to the stag on Monday.

In the middle of the day Subhan came, and said it would be well for himself and Phuttoo to start at once for the ground, and make a reconnaissance: to this I consented. After dinner I set out myself, and met the shepherd on the way, who whispered something in a peculiar manner to Mooktoo. On my enquiring what it was, he told me the bara sing was dead, shot by Subhan. I was exceedingly annoyed: the act was so altogether contrary to usage and orders. I was guided to the place, not more than two miles from my camp, and there lay the stag, a noble specimen with fine branching horns of great beauty, Subhan looking guilty and agitated, Phuttoo also putting on a demure look of doubtful expectation. Reprimanding my delinquent hunter, and much vexed, I went back and took up my night's quarters at the old wooden hut. From enquiry there appeared to be no chance of finding another bara sing; but there were numbers of bears, so I resolved to try and compass the destruction of some of those animals in the morning. As I sat cogitating over the fire, a woodcock came flitting about, uttering his peculiar grating croak. There was a plashy rivulet amid the rank vegetation just below us, which was a likely haunt for this long-billed visitor.

8th October. Though early astir, it was deemed useless to hunt before the sun had sufficiently displayed his power to warm the valley, and by melting the hoar frost rendered the herbage suitable for Bruin's early repast. So I first had breakfast, and then took my way up a narrow well-timbered valley in which the shepherd had, a few days since, viewed sixteen bears. There were plenty of tracks now, but only one bear seen far up on the hill-side. Having crossed much snow, we ascended a steep tortuous gorge which brought us to another long valley, where again signs of bears were abundant. After a considerable pause I descried one far up the hill-side. We watched him till he apparently retired to snooze. We then had to make a tremendous stiff ascent, terminating in a wall-like rock, up the face of which we had to pull ourselves by the bushes growing on the surface, hand over hand. At last we got over the spot we expected to find Bruin in, but fancying him gone began to talk, when a fierce growl answered us. I desired Phuttoo to throw a stone into the thicket, which done, out bolted Bruin, and growling savagely took up a grassy opening, leading straight to us. He was half covered by the long grass. I took a snap shot, and hit him hard, when, yelling out his extreme dissatisfaction, he made off down hill as fast as he could scuttle, and escaped.

We now returned straight for camp, and saw nothing more. On arrival I was informed that Captain Austen had passed and left two newspapers—one containing my extension of leave, he said. I eagerly enquired, "How much?" "A month," replied Abdoolah. I was all exultation—alas! soon reduced by the gazette proving that I had got but to the thirty-first instant. However, there was yet time, perhaps, to kill a bara sing. There was a good locality ahead.

9th October. A very hard frost, and difficult to attain comfortable warmth by the most rapid walking, till the sun helped one. Bold romantic scenery, but a horrid road—I really think the worst four miles yet encountered. We met Kamal with letters, papers, and fruit. I sat down to read the former; Errington confirms gazette,—all well at home, thank God!—two brothers in Switzerland.

The road improved as the valley widened. There was a good deal of cultivated land, but only a hovel or two here and there, the peasants, I believe, deserting this beautiful and fertile valley, in order to avoid the constant impressment they are subject to as coolies here on this highway to Iskardo and Ladâk. The walnut trees were very large and abundant. Bear sign everywhere. We halted at a picturesque hamlet from which every male, save an old infirm man, had fled to the jungle to escape being pressed for Austen's baggage, a quantity of which was here detained for lack of porters. This was a bad look out. I gave orders to make liberal promises to my Dras coolies to keep them in good humour, as I could not possibly discharge them. They remonstrated loudly; but there was no alternative.

10th October. Some ten coolies with one horse and yâk levanted during the night, and carried off Phuttoo's blanket; so he said. The silly fellows had thus sacrificed four days' hire. What could be done? The mukadam was found, and I got out of the way, leaving the energetic Abdoolah and the unscrupulous shikarries to practise such measures as they thought the case required.

I followed a charming path through woodlands skirting a river—the Scind, I believe—to a small hamlet shaded by enormous, umbrageous walnuts. This is but half a march; but from hence we start up the mountains after the bara sing. It is a famous ground, and we have news of the stags being in numbers bellowing there. A native of this place confirmed the intelligence, telling us that he had a field high up the hill, and being there at work four days ago he had heard the bellowing. I engaged him as guide.

Abdoolah and Co. had managed to obtain coolies and tats to bring in all the baggage, and from muttered conversation I fear that much oppression was exercised. However, I did not enquire too strictly into the case, but ordered liberal rewards. Arrangements were made to divide the party. Phuttoo goes on with the baggage to Sirinuggur. I take my bedding, canteen, a stew, &c., and Buddoo attends me. All the coolies were shut up in a house at night and guarded—a necessary precaution, but a most disagreeable one.

11th October. Up betimes, and parting directions given to Abdoolah to mind and pay the coolies liberally.

I ordered the two dogs to be laid hold of, but poor Sara put on so piteous an air of dejection, looking so disappointed and miserable that I could not refuse his mute appeal, and he bounded frantically to my side on the hint to come. We had a heavy climb of some three miles up a well-wooded mountain, occasionally passing over open glades richly cropped with rank grass, and so on to the lower crest, whence slope very steep, smooth, grassy sides to a ravine, the other side of which was a mountain equally steep, but covered as thickly as possible with fir and other trees from crest to base. Just as we reached the top our ears were saluted by the welcome bellow of a stag. I went a little further ahead, and then went down the slope and heard two or three more bellowing lustily. I had a good idea of the exact spot where these angry challengers were, and longed to be at them, but the jungle was said to be impracticable. One animal had evidently shifted his quarters. Subhan now joined me; and, mentioning what I had observed, I suggested a move towards the neighbourhood of the moving stag. He was all for it, too.

We gained the spot that we desired, and were greeted by lusty roars across a ravine, the voice issuing from the fir trees, now and again repeated. So on, for a couple of hours, when a gentle doe was spied amid the low bushes in the ravine. How stealthily and gently she moved about, her ears pricked, and restlessly reconnoitring all around! After a time she came a few yards up the slope, and, having paused under a tree, again took to the bushes and disappeared. Soon the stag's renewed bellowing betrayed him to be on the stir, seeking in agitation his flighty mistress, and he was suddenly viewed high up on our side the ravine, standing listening and looking for his lost mate. A rapid consultation and withdrawing from sight; and we then crept crouching to make a detour, and ascending the hill-side intercept our prey on a line it was thought that he would take. All was now subdued excitement. It was undoubtedly a bara sing of the largest size. We had some two hundred yards further to toil up, when suddenly a loud bellow resounded straight before us, proceeding from behind a clump of bushes crowning a knoll on our left. To drop and handle Whitworth was instantaneous. And hardly was I ready when Subhan whispered "there he comes", and truly, heralded by his huge antlers, he topped the rise, and was at once immersed in the bushes, his form too much concealed by boughs and foliage to risk a shot. Soon he emerged, forcing his way, and came on—verily, a royal beast! Once I aimed, but the inequality of the ground removed him. Then he again presented himself, almost fronting me. Now sped the deadly bolt, and over rolled this forest monarch; then, throwing himself violently forward, he struggled down the steep declivity, almost concealed in the high thick fern. Sara fearlessly rushed upon the prostrate beast, and assailed him in the rear, jumping about, and barking frantically, and now and again taking a bite at the haunch. The animal was quite safe; but, lest he might go to the bottom of the deep ravine, where his headlong struggles were leading him, I scrambled after him, and delivered three other shots, the last behind the neck, coming out at the mouth.

The butcher's work finished, we ascended towards our bivouac, taking up a position whence an extensive view of the hill-side was obtained. Other stags were still audible, and suddenly Mooktoo started, and following his eye we saw a stag which had come over from behind us, out of the fir jungle which covered that side of our ridge. He did not see us, and passed downwards at a quick walk, in the direction we had recently come from. Of course, we were soon rapidly pursuing. The hill was steep, and I leading had just gained the top of the slope, when I was aware of the presence of the stag which, having just caught a glimpse of me, was standing erect, gazing at me. He had apparently just turned on his tracks, and thus met us face to face. He had probably been scared by the smell of blood. He was about two hundred yards off, his chest towards me; but unfortunately I was now lying down, completely blown, and my hand, in consequence, so unsteady that I would not risk a shot, hoping that he might yet come on. But no: he turned, and trotted up to the crest of the ridge to take covert. The case being urgent, I rested the Whitworth on Subhan's shoulder, and aiming forward and high struck him somewhere behind the shoulder, but high. He was then on the sharp ridge, and apparently flinched, and fell to the shot. We speeded up as fast as the steepness allowed, expecting to view the animal; but he had dived down the precipitous bank into the jungle. We were soon on his tracks, easily found and followed by the blood which appeared to have been spurting out of the wound. We thought we were sure of him; but daylight failing, and the blood diminishing, we came to a fault, and, though hitting off the slot again, could not work it out, so reluctantly gave it up, resolved to take up the pursuit in the morning.

We climbed back, and made for our bivouac. It was now black dark, and our fires were blazing away famously, lighting up the black masses of firs in the midst of which was our camp. Dinner was soon ready. This was a bright hour of a hunter's existence. The day had been successful, and the morrow was full of hope and promise. The bivouac, with its romance of situation, its glowing fires, crackling and flickering, throwing a ruddy glare over all surrounding objects, and thereby revealing the black recesses of the forest—bringing prominently out the picturesque groups, the giant shadow of one or other of whom moving athwart, in execution of some culinary work, was occasionally cast across the scene—was in its way perfect. I adjourned to the fire, and chatted and planned with the two hunters: then retired to my lair, thinking in the words of the old song, "Oh! 'tis merry, 'tis merry, in good greenwood."

Mooktoo is to track up to-morrow with the guide and coolies; Subhan and I, Kamal attending, to look for fresh game. Subhan proposes going over the summit of the mountain in the middle of the day.

12th October. I was accoutring myself as day broke, and the two parties started together, our path being the same for some distance. We had not gone far ere Subhan spied a stag far down below us, standing up. He soon lay down, and there seemed a good chance of a successful stalk; but Subhan, the impetuous Subhan, taking the lead, descended straight down the steep slope towards the recumbent deer. I remonstrated at this barefaced attempt on so wary an animal—the wind was also unfavourable—but the wilful Subhan held on his course, sliding on his back, as did I and Kamal. Soon the stag showed signs of uneasiness, became restless, looked around him, then rose, and finally stept gracefully and quietly from our view. When we reached his ground, we found no clue to his retreat. Another was heard in the jungle, bellowing loudly, his deep, hoarse notes and powerful lungs bespeaking him a first-rate stag. I had noticed his voice yesterday in the same spot. Others were answering him. Thinking we might ascertain the precise spot he harboured in, and then stalk him through the jungle, we advanced on him, and lay down to listen and watch: from which time he kept mute. We remained thus about a couple of hours, and then returned to bivouac to breakfast.

Mooktoo came back, also unsuccessful. He had followed the track right down to the river at the foot of the mountain, where the thick shrubs and matted underwood frustrated any further attempt. In this heavy thicket, close to water, the stricken deer had doubtless taken refuge to die. Oh! for an Australian native, or a good hound! But these Cashmere hunters are wretched creatures on a trail.

I went down the slopes to listen. The stag before-noticed and others were again bellowing. I sat reading till Subhan called me, the coolies and whole party being on the way to the other place, and passing by me. I called attention to the fact of the certainty of game here, but Subhan said the place we were going to harboured more deer, and presented greater facilities for stalking, being more open and level, and the jungles so thin that if we heard a stag bellow we should certainly be able to approach and shoot him—and so forth. With great reluctance and serious misgivings I turned to leave this favourite haunt of the bara sing, where there could be no doubt of several harbouring, to proceed to one knew not what sort of place, notwithstanding the anticipations of the sanguine Subhan.

We had a tremendous pull up the mountain, from the summit of which was presented a magnificent panoramic view of the valley of Cashmere, of which the eye could embrace the greater extent. Down immediately below the spurs of this vast mountain lay smooth and glittering the Dal lake, not a ripple disturbing its mirror-like surface, the reflections of the small islands with their noble chunar trees only distinguishable from the realities by the inverted position. Across the lake was the city—a confusion of trees, water, and dimly seen buildings, shrouded in smoke and haze. It being mid-day, a glare and a haze obscured the distant features; through it, however, the opposite range of hills enclosing the valley, with its countless sunny peaks, was plainly defined. It was a glorious landscape. Nothing earthly, I should imagine, could surpass it.

Having gazed my fill, I thought of the shooting qualities of the new beat, and saw with disappointment that, though the slopes were extensive, they were very steep, and the ravines, though admirably adapted for coverts, were very rugged, precipitous, and inaccessible. There were probably many deer there, and we might see them; but to get at them, to cross from one slope to another, was out of the question. Many places, where deer had couched in the rank grass, were passed on the upper slopes, but still I felt a misgiving that we should do nothing there.

We turned off the ridge to the left, to our camp ground which overhung the valley we had come from. In the afternoon I went out to watch and listen, and heard a stag bellow. We got opposite his position, a ravine dividing us, when we were compelled to leave him as it was now dusk, and returned to camp with the understanding that we would beat up his quarters in the morning. I could hear the stags in the deep vale below, and regretted having given them up.

The night was very chill, and the forest damp with its dead leaves and decaying vegetation. But a rousing fire of dry fir spread a glow and warmth around. It is a delightful thing, a bright, crackling fire on a cold night in the forest. There are not many remaining for me to enjoy now, as to-morrow closes my hunting season: the next day is Sunday, and on Monday morning I must make tracks for Sirinuggur.

13th October. As previously agreed we were ready to start at earliest dawn, and on reaching the ravine, where we heard the stag last night, we stopped to listen. Ere long we were rewarded by the low bleat of a doe, which was once or twice repeated. Then came answering the hoarse cry of a stag. These animals would seem to be in some thick trees opposite us, across the ravine. Subhan, after a while, proposed that we should cross the head of the ravine to which we were close, and so reach the ridge over it, and above the deer, leaving Kamal and the guide who, when they saw us at a point determined, were to descend and move down the ravine; when, it was hoped, the deer alarmed would cross the ridge near us to enter another ravine. The plan was approved as the only one we could here adopt.

We put it in force and gained the ridge, along which Subhan was advancing, and passing a clear, open, grassy dell leading from the ravine in which were the deer, when Mooktoo, greatly excited, signalled the game: but at that very moment they became concealed by the fir trees fringing the ridge over which they went, and we arrived in time to see a fine stag and hind far below us in the bottom of the adjoining ravine. We now descended some distance, hoping to catch a sight of the deer—but in vain; and as it was, in all probability, useless to look for game elsewhere at this hour we resolved to take up our quarters here for the day, thus reserving the chance of the deer coming out to feed in the evening. I, therefore, selected a seat in the rocks under a bush—just space enough for me to sit in—and what with a fine fat wild-duck for breakfast, and my newspapers afterwards, contrived to pass the time without weariness.

About four o'clock we all roused ourselves to peer into the ravine, and Mooktoo soon detected a stag coming from under some trees. He, however, almost immediately passed from view downwards. Waiting some time without another glimpse of him, we moved upwards with the intention of trying to meet him, but found the sides of the hill so steep, and the dry herbage so noisy, that we thought it quite useless to proceed in that direction, so ascended to the top of the ridge, and moved along that downwards. Mooktoo and I went ahead of the others, and all took posts of observation. We two ere long saw a stag, in all probability that just seen. It appeared as though he would cross the ridge we were on far below us, so we hastened to intercept him. The ridge was sharp and rough, hardly giving space for the foot; but on we hastened, turning to the left as the ridge diverged at a right angle; now down some precipitous steps of rock, and we were over the dingle in which we had last observed the deer evidently making in this direction. We could not examine our side thoroughly from its roughness and extreme steepness. We could see nothing of the deer. Had he already crossed over? If so, he must have greatly quickened his pace. We went on a little, and then descended the slope a few yards to get a better view of the depths extending below us. Here I sat down, intending to await events, but Mooktoo urged me to go up again, and follow further on the ridge. We did so; but nothing could be seen of the deer. So, supposing he had in some manner given us the slip, we turned back, and were crossing the place where we first expected to meet him in his ascent, when little Sara, sniffing the air, all at once started off, taking short jumps into the air, and barking. Mooktoo ran after the dog, and in great excitement signalled the chase close at hand. The little dog gave tongue. I ran forward—but nothing was in sight. I paused for information, when from the bottom of the dell sounded the belling of the deer—a peculiar note, expressive, I fancy, of alarm and excitement. Only his head and back were visible above the high, thick fern. I hesitated to fire. He moved on up the opposite side, and as he paused, only showing his head and ridge of back, I fired. We thought him struck, as he drooped, and did not come in view for some seconds, when he was seen leisurely going off along the hill-side; but I believe the dip of the ground deceived us. There vanished my last chance of a bara sing. Sad, very sad, we wended our way back to camp, our last day's sport ended so unluckily.

CHAPTER XVII.

CASHMERE.

14th October. Sunday. I did not stir from the bivouac till the afternoon, passing the day reading, in pleasant enjoyment of my sylvan retreat. The coolies returned about 2 P.M., bringing some apples, pears, and grapes—a welcome supply, but the grapes small and flavourless. In the afternoon I rambled some distance downwards to a seat commanding, at the same time, the magnificent prospect of the valley spread out below, and some ravines and dells on either hand likely to contain bara sing. Here I sat long meditating—thinking over the incidents of my excursion, and casting reflections forward on my future route, and arrival below. Nothing was seen or heard. Retracing my steps, it occurred to me from examination of the range of hills I was traversing, that I might hunt the ravine tried yesterday, and descend from thence, while the coolies and traps took the ordinary and easier route. On proposing this, it was cordially welcomed by the two hunters. Buddoo and coolies would make straight for Shalimah Bagh to which a canal ran from the Dal lake. There he was to engage boats, and await our arrival.

15th October. We got away with earliest dawn—again heard the bara sing—again were they seen, and a shot all but obtained as they crossed the ridge as before. The guide was now sent down to drive the other ravine, and we kept along the ridge, and stopped in ambush a long time without seeing anything. Then, giving up, we resumed our downward course, and I had stopped to don another pair of grass sandals, when Mooktoo, looking down into the ravine, signalled game. On joining him, we saw a fine stag standing gazing at the guide who on the same level was trying to turn him up to us. But the provoking animal, as though quite up to the dodge and danger, preferred facing the guide and the stones he hurled to breasting the hill, and diving down took back up the bed of the river. This was the last episode of the chase of the bara sing.

A steep and slippery descent, not accomplished without some half-dozen tumbles, landed us in the bed of a ravine which crossed that we had been hunting at right-angles, and with its brawling torrent debouched on the open cultivated undulations lying over the Dal lake. A path leading through two villages, as usual shaded by fine chunars, brought us to the Shalimah Bagh, a monument of former magnificence and luxury, now neglected and desolate. Some patchwork repairs have been made this year to its buildings by the Maharajah, only enough to check ruin and decay here and there, to which everything here seems rapidly hastening. Following the now empty aqueduct, we reached the canal, and found two boats awaiting us, into one of which I stepped, and gladly extended myself on the soft namba spread for me. The passage from the Shalimah Bagh to my former bungalow occupied about an hour and three-quarters. The Jhelum was now some six or seven feet lower than before, and the stream proportionably moderate. I found all my baggage stowed in the bungalow, and ordered it to be ready for a start on the seventeenth, intending to get off myself, if possible, on the eighteenth.

16th October. After breakfast I took boat, and went first to a shawl merchant's, Mirza Mahomed Shah, and purchased articles for presents to dear ones at home; then to a papier-machè shop. Coming back, I found a card from Captain Tulloh, 21st P.N.I. He left to-day, I understood. But as I was sitting shut up for the night, and reading, I heard sounds as of an arrival, and voices as of a saheb, and sure enough there was Tulloh come to claim shelter, as his jan-pan broke down shortly after starting. We sat long chatting over our mutual excursions.

17th October. Both of us astir early. A merchant employed by Tulloh had brought his own horse to take him to Ramoo, and on my mentioning a difficulty in procuring money, he readily engaged to supply. Tulloh off, I had a talk with the merchant, Samhed Shah, a most respectable-looking and pleasant-mannered man. I agreed to go to his shop after breakfast, and was aggravated into buying a scarf, caps, and black choga—the latter not yet ready. All my baggage left this morning; Murad and party also. Abdoolah and Buddoo only remain with me. Suleiman informed me that the Rajah of Kopalu was here, and had received the Testaments. He would like to see me, but feared the jealousy of the Maharajah.

On my arrival I had been visited by an Affghan to whom I had before given ten rupees. He was, by his own report and that of many testimonials apparently genuine, of great service to our sick and wounded at the time of the Affghan disaster, for which humanity he had to flee his country on the withdrawal of the British troops, and (strange to say) has never been adequately rewarded by our Government, though his case has been brought forward and published. I promised to represent the matter to Sir R. Montgomery, in hopes of something being yet done for his benefit.

18th October. Samhed Shah not appearing by ten o'clock, I took boat and went down the river, and sent a man to his shop from which came a brother or partner and told me that the black choga would not be ready for three or four hours. On representing the delay and uncertainty to Abdoolah, he recommended putting off the start till to-morrow, and fetching Shupyim in one march. I now took leave of my three shikarries who had remained in order to escort me some miles out, but this further delay was too much for them, naturally enough as they had been more than five months absent from their families. I also took leave of the Baboo whose services have been invaluable. He refused any pecuniary reward, and I had difficulty in getting him to name any present from below that would be acceptable to him. After some time I suggested a revolver. This seemed to please him, so having two with my baggage, I engaged to send him one of them, and so we shook hands and parted. He has got a nag for me to take me to Ramoo, from the Maharajah's stud, he says. And now I have parted, I think, on the most friendly terms with my Cashmere allies and retainers.

At length came the long expected choga, just from the dyer's and still moist, so it had to be hung up. And now this busy day draws to a close, and to-morrow I quit this lovely country, so full of natural charms, but through bad government with its vast resources so little developed. Would that it might fall into the hands of the British, without either usurpation or fraud such as we have been in the habit in India of pleasantly designating political necessity!

19th October. As I was still within the outskirts of Sirinuggur, a man halloaed to me to loose my dogs, little Sara and Fan, as there was shikar before me, and, looking up, there was a fine fox with a splendid brush scudding over the maidan, a great cur far behind him. My two little animals made a dash for him, but he just then crossed a bank; and they came back. I suppose the animal had escaped from trap or cage.

I arrived at Ramoo heartily tired of the native saddle, and was glad to mount my own Cabulli. My saddle was like an armchair after the other, and though the mid-day sun was hot I jogged on contentedly to Shupyim, where all my baggage still waited. It was now three o'clock, and I immediately directed all to move to Heerpoor, in order to reach Alliahabad to-morrow, where I shall join them. The old kotwal, a most obliging old fellow, welcomed me warmly, mindful of former backsheesh. Buddoo and baggage not arriving till nine, he sent me his charpoy and bedding, and placed his choga from his own shoulders on to mine, notwithstanding my protestations against his so denuding himself. He insisted, having plenty more, he said, at home. Abdoolah cooked me some chops, so altogether I fared admirably, and was just turning in, when Buddoo arrived. He had been detained by the delay and difficulty in obtaining a change of coolies at Serai.

20th October. Up ere dawn, and everything made ready for a start, the kotwal very busy, lending a helping hand. I gave him a long certificate, of which testimonials he has hundreds, and takes much pleasure in exhibiting them to any saheb who may have sufficient patience and good temper to humour him. With a friendly farewell I set off on foot, and enjoyed a delightful march to Heerpoor, where I mounted Yarkandi who was full of spirits, and when in such a mood is very absurd with his clumsy frisking. The weather was lovely and scenery beautiful, admiring which and often dismounting from the very rocky and steep nature of the ground, I reached Alliahabad. My servants and coolies had been there some time. I ordered out my tent, but had better have put up in the old serai, for the wind outside was biting. The season, though, is much less advanced than last year, when the ground was covered with snow, and the undergrowth in the forests dead and prostrate as in mid-winter. Now the vegetation is only beginning to yield to the remorseless gripe of Jack Frost, enough still remaining to shelter a bear; though I saw none of those animals now, whereas last year I spied three on the bare ground.

The wind was wondrous shrewd, and put me in mind of Karakorum. I gave orders to halt here to-morrow, Sunday.

21st October. A severe frost, and bitter cold wind. I kept my tent, and breakfasted within. Finding I had no less than forty coolies—just fifteen more than I required in coming up, with my full supply of liquors, stores, lead, shot, and books,

&c.—in spite of Abdoolah's reluctance, I ordered all the baggage together, and examined the contents of the kheltas, when I found that I could with ease reduce the number of loads to thirty-five. Such a lot of rubbish of Abdoolah's stowed away; some in every khelta, I think. Excepting the above slight disturbance, I passed a pleasant, cheerful day.

22nd October. Much fuss and bawling at a very untimely hour, yet the baggage not off as early as intended. The coolies took such a time to fit their loads to their fancies that I passed them all within a mile of camp, and trudged steadily on for the Pir—a heavy, steady pull of three miles or so. Thence I enjoyed the superb view—the whole valley, through which my homeward route lies, being unrolled in all its windings before me. And beautiful it looked, now just lit up by the risen sun. A few minutes to take an impression, and down I sped, the path—bad enough in itself—made more difficult than usual by the number of tattoos and bullocks which appear at this season to throng the narrow paths. It took me about an hour to reach the bottom. I was surprised to find the huge snowdrift, which I thought to be inconsumable—some always remaining to be renewed each winter—entirely dissolved; the mass of earth and stones it had collected alone remaining to mark its position. I scrambled from the bed of the torrent up that horrid bit of road immediately above it, and there was completely checked by a continuous string of some two hundred laden bullocks. As it was very possible to be sent rolling down the precipitous bank by a rude shock from their hard mass of salt, I pulled up for half an hour, and then on to Possianah, where I was welcomed by the man and woman who attend to the wants of wayfarers. Though I carried my usual hunter's breakfast, I gratified the old importunate couple by directing some chupatties and eggs to be prepared, and did not fail to do justice to them. I gave the old fellow a pukka rupee, for which liberal donation the pair pretended to offer up prayers on my behalf. Alas! the hypocrites! When Abdoolah arrived, they claimed payment of him for my refreshment, assuring him that such was my order. But Abdoolah knew my ways better, and was not deceived, though the man followed him a long distance, urging his claim. I walked the whole distance to Byramgullah, and enjoyed the exercise amid such lovely scenery. On the arrival of Abdoolah, and learning from him the attempted fraud of the Possianah 'traiteur,' I ordered the kotwal to be informed of it, that he might be fined and checked in such malpractices.

23rd October. On setting off I was accosted by the old delinquent of Possianah, who, it seems, had been immediately on my report brought with his wife to answer the charge. They were astonished and terrified at the position into which they had brought themselves, and were profuse in all sorts of asseverations of innocent intention. They stated that my servants had been supplied after me, and for this they demanded remuneration, considering my rupee as my individual backsheesh, as indeed it was. If this were true, they had right on their side, and it is very probable that such were the facts. But it is impossible to arrive at the truth in such a case, the Hindoo servants being as great adepts at lying as these people, especially where their interests are at stake. I could not even rely upon Abdoolah in such a case. I desired the kotwal to pardon them; but they are sure to be forced to give up the rupee.

This disposed of, I continued my progress, and was attended by a well-looking black-and-tan dog of the Ladâk breed, whose evident familiarity with Europeans made me think him a stray dog of the Survey department. He left me at the foot of the Rattan Panjal; up which steep mountain I ascended, and pausing to take a mental photograph of the splendid view presented from the top again pushed on, enjoying the beautiful scenery, varied at each turn of the winding path. I think nothing in the whole journey surpasses this. The forms of the hills are so fine and diversified, and the foliage so rich and abundant. I stopped by a bright gurgling stream in an enchanting spot. Reposing on a thick, soft turf, and canopied by sweet-smelling shrubs, I awaited the arrival of breakfast. In this locality, and on to Thanna, still bloom some deliciously-fragrant creepers, yielding a perfume like woodbine. With this exception, one misses the abounding fragrance enjoyed early in the year—one of the greatest charms of the journey to my mind.

I finished the remaining mile or two riding. There was a very perceptible change of temperature here, which induced me on arrival of my traps to effect a thorough change of costume. I was well remembered and pestered by beggars—one, a blind man, with a fearful goitre: one sees but few so afflicted in these mountain regions. My servants, to my surprise, brought with them the Ladâk dog. He had followed them, and was so pleased with my notice that, feeling sure I was not committing a theft, but only securing a truant or wanderer, I ordered him to be tied up, and to be enrolled on our strength for rations. Poor Sara is so dreadfully jealous that he has gone and secluded himself in the tent, and actually shed tears in his distress: he refused his dinner also, till I took it into the tent for him, and coaxed him to eat it.

A row just took place between the Maharajah's moonshi, or tax-gatherer, and some of my followers. I heard angry voices for some time, Suleiman appearing to be much aggrieved and loud in indignation. After repeatedly intimating his intention of appealing to me, he came and reported the said moonshi to be exceedingly intrusive and impertinent, insisting upon an examination of his bundles, and persevering therein in spite of his remonstrances and those of Abdoolah, as well as threats of my vengeance. This representation Abdoolah confirmed, and assured me that no obstacle had been placed in the way of the moonshi inspecting the goods of the numerous hangers-on of my party. So I sallied forth, and calling to the moonshi ordered him to approach, and he hesitating to obey, I sent my sepoys to bring him to me. He then advanced amid a general bully-ragging. Suleiman accused him of abusing him. Believing there had been loss of temper on both sides, I asked the moonshi if he had any complaint to make, or if any of the strangers, who had attached themselves to my company, had attempted to evade his scrutiny. He replied, 'No:' so I cautioned him to execute his duties in a more becoming manner, and not to interfere where he had no authority. And so amid general clamour the party dispersed, the moonshi strutting off with his myrmidons, with an air of immense importance and offended dignity. Suleiman did not meet with any of the enquiries met with when coming up. He was told they had dispersed here and there, in one employment or other. The Ladâk dog, dubbed 'Bhoota,' has taken to his new quarters by my tent, and commenced his duties as watch-dog, barking in a fine rich base voice. Sara still in the dumps.

24th October. A pleasant march to Rijaori. Excepting a few stony places, this is a tolerable path, much the best of the whole route. Once again I reclined under those fine chunars—the last I shall see, as they are the first when coming. The young fishermen were soon in attendance with bait, and gave me a full account of the great success of Bucksby White saheb (24th) who stopped here eight days, and caught many fish, some very large, but nothing like mine. They dwelt forcibly on his giving them five rupees, backsheesh—pukka rupees, too. I got my tackle in order, but from the report of the low state of the river and clearness of the water did not anticipate sport; still thought I ought to try, so started off at four, and tried two favourite pools which were so still and clear that I remained but a short time, judging that all attempts would be vain to catch a big one, and I cared not for a small one. So I wound up and returned, no ways disappointed, the sun now setting and the effects charming.

I read to-day in a back number of the *Lahore Chronicle* a letter signed 'Traveller,' purporting to be a just representation of the condition of the Cashmiries under the Maharajah's rule, which he describes to be most satisfactory—the whole country highly cultivated, inhabitants well off and contented, and signs of good government and prosperity everywhere. A man of small powers of observation might possibly be deceived to such an extent, however difficult, but when this scribbler comes to draw comparisons between the Maharajah's and the British government favourable to the former, especially in the matter of the repair of roads—a process altogether unknown in the Maharajah's dominions—one cannot help suspecting the writer to have been tempted by a douceur; to have been engaged by the Maharajah specially thus to misrepresent facts, and give a false colour to realities in Cashmere, in order to mislead the public, and blind distant enquirers as to the nature of the Maharajah's rule and the condition of his people. I can imagine no other reason for such a palpable perversion of truth than seeing objects through the golden hues of the Maharajah's spectacles.

25th October. I got a considerable wetting crossing the river which though now so low is full of irregularities, deep holes, and terrible smooth round stones. It is certainly a very awkward ford at the best of times. I discovered some duck in a deep pool, and dropped one wounded. The two little dogs gave chase, little Fan first plunging into the deep water at which the usually forward Sara hesitated. Away they went, and there was a grand duck hunt. The bird, as the dogs neared it, dived, and so crossed the width of the pool to my side, its course discovered by the tell-tale bubbles, and there it took refuge under the thick bushes fringing the bank. Now in plunged the sporting syce, Ruttoo, and was immediately up to his neck. He peered under the bushes as I made my way above, and we had gone their length without retrieving the bird, when a violent hurry-scurry took place forward, and the little dogs were full cry after their poor, quacking, hobbling victim which was secured just as it regained the brink of the water. There were a good many black partridges about here, and many fine fish seen basking. The Yarkandi lost a shoe, and believing him to be lame I dismounted, but think the cunning old fellow did it on purpose to humbug me as I noticed that he went all right when I was off him. Reaching the old Serai, I found a new baraduri erected on a fine airy prominence over the river, a great convenience to travellers. A havildar and six sepoys turned out in full fig to salute me, looking very clean and smart. I had a long chat with the havildar, a very civil fellow: he begged some powder as he is fond of shikar, and there are pea-fowl, wild-duck, jungle-fowl, and partridge in the neighbouring jungle.

26th October. The havildar provided me with a chuprassee who was to shew me a different and better road than that I had come by. But, excepting about a mile immediately on quitting the baraduri which lay by the river-side, he took me by the old stony route, there being no better, I presume. The skeleton of the murderer appeared to have fallen from the ropes which had suspended it, relieving the public of a most repulsive spectacle. I took up my old camp ground in preference to going on to the baraduri, at which, however, I understand all travellers stop and are satisfied.

27th October. In consequence of the increasing heat of the sun as we neared the plains, I made an earlier start than usual. It was still far from light as I crossed the river which, to my surprise, I was able to do on stepping stones, so low is it from the absence of rain, I suppose. As I was crossing, two duck flew by within easy shot, and as they returned I got my gun ready, and dropped one which fell some way off up stream. Reloading I went after it, and had almost given it up, when Sara tracked it up, and a hunt took place in the water, the two little dogs working well and securing the game. Mounting the hill I hailed the old couple at top, and ordered some milk: the old woman came forth with it, and we had a chat. These poor people were robbed of all their little wealth not long before I came this way, and have recovered nothing. The thief was one upon whom they had bestowed hospitality, a sort of faquir who are one and all impostors, if not rogues. The old lady, as though pleased with our colloquy, brought some ripe plantains, evidently rarities in these regions.

Crossing another stream, a small flock of wild fowl flew over. I dismounted, and got my gun, and as good luck would have it they came back overhead, and firing both barrels one bird fell dead, a fine grey widgeon. Then I jogged on to Saidabad. It is now very hot in the middle of the day, so I put up in the baraduri, though there are many objections—a number of hornets in the roof, and a noisy party of natives in an adjoining part.

Halting here the next day (Sunday), I was off on Monday morning ere the stars had disappeared, and surmounted the long and rugged ascent. The descent was tiresome—long, stony, and steep—but I hastened on without a pause till I emerged from the narrow ravine opening on to the level cultivated lands, the commencement of the interminable plains of the Punjab. I arrived in good time at Bhimber, and found to my satisfaction a chowdree from Lahore stationed here to arrange dâks for officers coming from Cashmere—a capital and considerate plan. My servants and baggage arriving, I arranged things for the journey, keeping the head with me; settled with servants and coolies, tipped sepoys, packed up the revolver with a letter for the Baboo, and having dined on wild duck, and taking an ample supply of 'vivers' for the road, entered my dooly, and was borne off with the uncomfortable prospect of a tedious and dusty two days' journey to Amritsir. And here I conclude my diary, having succeeded far beyond my expectations in maintaining it in some order and method.

* * * * *

NOTE.—The skull, on being examined by medical men, was pronounced to be that of an Asiatic.

END OF DIARY.

The sad task now remains of recording the death of the writer, which took place at Meean Meer on the 23rd of August, 1861, under the circumstances mentioned in the following extract from the *Lahore Chronicle*:—

> "It is with deep grief that we announce the death last night from cholera of that admirable officer and most excellent man, AUGUSTUS HENRY IRBY, Lieutenant-Colonel Commanding the 51st King's Own Light Infantry. In him the public service and society have lost one of its most honourable members, and the officers and men whom he commanded one they esteemed as a warm-hearted comrade and true friend. In all relations of life, Colonel IRBY had won the esteem of those with whom he had connection. He knew his duty thoroughly and did it; when his regiment moved out of the cantonments to escape, if possible, from the pestilence which has struck down more than one hundred and twenty of them, he remained with the sick, caught the contagion, and died at his post."

9 789358 007374

Printed by Libri Plureos GmbH in Hamburg, Germany